**MULTICULTURAL MARKETING
AND BUSINESS CONSULTING**

Multicultural Marketing

AND

Business Consulting

Thaddeus Spratlen

Leslie Lum

Detra Y. Montoya

Michael Verchot

BUSINESS AND ECONOMIC DEVELOPMENT CENTER

Foster School of Business   University of Washington

DISTRIBUTED BY THE UNIVERSITY OF WASHINGTON PRESS

BEDC, Foster School of Business
University of Washington, Box 353200
Seattle, WA 98195-3200
http://foster.washington.edu/bedc

Distributed by
University of Washington Press
PO Box 50096, Seattle, WA 98145, USA
www.washington.edu/uwpress

Design by Ashley Saleeba and Tom Eykemans
Composition by Integrated Composition Systems,
Spokane, Washington
Printed in the United States of America

The paper used in this publication meets the minimum requirements
of American National Standard for Information Sciences—Permanence
of Paper for Printed Library Materials, ANSI Z39.48-1984.∞

Library of Congress Cataloging-in-Publication Data
Multicultural marketing and business consulting / Thaddeus
Spratlen . . . [et al.].
p. cm.
Includes bibliographical references and index.
ISBN 978-0-295-99239-6 (paper-over-boards : alk. paper)
1. Marketing—Cross-cultural studies.   2. Multiculturalism
in advertising.   3. Marketing consultants.   4. Business
consultants.   I. Spratlen, Thaddeus, 1930–
HF5415.M755   2012
658.8008—dc23   2012037029

Contents

vii

Preface

The Business and Economic Development Center (BEDC) was founded in 1995 under the leadership of then dean of the Foster School of Business at the University of Washington William Bradford. It was officially launched as a partnership among the UW Foster School, community-based organizations, small business owners, leaders of Seattle's corporate community, and elected officials. Its mission is to assist historically underserved businesses, which include small businesses in economically distressed communities and minority-, veteran-, and women-owned businesses.

Work to build the BEDC began in the summer of 1994 when a team of faculty led by Thaddeus Spratlen and David Gautschi worked with MBA students to identify the components of a comprehensive inner-city economic development system. The model that evolved matched student teams, faculty, and industry advisors, including alumni, with underserved businesses and nonprofit organizations. Although the center's services are not limited to minority business enterprises (MBEs), those MBEs constitute a large proportion of the businesses served. The BEDC now enables undergraduate and graduate students to provide intensive consulting services to emerging, underserved businesses that seek to capture a new growth opportunity or solve a pressing business problem.

For more information about the University of Washington Foster School's Business and Economic Development Center, visit the website at www.Foster.Washington.edu/BEDC.

ACKNOWLEDGMENTS

The BEDC and the coauthors of this book are grateful for financial support from the JPMorgan Chase Foundation, without which this book would not have been possible. We also want to give special thanks to Jennifer Bauermeister and Jesse Robbins, who helped bring the book to completion.

The University of Washington Foster School has consistently provided strong support to the Business and Economic Development Center. Thanks to the numerous enterprises, nonprofit entities, and individuals whose funding and other forms of support have contributed to the BEDC's success. Kudos to the Rotary Club of Seattle for providing mentors and to the UW alumni and professional advisors who provided valuable feedback on effective problem solving and pedagogy. Last but certainly not least, our gratitude to the many students who offered deeply reflective evaluations of our teaching and writing in this textbook. They were invaluable to our understanding of how students learn.

ABOUT THE AUTHORS

Thaddeus Spratlen is professor emeritus of marketing at the University of Washington and founder of the Business and Economic Development Center. He has authored numerous articles and is considered one of the nation's experts on multicultural marketing and business assistance for urban enterprises. The American Marketing Association Foundation established the Williams-Qualls-Spratlen Multicultural Mentoring Award of Excellence, named equally for Spratlen, Jerome D. Williams, and William Qualls, for their pioneering work in mentoring multicultural students and junior faculty and doing advanced research on issues of racial, ethnic, and cultural diversity.

Leslie Lum has worked in corporate development for a Fortune 100 company as part of the team that restructured the company from manufacturing to financial services. She has worked in mergers and acquisitions with HSBC (the global bank) and has been general manager for a retail start-up. Her print and web book *Personal Investing*, which teaches novices how to invest, was published by South-Western in 2002. Since 2002 she has led student teams at Bellevue College in Washington, where the program won a 2004 award from the Community College National Center for Community Engagement.

Detra Y. Montoya is clinical associate professor in the W. P. Carey School of Business at Arizona State University. Her research focuses on multicultural consumer behavior. She has worked in Procter and Gamble's multicultural business development organization, with an emphasis on developing national multicultural merchandising programs. She has taught student consulting teams at the University of Washington as part of the Business and Economic Development Center's Student Consulting Program. In addition, she has taught marketing courses to small business owners across the state of Washington.

Michael Verchot is the founding director of the Business and Economic Development Center at the University of Washington Foster School of Business. Under his leadership, the program has moved from a start-up to a major focal point for minority business enterprises in the Pacific Northwest. Among its numerous programs are the Minority Business Awards with the *Puget Sound Business Journal,* the minority business summit of the largest businesses in Washington State, and an extensive consulting program in which teams of students and industry mentors have worked with more than 250 MBEs, generated $85 million in revenues, and created and retained more than 6,000 jobs between 1995 and 2012. The BEDC is considered the definitive expert on minority markets and businesses in the Pacific Northwest and has been featured in numerous articles in the general and business press. It has won the SBA Vision Award. Michael Verchot won the national Minority Business Advocate of the Year Award in 2004 from the US Department of Commerce.

**MULTICULTURAL MARKETING
AND BUSINESS CONSULTING**

1. Multicultural Markets

ABOUT THIS MODULE

Several developments in the US economy and society help to explain the emergence of multicultural markets as an important aspect of the current business environment. The growth of multicultural populations is outpacing that of non-Hispanic whites and is projected to do so until midcentury, when minorities will outnumber non-Hispanic whites. There is a growing recognition in mainstream business of the significant spending power of multicultural communities. According to the Selig Center for Economic Growth, total annual buying power of African Americans, Asians, American Indians, and Hispanics in 2010 amounted to $2.7 trillion and is expected to reach $14.1 trillion in 2015. This represents a 188% increase over 1990. The trend toward greater cultural diversity in the population is creating new opportunities for businesses.

This module presents an overview of the size and characteristics of the larger multicultural markets, including African Americans (also referred to as blacks), Hispanics (also referred to as Latinos), Asians, and American Indians (also referred to as Native Americans). American Indians and Alaska Natives may be referred to by the US Census acronym AIAN. In most of this book, the term *American Indians* is used. Native Hawaiians and Pacific Islanders may be referred to by the US Census acronym NHPI. White populations that do not include individuals of Hispanic ethnicity are often compared with these groups; according to US Census terminology, they are referred to as non-Hispanic whites. Historically, they have been referred to as the dominant or majority population.

As generally understood, culture includes language, the arts, customs, beliefs, institutions, and patterns of behavior in society. We recognize that categories of people (based on race, ethnicity, national origin, and other characteristics) differ culturally from the majority population. They may also embrace or share many of the elements of the dominant culture. However, the study of marketplaces has been multiplied by the number of different cultures within US society. Not only is it important to know the demographics of multicultural groups, it has become mandatory to include the cultural context and the political, legal, and social factors of each of these groups. Racism is an example of a process of racial/ethnic bias and related forms of discrimination that adversely affect many facets of our society with respect to the large cultural groups that we describe. All these factors must be included in a comprehensive understanding of the multicultural marketplace and the new paradigms that may emerge out of this change.

After Studying This Module

This module provides basic knowledge of multicultural markets. It provides a starting point for students to explore the complexity of these and other groups. After studying this module, students should be able to:

- Explain the size and market potential of selected multicultural populations and project population trends in each group.
- Understand the environment in which multicultural populations have come to exist and thrive in the United States.
- Quantify and analyze the impact of multicultural populations on the marketplace.
- Describe the demography, geographic location, and purchasing power of the larger multicultural groups.
- Interpret other salient characteristics of multicultural populations that may affect the marketplace.

MULTICULTURAL MARKETS

Multicultural Marketing

Multicultural marketing has evolved since the early 1990s. Prior to that time, marketing to diverse racial and ethnic groups was generally referred to as minority marketing. While the phrase *marketing to minorities* is still used to refer to the targeting of racial/ethnic groups, diversity in multicultural terms extends far beyond race and ethnicity to embrace lifestyles such as sexual orientation, distinctive value orientations associated with dietary practices (e.g., vegetarian and organic food preferences), or catering to disability populations. Broadly, multicultural marketing can be defined as the *process of using market exchange concepts, methods, and techniques to recognize and respond to culturally distinct group characteristics and preferences of individuals, organizations, and communities.*

The essence of multicultural marketing requires culture and its complexities to be at the core of management and strategy. Cultural distinctiveness of target groups is emphasized in contrast to the dominant and relatively standardized European American norms of traditional marketing. Cultural diversity is emphasized over cultural homogeneity. Whereas traditional marketing generally assumes assimilation into the dominant culture, multicultural marketing recognizes differences from the dominant culture in many forms—language, customs, music, food, folk art, and other forms of cultural expression.

The language characteristics and cultural traditions of many immigrant groups commonly lead to "high-context" relationships that foster a group-centeredness, stronger social bonds, and more close-knit interactions than typically occur in the dominant culture. They have not assimilated into European American culture; indeed, attempts to persuade, seduce, or even force groups to assimilate have led to external and internal conflicts among minorities. As America becomes more diverse, it is the model of acculturation—where cultures exist side by side and influence each other—that may be more effective. The marketing implications that follow are that communications media in languages other than English are needed to prevent market isolation because of language. Or, if English is the appropriate language, the focus might be on media that serve a community of color. There could be an emphasis on word-of-mouth messages or, alternatively, less emphasis on individualistic and self-centered messages and themes.

Multicultural marketing also embraces changing cultural traditions in the United States. Another reflection of the shift to multicultural marketing is illustrated in responses to changing demographics and increased market power of culturally distinct groups of consumers. For example, the growing presence and importance of Southeast Asians and Hispanics in Southern California have brought about noticeable marketing changes. Retailers in malls serving Southeast Asians have altered their merchandise assortments to reflect substantially higher proportions of petite sizes than in stores serving other population groups. Supermarkets catering to Hispanics (especially Mexican Americans) frequently alter store decor and musical programs and incorporate Spanish-language signage into their store operations. Such responses illustrate how multicultural marketing benefits both consumers and enterprises. Consumers are better served with more appropriate choices in goods and services. Enterprises benefit by increased patronage and more competitive performance in their operations.

Along with culture, other factors that have shaped a group's history in America must be considered and understood. Racism is an integral part of the treatment and experiences of groups based on racial/ethnic and color differences as well as language and country of origin. It stems from beliefs, attitudes, and actions that consider norms, institutions, and other elements of the dominant majority culture to be superior. Conversely, people of color and many of their characteristics are considered and treated as if they are inferior. When put into behavior and social interaction involving these groups, racism results in discrimination, disparity, and other negative outcomes. Historically, consider three of its most extreme forms—enslavement of African Americans, subjugation and genocide of American Indians, and internment of Japanese Americans during World War II. These are forms of institutional racism, since they go beyond individual bias and behavior to represent actions taken on an organizational and systemic or national level. In the present, it is evident in many forms of racial/ethnic profiling that lead to the highly disproportionate incarceration of African American and Hispanic males. Racism helps to explain the stark deprivation of large proportions of American Indians on most reservations and the glass ceiling commonly faced by the most well-endowed Asian Americans. Moreover, many statistical measures of the differences between these groups and those in the historically larger majority population reflect the continued

CHANGES IN MARKETING PROCESS

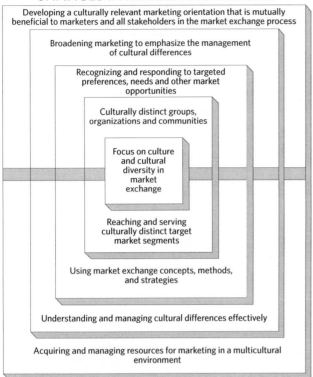

Developing a culturally relevant marketing orientation that is mutually beneficial to marketers and all stakeholders in the market exchange process

Broadening marketing to emphasize the management of cultural differences

Recognizing and responding to targeted preferences, needs and other market opportunities

Culturally distinct groups, organizations and communities

Focus on culture and cultural diversity in market exchange

Reaching and serving culturally distinct target market segments

Using market exchange concepts, methods, and strategies

Understanding and managing cultural differences effectively

Acquiring and managing resources for marketing in a multicultural environment

CHANGES IN MARKETING PRACTICE

FIGURE 1-1. Conceptual Framework for Multicultural Marketing
© 2000 Thaddeus Spratlen

influence of racism on multicultural groups in education, income, poverty, wealth, health, and crime.

Multicultural marketing broadens the field in several ways. It assigns meaning and importance to groups and communities that have been neglected and traditionally underserved. Marketing becomes more culturally sensitive, inclusive, pluralistic, and progressive than was and is the case in traditional marketing. Multicultural marketing represents a forward-looking perspective in the theory and practice of marketing.

The main concepts and changes associated with multicultural marketing are illustrated in Figure 1-1.

Context of Multicultural Markets

In terms of overall percentage of consumer groups, multicultural markets comprise as much as 60% or more of the US marketplace. One in five people in the United States speaks a language other than English at home. Racial ethnic groups constitute over 40%, segments by sexual orientation make up another 10 to 15%, and disability populations yet another 5% of the overall US pop-

ulation. Other lifestyle segments could increase the proportion up to at least 60%. This proportion grows larger if the market is defined to include younger age groups.

The hallmark of embracing multicultural marketing still incorrectly focuses mainly on four groups: Hispanics, African Americans, Asians, and American Indians. Historically, mainstream business has not paid much attention to multicultural markets because they were considered to be relatively small and seemingly difficult for business strategists of a predominantly white, non-Hispanic culture to understand.

As evidence for this, government and business have yet to come up with an effective means of categorizing these growing populations. In fact, the category "white" includes most Hispanics, while black commingles individuals born in or outside America of African, Caribbean, or South American descent. Asians originate from over twenty countries with different languages, cultures, and histories. Populations that immigrated from South America, Central America, and Mexico are labeled Hispanic even though these individuals are not from Spain. Similarly, other indigenous people of the United States such as American Indians and Alaska Natives are categorized together although they represent over 500 tribes of different languages, cultures, and sovereign governments. The term *minority* is itself quickly becoming a misnomer because it suggests that there is a homogeneous majority population.

Until recently, mainstream business did not focus on these populations because they were small in number relative to the more established white non-Hispanic population of mainly European origin or heritage. These more established populations had several generations to learn English and create the social and political infrastructure that supported business development. Over the years, the fusions of these originally multiethnic groups created a relatively homogeneous American culture that was approached by businesses using national demographics.

European populations were established in the United States through immigration. The first wave of immigrants from the mid- to late 1800s included the Irish and Germans. This was followed by the Italians in the early 1900s. European immigrants came to the United States to escape harsh economic conditions, wars, or persecution. Race-based exclusion laws prevented the same scale of immigration from other parts of the world. In 1882 the US Congress passed the Chinese Exclusion Act, which was later extended to all Asians until 1943, when it was repealed. Immigration quotas in the Immigration Act

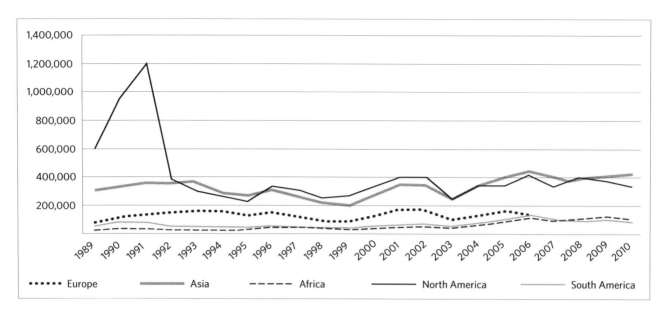

FIGURE 1-2. Immigrants by Region
Source: Yearbook of Immigration Statistics, 2003 and 2010 Numbers after 2003 are immigrants
with permanent residence status only. ImmigrationStatistics.xlsx

of 1924 effectively limited immigration until the 1965 Hart-Cellar Act lifted the discriminatory quotas. For many generations, racially oppressive policies prevented African Americans and American Indians from providing much more than low-wage labor.

Twentieth-century immigration after World War II showed a dramatic shift, with increased immigration from Asian countries such as China, India, Korea, the Philippines, and Vietnam, which had been engaged in conflicts such as the Korean and Vietnam wars. Immigration also increased from the Caribbean, Central America, South America, and particularly Mexico, which accounted for the bulk of the spike in 1991.

Multicultural Population Growth

Evidence to support and explain the shift to multicultural marketing is clear and convincing. In terms of overall size, the five largest racial/ethnic groups that are referred to

as minority groups comprise about 116 million, or 38% of the population as of the 2010 census. African Americans (alone or in combination) number about 42 million, and Hispanics number about 50.5 million. Asians account for another 17.3 million, while American Indians (Native Americans and Alaska Natives) total almost 5.2 million. Native Hawaiians and other Pacific Islanders account for 1.2 million. Multiple-race Americans, first allowed as a category in the 2000 census, now number close to 9 million. About 21.7 million identified themselves as some other race.

Figure 1-3 shows that the growth rates for Hispanics, Asians, and mixed-race groups are the highest, while the non-Hispanic white population has very little growth for the ten years ending in 2010. In fact, the Hispanic population accounted for 56% of the growth in population between 2000 and 2010, while African Americans and Asians accounted for 16% each.

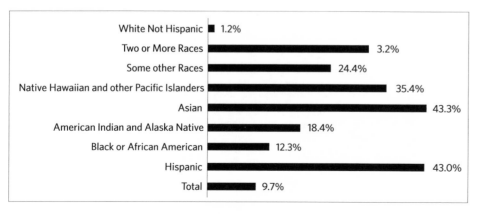

FIGURE 1-3. Multicultural Population Growth
Source: 2010 Census Briefs, Overview of Race and Hispanic Origin: 2010 Population_2000_2010_2050.xlsx

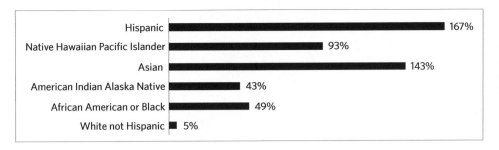

FIGURE 1-4. Population
Growth Projections

Source: National Population Projections,
released 2008 http://www.census.gov/
population/www/projections/summary
tables.html Population_2000_2010_2050
.xlsx

According to the Selig Center for Economic Growth at the University of Georgia, African Americans, Hispanics, Asians, and American Indians accounted for $2.2 trillion, or close to 20% of US purchasing power in 2010. In addition to the impressive dollar amount of spending power, marketers are attracted to the often disproportionate patterns of spending associated with specific groups. For example, African American consumption rates of apparel, shoes, cosmetics, and soft drinks can be up to three times their population proportion.

Going forward, the same patterns will persist. The US Census projects that Hispanic and Asian populations will account for 90% of the growth in population in the next 50 years. In fact, it is projected that after 2030, the non-Hispanic white population will actually be in decline.

Perhaps most telling is the shift in population of younger consumers or those most coveted by marketers. According to projections for 2050, minorities will dominate the younger age categories, while non-Hispanic whites will constitute most of the older or retired population. In fact, if it were not for minorities, the median age in the United States at midcentury would be 44 years. If that were the case, the United States would face the same problems that Japan and European countries face with a rapidly aging population. The median age of developed countries is expected to reach 46.4 years by 2050. Japan, Italy, Switzerland, Germany, and Sweden already have median ages over 40. Some western Euro-

pean countries and Japan look to a median age in the 50s by midcentury.[1] Without its diverse population, the United States would be in the same predicament.

This is not to say that major change is expected only in the mid-twenty-first century. Already major urban areas, which are often the leading edge of demographic and cultural change, have shifted to become multicultural areas in which no single cultural group dominates. Of the three largest US cities, New York, Los Angeles, and Chicago,[2] all have non-Hispanic whites constituting less than one-quarter of their populations in 2010.

It is a misconception that minority populations are static. Although they may suffer an economic disadvantage because of exclusion, discrimination, lack of language skills, or other resources, these populations are dynamic and quick to learn. Education levels have risen over the past 20 years and will continue to increase for populations that currently lag the white non-Hispanic population. Major developments such as the rise of educational institutions that are run by black or American Indian educators for black or American Indian students have shown success rates exceeding those of mainstream educational institutions. Additionally, first-generation Hispanics are finding community colleges to be an effective gateway to education. It is anticipated that with more time in the United States, their education levels will continue to accelerate, as shown in Figure 1-5.

Increases in education levels are often coupled with an increase in income. Median household income, as shown in Figure 1-6, grew more for minorities than it did for non-Hispanic whites. As rates of college education accelerate and as more role models emerge within their own communities, income levels can rise to close to parity with non-Hispanic whites.

When the demographic trends are combined with the

TABLE 1-1. Median Age

	2010	2050
Two races	19.9	24.7
Hispanic	27.5	31.2
Native Hawaiian Pacific Islander	28.2	33.4
American Indian Alaskan Native	30.0	34.1
African American or black	30.7	36.3
Asian	34.3	40.9
Non-Hispanic white	41.3	44.6

Source: US Census Bureau, 2010. Population_2000_2010_2050.xlsx

1   *CIA World Factbook*, 2010. Retrieved 12/20/11 from http://www
    .cia.gov.
2   US Census Bureau, *American Factfinder*, 2009. Retrieved 12/20/11
    from http://www.census.gov.

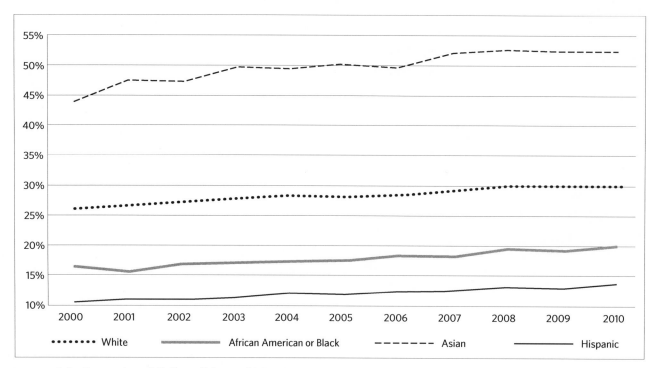

FIGURE 1-5. Proportion of College-Educated Minorities.

Source: US Census http://www.census.gov/hhes/socdemo/education/data/cps/2010/tables.html
EducationalAttainmentHistoical.xlsx

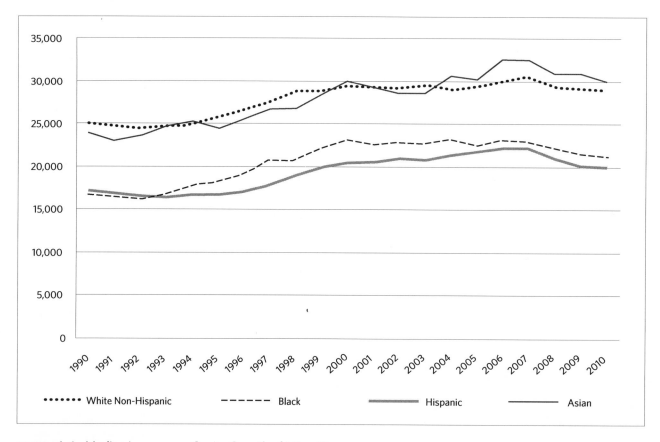

FIGURE 1-6. Median Income per Capita Growth of Minorities

Source: US Census http://www.census.gov/hhes/www/income/data/historical/people/index.html edianIncomebyRace.xlsx

data on spending power, it is clear that multicultural markets represent a tremendous opportunity for both mainstream and minority businesses. It is also generally the case that minority markets are underserved. In some instances brand loyalty has not been established for many of these segments. In addition, minority populations are already a major factor in the youth market and promise to increase their prominence in the years to come.

Multicultural Purchasing Power

Minority populations still lag the white population in income levels, but the purchasing power (as measured by personal disposable income) of Hispanic, African American, Asian, American Indian, and multiracial populations is significant, accounting for more than $2.7 trillion in 2010, or 24% of total buying power, according to the Selig Center for Economic Growth. This is projected to grow 38% by 2015 to almost $3.8 trillion. At current levels of minority income, this purchasing power translates to 35% of the growth in overall purchasing power in the next five years.

The geographic concentration and cultural traditions of Hispanics and African Americans as well as Asians and American Indians give them substantial market potential in a variety of local and regional markets as well as in ethnically focused product categories. "Getting it" in the context of multicultural communities means understanding the potential and actual spending of customers who are members of diverse racial/ethnic groups so that targeted marketing efforts are more likely to be effective. "Getting it" also means acknowledging, responding to, and respecting that these individuals (regardless of their income, wealth, and class) should not be considered to be "Caucasians in other than white skin." In order to be successful in the new America, there is no doubt that business enterprises must "get it" and respond to opportunities in expanding multicultural markets.

TABLE 1-2. Multicultural Purchasing Power

$ Billions	2010	2015	Difference	Percent Change
Total	11,124	14,119	2,995	26
Hispanic	1,036	1,482	446	43
Black	957	1,247	290	30
American Indian	68	90	23	33
Asian	543	775	232	43
Multiracial	116	165	49	43%

Source: Selig Center for Economic Growth, *The Multicultural Economy, 2010.* Athens, GA: Selig Center for Economic Growth, 2010. SeligBuyingPower.xlsx

The goal of segmentation is to identify groups of customers that might not be served by other competitors. Market niches can be attractive because they have characteristics that lend themselves to profitability or more frequent buying. Sometimes they are attractive simply because no other competitor has sufficiently served that market. All these arguments hold for multicultural markets. In the past, mainstream enterprises have not effectively targeted these populations because they were considered of insufficient size to be profitable or because they are difficult for mainstream marketers to understand. Large enterprises look for sales in the hundreds of millions as attractive potential markets. African American, Hispanic, and Asian/Pacific Islander markets are now of significant enough size to draw the attention of these large national and multinational firms.

In addition, all these groups have faced discrimination as customers. There is a large body of research showing discrimination in major consumer purchasing such as housing and cars. A review of consumer racial profiling court cases outlined increasing discrimination ranging from subtle degradation to overt denial of goods or services.[3]

This section describes the larger segments of the multicultural market. It does so using the determinants of segmentation practiced in single culture mass marketing, including demographics, geography, psychographic factors, and buying behavior. However, multicultural markets include myriad dimensions that define each culture and its relationship to the dominant culture. Such dimensions include sociological, psychological, and economic factors and racism. These all play a role in communicating to and determining the needs of the segment. The complexity of these other dimensions cannot be contained in this small space. Nor can it be inclusive of the many cultures that make up the United States. Rather, this section attempts to provide a brief overview for further exploration.

AFRICAN AMERICANS
Demographics

The 2010 US Census counted 42 million African Americans, including the 2.3 million who identified as African American in combination with another race. Between

3 A. G. Harris, G. R. Henderson, and J. D. Williams, "Courting Customers: Assessing Consumer Racial Profiling and Other Marketplace Discrimination." Journal of Public Policy and Marketing, vol. 24, no. 1 (2005): 163–71.

2000 and 2010, those who counted black or African American as their only race grew 12.3% versus 9.7% for the total population. As with other races and ethnicities, the definition of the segment is itself a complex task. Of those who identify their race as African American alone, about 1.2 million are Hispanic blacks. Of those who identify themselves as black along with another race, the largest combination was black with white (1.8 million). Although it is estimated that up to one-third of African Americans are of multiple race, the struggle for lineage acknowledgment reaches as far back as the black descendants of Thomas Jefferson. In America's dominant culture, people with any portion of black heritage are typically identified as black.

Immigration from Africa is increasing relative to historical rates. Almost 1.3 million Africans immigrated to the United States from 1990 to 2010, more than six times more than in the preceding 200 years. This tally of immigration, of course, excludes the estimated 8 million Africans who were forcibly brought to the Americas as part of the slave trade.

The gender split between male and female African Americans is 48% male and 52% female compared with 49% male and 51% female for the general population. African American males actually outnumber females until age 20. After that point the number of females outpaces the number of males by a large margin. Although the same trend occurs in the white population, it does not start as early (females outnumber males starting at age 45), nor is the difference so pronounced until age 60. The smaller proportion of African American men plays itself out in family structure. Women head 44% of African American households and, similar to women in other groups, control more than two-thirds of the buying decisions.[4]

The median age of all US males is 35.5, while black males have a median age of 29.9. Black females also have a lower median age of 33.3 as compared with all US females at 38.1.[5] A number of sociological factors, from lower access to health care to heightened victimization from crime, may account for these differences.

As a population, African Americans have more health risks as manifested by an average life expectancy of 70 years for African American males versus 75.6 for all US males and infant mortality rates of 13.3 per 1,000 births as compared with 5.63 for the white population.[6] These disparities are often caused by discrimination, cultural barriers, and lack of access to health care. Research documents the lack of access to healthy foods and the preponderance of environmentally unsafe conditions in both urban and rural areas where blacks live. Blacks are more likely to be obese (37.7% for black males and 51.8% for black females versus 34.7% for the general population).[7] Other studies have documented the preponderance of fast-food advertising in predominantly black areas.[8] There is a market opportunity for enterprises to provide products that address health needs specific to the African American population.

On average, African American households are slightly larger (2.7 persons per household) than whites (2.5) and are more likely to have children under age 18. Black women have a slightly higher fertility rate (56:1,000 gave birth versus 50:1,000 for white non-Hispanic women), and 60% of these women were unmarried compared with 20% of non-Hispanic white women. Non-Hispanic whites are more likely to be married (57%) as compared to blacks (34%). About 30% of black households have female heads as compared with 9% of non-Hispanic whites. Nearly 7% of blacks aged 30 and older are grandparents living with their grandchildren as compared with only 2% of non-Hispanic whites. Approximately 52% of black grandparents were responsible for the care of their grandchildren as compared with 45% of non-Hispanic whites. About 26.7% of blacks are in management and professional occupations as compared with 37.6% of non-Hispanic whites.[9]

African Americans continue to lag behind the white population in educational attainment (see Figure 1-7), and this is of concern because education is one of the main determinants of wealth. It was only after the US Supreme

4 M. Miley and A. Mack, "The New Female Consumer: The Rise of the New Mom," Advertising Age, White Paper, November 16, 2009.

5 US Census Bureau, The Black Population in the US, 2008. Retrieved 12/20/11 from http://www.census.gov/population/www/socdemo/race/Black-slide-presentation.html.

6 Centers for Disease Control and Prevention, National Vital Statistics Reports, vol. 59, no. 6, June 29, 2011. Retrieved 12/20/11 from http://www.cdc.gov/nchs/data/nvsr/nvsr59/nvsr59_06.pdf.

7 Centers for Disease Control and Prevention, "Health, United States 2010." Retrieved 12/20/11 from http://www.cdc.gov/nchs/fastats/black_health.htm.

8 J. D. Williams and S. K. Kumanyika, "Is Social Marketing an Effective Tool to Reduce Health Disparities?" Social Marketing Quarterly, vol. 7, no. 4 (Winter 2002).

9 US Census Bureau, The American Community—Blacks: 2004. American Community Survey Report, February 2007.

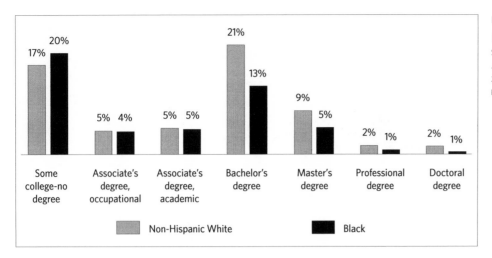

FIGURE 1-7. African American
Education Attainment
Source: US Census Bureau. http://www.census
.gov/hhes/socdemo/education/data/cps/
2010/tables.html EducationalAttainmentby
Race.xlsx

Court's decision in *Brown v. Board of Education* in 1954 that the government started to enforce equal access to education. Many young African American students continue to learn under conditions that severely constrain their ability to perform. These include attending substandard schools or schools with far fewer resources than those in white neighborhoods. Being first in their families to attend higher education handicaps them in navigating a complex, confusing, and expensive system.

The number of college-educated African Americans has increased by 135% since 1980 compared with 75% for the white population. There are nearly 105 historically black colleges and universities (HBCUs),[10] such as Howard University and Morehouse (the alma mater of Martin Luther King Jr.). These universities graduate 25% of all African American degree holders while accounting for only 3% of higher education institutions. More than half of African American professionals are graduates of HBCUs.[11] However, disparities still persist. Blacks make up 8% of first-year medical students, only 1% more than in 1975 and half their proportion in the population. Studies have shown that if personal factors are held constant, blacks are more likely to both enter and graduate from college.[12] The disparities continue because of pre-college personal factors such as parents' educational levels and

attending schools with lower per-pupil spending, higher poverty rates, and lower average standardized test scores.

It is projected that educational attainment will continue to rise as African American youth find more role models among the increasing ranks of college-educated blacks. Blacks continue to secure a broad spectrum of high-level, high-profile government and corporate positions, and this will also do much to raise the aspirations of the young. Similar to other multicultural segments, the demographics of this group is dynamic, fast changing, and often overlooked by mainstream marketers.

With rising educational levels over the long term, African American income levels are rising as well. This is particularly true for families with incomes of more than $75,000. As can be seen in Figure 1-8, the proportion of African American households with incomes from $75,000 to $99,999 grew 31% between 1990 and 2005 as compared with 5.3% increase for non-Hispanics whites; black households with incomes $100,000 and over grew 59% versus 49% for non-Hispanic whites.

Although every downturn results in economic decline for all groups, minorities are affected to a greater extent. The 2007–2008 recession had a disproportionate impact on African American wealth. In 2009 the median wealth of white households ($113,149) was 20 times that of black households ($5,677).[13] From 2005 to 2009, median net worth fell 53% for black households versus a 16% drop for white households. Black households were not affected as much as Hispanic and Asian households in the drop of

10 White House Initiative on Historically Black Colleges and Universities. Retrieved 12/20/11 from http://www2.ed.gov/about/inits/list/whhbcu/edlite-index.html.

11 United Negro College Fund. Retrieved 12/20/11 from http://www.uncf.org/aboutus/hbcus.asp.

12 I. Hinton, J. Howell, E. Merwin, S. Stern, S. Turner, I. Williams, and M. Wilson, "The Educational Pipeline for Health Care Professionals: Understanding the Source of Racial Differences," *Journal of Human Resources*, vol. 451, no. 5 (2010): 116.

13 P. Taylor, R. Fry, and R. Kochhar, "Wealth Gaps Rise to Record Highs between Whites, Blacks, Hispanics." Pew Research Center, July 26, 2011. http://pewsocialtrends.org/2011/07/26/wealth-gaps-rise-to-record-highs-between-whites-blacks-hispanics/.

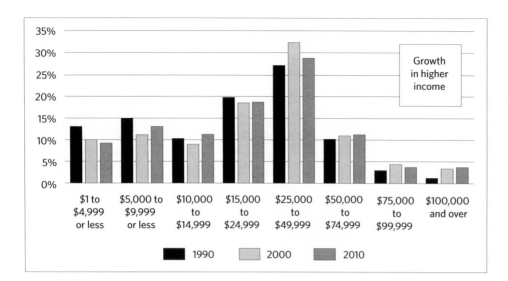

FIGURE 1-8. Comparative Income Growth of African American Families

Source: US Census Bureau, 2010 http://www.census.gov/hhes/www/income/data/historical/household/index.html HouseholdIncomebyRace.xlsx

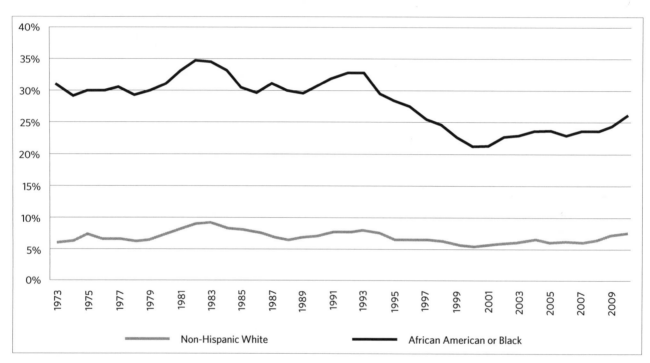

FIGURE 1-9. Poverty Rates of African Americans

Source: US Census Bureau. http://www.census.gov/hhes/www/poverty/data/historical/people.html Poverty_2010.xlsx

real estate values; however, black households did experience drops in retirement accounts and in the values of the businesses they owned.

African Americans made significant inroads in reducing poverty rates in the 1990s, as can be seen in Figure 1-9. Black poverty rates still remain significantly higher than those of the white population. In 2010, black poverty at 27%[14] was slightly higher than for Hispanics at 26%, while whites had a 9.9% poverty level and Asians 12.1%.[15] The large proportion of single female heads in black households partially explains this. Within any group, families headed by single females tend to have a higher rate of poverty. As with Hispanic Americans, recessions tend to take a larger toll on African Americans, throwing more into poverty and stagnating income growth.

14 US Census Bureau, "Poverty," 2011. Retrieved 12/20/11 from http://www.census.gov/hhes/www/poverty/histpov/hstpov2.html.

15 S. Travernise, "Soaring Poverty Casts Spotlight on 'Lost Decade,'" *New York Times*, September 13, 2011. http://www.nytimes.com/2011/09/14/us/14census.html?scp=3&sq=poverty&st=cse.

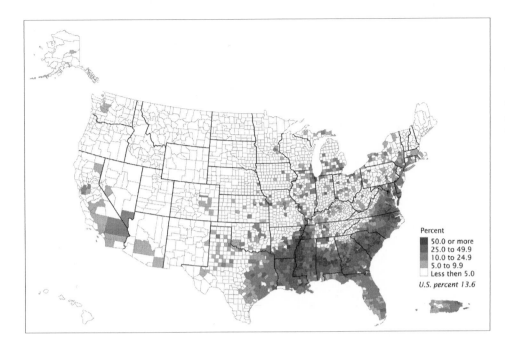

FIGURE 1-10. Black or African American Population as a Percent of County Population, 2010

Source: US Census Bureau. http://www.census.gov/population/www/socdemo/race/Black-slide-presentation.html

Geographics

African Americans tend to cluster in certain regions of the country. More than 55% of African Americans live in the south.[16] The US Census map (Figure 1-10) shows the high concentration of African Americans as a percent of the population in the mid-Atlantic and southeast. The largest numbers of African Americans live in New York, Florida, Georgia, Texas, and California. The states that experienced the greatest growth in African American population from 2000 to 2008 were Arizona, Nevada, Minnesota, Washington, and Georgia.

African Americans are more likely to be living in metropolitan areas than the population as a whole. The cities with the largest African American populations are New York, Chicago, Detroit, Philadelphia, and Houston, totaling about 5 million. African Americans play a prominent political role in the cities where they have higher populations. Of the major cities, six have African American mayors. According to the National Conference of Black Mayors, 650 US cities have black mayors representing more than 48 million citizens.[17] As of 2009, there were 41 black members of Congress and 1 black senator as compared with 23 Hispanic members of Congress and 3 senators. Asians lag with only 8 members of Congress and 1 senator.[18]

Other Factors

Along with the strong political involvement of African Americans, other psychological and sociological factors play into the population. Poverty, criminal records, and single-female-headed households are more prevalent than in other groups. One in 15 black males has spent time in a correctional institution as compared with one in 106 for white males and one in 36 for Hispanic males.[19] In large part, this was due to the war on drugs. Studies have documented the wrongful convictions, lack of adequate legal representation, and racial profiling, particularly in the war on drugs. The 2001 Sentencing Report stated that African Americans constituted 13% of drug users but 35% of arrests and 53% of those convicted.[20]

---

16 US Census Bureau, *The American Community-Blacks: 2004*. February 2007. American Community Survey Report.

17 National Conference of Black Mayors. Retrieved 12/20/11 from http://ncbm.org/2009/04/our-mission.

18 US Census Bureau, *The 2011 Statistical Abstract*. Retrieved 12/20/11 from http://www.census.gov/compendia/statab/cats/elections/elected_public_officials—characteristics.html.

19 J. Waren, A. Gelb, J. Horowitz, and J. Riordan, "One in 100: Behind Bars in 2008." Pew Center for the States, 2008. Retrieved 12/20/11 from http://www.pewcenteronthestates.org/uploadedFiles/8015PCTS_Prison08_FINAL_2-1-1_FORWEB.pdf.

20 US Sentencing Commission, *Sourcebook of Federal Sentencing Statistics*, 2001. Retrieved 12/20/11 from http://www.ussc.gov/Data_and_Statistics/Annual_Reports_and_Sourcebooks/2001/SBTOC01.htm.

A criminal conviction has multiplier effects on families and household accumulation of wealth. It dismantles family structure and precludes higher-paying jobs.

Racism is a reality in the lives of most minority populations, and the competent enterprise will acknowledge and understand that it is a part of the complexity of marketing to minority cultures in the United States. This also represents an opportunity because most minorities do not feel that their needs are currently being served in the marketplace. Most African Americans consider racial discrimination to be an important issue; 44% of African Americans report that they or a family member had experienced racial discrimination in the last few years.[21] African Americans overwhelmingly feel that they experience more discrimination than other groups. With regard to the enterprises that serve the African American population, the discrimination experienced has been widely documented. In particular, studies of lending practices have shown that black consumers are unfairly denied credit or charged rates disproportionate to their credit risk.

Home ownership is lower among blacks, with 44.2% owning homes versus 73.4% for non-Hispanic whites. The gap is the largest since 1994.[22] Blacks had made major gains in home ownership, moving up to 49.7% in mid-2004. However, they were targeted by subprime lenders. In 1993, subprime refinancing loans accounted for 8% of home loans in African American neighborhoods and 1% in white neighborhoods. By 1998, 51% of the total loans in African American neighborhoods were subprime compared with 9% in white neighborhoods. This proportion remained constant until 2005 when 52% of loans in African American neighborhoods were subprime.[23]

According to the Consumer Finance Survey,[24] home equity continues to be the largest component of household wealth. The barriers that restricted black home

ownership and the comparatively lower appreciation of homes in predominantly black neighborhoods as compared with white neighborhoods are the same barriers that stifle the accumulation of African American wealth. Predatory subprime lending and subsequent foreclosures inordinately set African American families back in their quest to build a secure financial future.

Religion, and particularly the church, has played a major role in the lives of African Americans from the times of slavery until today. Eight historically black denominations represent 65,000 churches and membership of more than 20 million people.[25] These denominations are: African Methodist Episcopal, African Methodist Episcopal Zion, Christian Methodist Episcopal, Church of God in Christ, National Baptist Convention of America, Inc., National Baptist Convention, USA, Inc., National Missionary Baptist Convention of America, and Progressive National Baptist Convention, Inc.[26] In addition to the customary role churches assume in other cultures, these ministries promote justice, affiliate relations, children and family development, economic development, anti-drug and anti-violence campaigns, health issues, voter education, and leadership development. They continue to be a major means of communicating to the black population.

As with other minorities, the history, culture, and traditions of African Americans are not common knowledge to the American public because of the lack of inclusion in most school curriculums. Over the past four decades, Kwanzaa has emerged as a post-Christmas celebration among African Americans. Many individuals and families may celebrate both Christmas and Kwanzaa. Some have chosen to celebrate only or mainly Kwanzaa. In celebrating Kwanzaa (a Swahili word for "first fruits") between December 26 and January 1, much less emphasis is placed on giving presents. Greater emphasis is placed on family and community values. There are many examples of cultural differences in weddings, births, and other life events that spawn a host of new products and services—most of these provided by African American businesses that understand these customs and customer preferences.

21 Pew Hispanic Center and Kaiser Family Foundation, *2002 National Survey of Latinos*. Retrieved 12/20/11 from http://pewhispanic.org/files/reports/15.pdf.

22 US Census Bureau. "Housing." Retrieved 12/20/11 from http://www.census.gov/hhes/www/housing/hvs/historic/index.html.

23 C. L. Nier, "The Shadow of Credit: The Historical Origins of Racial Predatory Lending and Its Impact upon African American Wealth Accumulation," *Journal of Law and Social Change*, vol. 11 (2007): 131–94.

24 Brian K. Bucks, Arthur B. Kennickell, Traci L. Mach, and Kevin B. Moore, "Changes in U.S. Family Finances from 2004 to 2007: Evidence from the Survey of Consumer Finances," *Federal Reserve Bulletin*, vol. 95 (February 2009): A1–A55.

25 US Census Bureau, *2011 Statistical Abstract, Population*. Table 76: Religious Bodies—Selected Data. Retrieved 12/20/11 from http://www.census.gov/compendia/statab/cats/population/religion.html.

26 C. Eric Lincoln and Lawrence H. Mamiya, *The Black Church in the African American Experience*. Durham, NC: Duke University Press, 1990.

TABLE 1-3. Comparative Consumer Spending: Blacks versus All

Item	All Consumer Units	Black or African American	All Consumer Units, Percent of Total	Black or African American, Percent of Total	Difference
Number of consumer units (in thousands)	120,847	14,432			
Average Annual Expenditures	$49,067	$35,198			
Food at home	$3,753	$2,875	7.6	8.2	0.5%
Food away from home	$2,619	$1,649	5.3	4.7	-0.7%
Alcoholic beverages	$435	$201	0.9	0.6	-0.3%
Housing	$16,895	$13,409	34.4	38.1	**3.7%**
Shelter	$10,075	$7,847	20.5	22.3	**1.8%**
Utilities, fuels, and public services	$3,645	$3,660	7.4	10.4	**3.0%**
Household operations	$1,011	$618	2.1	1.8	-0.3%
Housekeeping supplies	$659	$434	1.3	1.2	-0.1%
Household furnishings and equipment	$1,506	$850	3.1	2.4	-0.7%
Apparel and services	$1,725	$1,761	3.5	5.0	**1.5%**
Transportation	$7,658	$5,269	15.6	15.0	-0.6%
Health care	$3,126	$1,762	6.4	5.0	-1.4%
Entertainment	$2,693	$1,406	5.5	4.0	-1.5%
Personal care products and services	$596	$536	1.2	1.5	0.3%
Reading	$110	$47	0.2	0.1	-0.1%
Education	$1,068	$599	2.2	1.7	-0.5%
Tobacco products and smoking supplies	$380	$232	0.8	0.7	-0.1%
Miscellaneous	$816	$633	1.7	1.8	0.1%
Cash contributions	$1,723	$1,277	3.5	3.6	0.1%
Personal insurance and pensions	$5,471	$3,542	11.2	10.1	-1.1%

Source: 2008 Consumer Expenditure Survey. http://www.bls.gov/cex/home.htm#tables ConsumerExpenditure2008.xlsx
Note: Bold figures are larger expenditures as compared to general consumer.

Purchasing Power

The Consumer Expenditure Survey[27] for 2008 showed that, despite their lower income, African Americans spent more on telephone services, utilities, shoes, and children's apparel than whites. As a proportion of their total household income, blacks spend more on groceries, housing, utilities, apparel, and transportation. They spend less on alcohol, health care, entertainment, personal insurance, and pensions.

Media

The ethnic press has long been a means for marginalized communities to give voice to their concerns and stories. As mainstream media become more concentrated, ethnic media perform an even more crucial role in providing dif-ferent perspectives. Unfortunately, the contraction of print media is also having its impact on ethnic print media. About 30% of African Americans report getting their news from newspapers, similar to the general public. Nearly 86% of blacks receive their news from television as compared with 64% of whites, according to a December 2010 Pew Research Center for the People and the Press survey.[28] The Black Press of America identifies 200 black-owned newspapers, including the *Los Angeles Sentinel*, the *Chicago Defender*, and the *Washington Afro American*. These newspapers cover recent news events from the black perspective. There are no remaining print dailies. In 2010, African American newspapers did increase their circulation.[29]

27 Consumer Expenditure Survey, "Race of Reference Person: Average Annual Expenditures and Characteristics," 2009. Downloaded from http://www.bls.gov/cex/tables.htm 9/24/11.

28 State of the News Media, "African American Media: Evolving in the New Era." Pew Research Center, Project for Excellence in Journalism. Retrieved 12/20/11 from stateofthemedia.org/2011/African-american/.

29 Ibid.

Of the diverse magazines targeting black readers, five dominate. *Ebony* (1.25 million circulation) claims a readership of 11 million with a breakdown of 54% women and 46% men, of which over 60% are college educated. *Jet* magazine (900,000 circulation) has 62% female readership, a mean age of 39.4, and a household income of about $59,000.[30] *Essence* (1.1 million circulation) is a magazine geared toward African American women. Its readership has a median age of 39 and median household income of $54,000.[31] *Black Enterprise* (500,000 circulation) covers African American businesses and provides an annual ranking of the 100 largest black-owned businesses. *Uptown* (225,000 circulation) is a national magazine with regional editions in New York, Philadelphia, Washington, DC, Charlotte, Atlanta, Detroit, and Chicago.

In other media, the Black Entertainment Television (BET) network, a subsidiary of Viacom Inc., is broadcast to 89 million homes in the United States, Canada, and the Caribbean.[32] The BET brand includes CENTRIC, which reflects the newer trends in music, culture, and lifestyles, and BET Gospel, which provides inspirational programming. Its demographic tends to be 18 to 34 year olds with incomes less than $30,000. TV One is another black cable station, and the Oprah Winfrey Network (OWN), although geared toward a general audience, made its debut in 2010. Black cable subscriptions increased in 2010 as compared with drops in all other groups.

Several hundred black radio stations feature news and commentary by well-known personalities such as Tom Joyner and Tavis Smiley, as well as various genres of black music, including Gospel, Hip Hop, R&B, Jazz and Blues, and Caribbean.[33] Many of these are owned by large conglomerates that seek to target the black demographic and, given the ability of radio media to broadcast globally on the Internet, are reaching markets in Africa and the rest of the world. The number of black-owned stations peaked at 274 in 1995 and currently is about 220.[34]

In 2010, 42% of African Americans found their news online as compared with 35% the year before, the largest gain in research done by the Pew Internet and American Life Project. African Americans are more socially active online than other ethnic groups. In 2010, 71% used social networking as compared with 58% of whites, 25% used tweeting as compared with 15% of whites, and 22% blogged as compared with 14% of whites.

HISPANIC AMERICANS
Demographics

Hispanic Americans have recently attracted the most attention among minority groups because of their high population growth rate and the fact that they surpassed African Americans as the largest minority group. This is fueled by both immigration since 1965 and higher birth rates than the overall US population. Hispanic is classified as an ethnic category (as opposed to race used for whites, African Americans, Asians, American Indians and Alaska Natives, and Native Hawaiian and Pacific Islanders) by the government to capture Spanish-speaking populations and persons from Brazil. Sometimes the term *Latino* is used since it does not exclude non-Spanish-speaking South American countries such as Brazil. According to the 2010 census, the group numbered more than 50.5 million and constituted 16.3% of the population. The Hispanic population grew 43% between 2000 and 2010, and more than half the total growth in the US population in that decade was due to the increase in the Hispanic population.

The term *Hispanic*, although used extensively by the government, media, and enterprises, is not a relevant term to the groups it categorizes. In fact, these populations identify most strongly with their country of origin. They include people hailing from Mexico, South and Central America, and the Caribbean, as can be seen in Table 1-4. With regard to race, about 63% of Hispanics identify themselves as white alone. Approximately 30% identify themselves as some other race alone, while 5% identify themselves as two or more races.

With regard to gender, differences exist between Hispanic and white populations. Hispanic males account for 51% of the group versus 49% for whites. Young adult males outnumber females in the prime working age groups from 15 to 40. This is similar to immigration patterns in Asian populations, where male workers predominated prior to 1980 due to restrictive immigration policies that prohibited the immigration of families.

30 *Ebony/Jet*, Media Kit. Retrieved 12/20/11 from http://www.ebony.com/downloads/EBMK_2011.pdf.
31 *Essence*, Media Kit. Retrieved 12/20/11 from http://packages.essence.com/mediakit/expanding.html.
32 BET Media Room. Retrieved 12/20/11 from http://bet.mediaroom.com/index.php?s=45.
33 Listing of radio stations retrieved 12/20/11 from http://www.radioblack.com/.
34 National Association of Black Owned Broadcasters. Retrieved 12/20/11 from http://www.nabob.org/mission.html.

TABLE 1-4. Hispanic Groups by National Origin

Origin and Type	2000 Number	2000 Percent of Total	2010 Number	2010 Percent of Total	Change 2000 to 2010 Number	Change 2000 to 2010 Percent Change
Mexican	20,640,711	58.5	31,798,258	63	11,157,547	54.1
Puerto Rican	3,406,178	9.6	4,623,716	9.2	1,217,538	35.7
Cuban	1,241,685	3.5	1,785,547	3.5	543,862	43.8
Other Hispanic	10,017,244	28.4	12,270,073	24.3	2,252,829	22.5
Dominican	764,945	2.2	1,414,703	2.8	649,758	84.9
Central American	1,686,937	4.8	3,998,280	7.9	2,311,343	137
Costa Rican	68,588	0.2	126,418	0.3	57,830	84.3
Guatemalan	372,487	1.1	1,044,209	2.1	671,722	180.3
Honduran	217,569	0.6	633,401	1.3	415,832	191.1
Nicaraguan	177,684	0.5	348,202	0.7	170,518	96
Panamanian	91,723	0.3	165,456	0.3	73,733	80.4
Salvadoran	655,165	1.9	1,648,968	3.3	993,803	151.7
Other Central American	103,721	0.3	31,626	0.1	-72,095	-69.5
South American	1,353,562	3.8	2,769,434	5.5	1,415,872	104.6
Argentinean	100,864	0.3	224,952	0.4	124,088	123
Bolivian	42,068	0.1	99,210	0.2	57,142	135.8
Chilean	68,849	0.2	126,810	0.3	57,961	84.2
Colombian	470,684	1.3	908,734	1.8	438,050	93.1
Ecuadoran	260,559	0.7	564,631	1.1	304,072	116.7
Paraguayan	8,769	–	20,023	–	11,254	128.3
Peruvian	233,926	0.7	531,358	1.1	297,432	127.1
Uruguayan	18,804	0.1	56,884	0.1	38,080	202.5
Venezuelan	91,507	0.3	215,023	0.4	123,516	135
Other South American	57,532	0.2	21,809		-35,723	-62.1
Spaniard	100,135	0.3	635,253	1.3	535,118	534.4
All other Hispanic	6,111,665	17.3	3,452,403	6.8	-2,659,262	-43.5

Source: 2010 Census Briefs. *The Hispanic Population: 2010.* May 2011 http://www.census.gov/prod/cen2010/briefs/c2010br-04.pdfHispanicPopulation.xlsx

The Hispanic population is younger than whites, African Americans, and Asians, although differences exist within Hispanic groups. In 2004, the median age for Mexicans was 26.9, while for Cubans it was 40.6, a median age that is higher than the non-Hispanic white median age of 40.1. Other Central American groups had median ages from 28 to 29. South American groups had median ages from 31 to 35.[35] Hispanic youth (numbering 14 million in 2006)[36] constitute the largest ethnic segment (20%) of the under-18 population in the United States.

Hispanic families are larger, with a median household size of 3.4 versus 2.45 for the non-Hispanic white family. Mexicans have the highest average household size at 3.7. The lowest are Cubans at 2.7. The marriage rate of 49.6% is lower than the 53.5% for non-Hispanic whites. Hispanic households have a larger number of single-parent households, with 18.8% having a female head of house-

35 All data on Hispanic demographics are from the 2007 US Census, *The American Community—Hispanics: 2004,* and *American Community Survey Reports,* February.

36 US Census Bureau, 2009. Retrieved 12/20/11 from http://factfinder.census.gov.

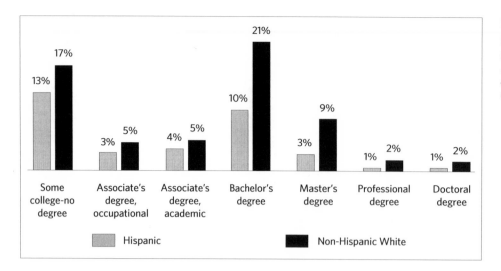

FIGURE 1-11. Hispanic Educational Attainment

Source: US Census Bureau. http://www .census.gov/hhes/socdemo/education/ data/cps/2010/tables.html Education byRace2010.xlsx

hold versus 8.9% for non-Hispanic whites, and 8.8% have a male head of household versus 3.5% for non-Hispanic whites. They have higher fertility rates of 75 per 1,000 women versus 50 per thousand for non-Hispanic whites. Hispanics out-marry in significant numbers, with nearly 20% marrying non-Hispanics.

The majority (96.2%) of non-Hispanic whites are native US citizens, compared with only 60.8% of Hispanic Americans. Approximately one-third of all other Hispanic groups, except Puerto Ricans (births in Puerto Rico are classified as native US births), are native US citizens. Of the foreign born, 45% entered the United States before 1990, 35% during the 1990s, and 20% in the year 2000 or later. The relatively recent immigration of most Hispanic Americans is a major reason for their lag in educational attainment. When coming to the United States, Hispanics have to grapple with a different language and social system. Because of this, Hispanics did not have the same growth rates in educational attainment as African Americans.

However, it is important not to discount the dynamism of minority populations. In 2010, an increase of 349,000 Hispanic students enrolled in college, bringing their total to 1.8 million, or 15% of the overall enrollment of 18- to 24-year-olds in two- or four-year colleges. In this age group, 31.9% of Hispanics were enrolled, as well as 38% of blacks, 43.3% of whites, and 62.2% of Asians.[37] The growth in the Hispanic population did not explain the entire increase in enrollment. The Pew His-

panic Center noted that Hispanic youth have increased their high school graduation rates from 70% to 73%. High unemployment in this age group was a factor in rising enrollment among blacks and Asians. However, Hispanics tend to favor community colleges, which accounted for 46% of their enrollment as compared with less than 30% for whites and Asians and less than 40% for blacks.[38] The low college completion rate of Hispanics reflects the lower educational attainment of immigrants. The rate of college completion for US-born Hispanics 25 to 29 years old is 20%, which is similar to the 19% for blacks.

The strong correlation between education and income is reflected in the Hispanic population. In 2010, the Hispanic median income of $39,539 was lower than non-Hispanic whites' median income of $68,961.[39] From 1990 to 2000, approximately 6% of Hispanics increased income from below $15,000 to higher levels. Almost 2% moved into income levels over $50,000 between 1990 and 2000. A 1% increase in this group occurred between 2000 and 2010; however, 4% of households fell to below $15,000. The 2008 recession had its greatest impact on middle-income Hispanic households.

While Hispanic income levels are 60% of those of non-Hispanic whites, it is important to note that Hispanic wealth (2009 median net worth $6,325) is one-eighteenth of non-Hispanic whites ($113,149).[40] Hispanics

37 Richard Fry, "24 Percent Growth from 2009 to 2010: Hispanic College Enrollment Spikes, Narrowing Gaps with Other Groups." Pew Hispanic Center, August 25, 2011. http://pewhispanic.org/ files/reports/146.pdf.

38 Ibid.

39 US Census Bureau, "Income." Retrieved 12/20/11 from http:// www.census.gov/hhes/www/income/data/historical/families/ index.html.

40 P. Taylor, R. Fry, and R. Kochhar, "Wealth Gaps Rise to Record Highs between Whites, Blacks, Hispanics." Pew Research Center,

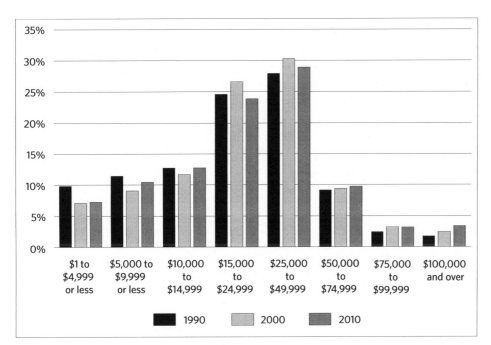

FIGURE 1-12. Hispanic Income Distribution

Source: US Census Bureau, 2010 http://www.census.gov/hhes/www/income/data/historical/household/index.html Household IncomebyRace.xlsx

Chart legend: 1990, 2000, 2010

X-axis categories: $1 to $4,999 or less | $5,000 to $9,999 or less | $10,000 to $14,999 | $15,000 to $24,999 | $25,000 to $49,999 | $50,000 to $74,999 | $75,000 to $99,999 | $100,000 and over

experienced a 66% drop in median net worth as compared to a 16% drop for whites between 2005 and 2009. More than one-third of Hispanic households had zero or negative net worth in 2009. Home ownership is the major component in net worth, and the median level of home equity for Hispanics fell from $99,983 in 2005 to $49,145 in 2009. The geographical concentration of Hispanics in California, Florida, Nevada, and Arizona, the states that suffered the steepest decline in housing values when the housing bubble burst in 2007, accounts for this drop.

Immigration

Approximately 63% of the Hispanic population comes from Mexico. Much of the Mexican-ancestry population preceded the English-speaking population in the Southwest, with Spanish-speaking settlers arriving in New Mexico as early as the 1600s, in Arizona and Texas in the late 1700s, and in California and Colorado in the early 1800s. These states continue to have high Hispanic populations, with 37.6% of Californians, 29.6% of Arizonians, 46% of New Mexicans, and 37.6% of Texans being Hispanic.

The Southwest experienced huge influxes of immigrants after the 1910 revolution in Mexico, providing the origins of the established Hispanic population. These set-

tlers moved into the Midwest in the 1920s, where the Hispanic population of Chicago began to grow. Since 1965, and particularly in the 1990s, Mexican immigration has grown, with most of that new population settling in the Southwest and West.

Puerto Ricans (4.6 million in 2010) account for 9.2% of the total US Hispanic population. They began settling in the United States after Spain ceded that island as a result of the Spanish-American War of 1898. The first major settlements occurred in New York City in the 1920s. A large migration occurred after World War II. New York drew the most, but by the 1960s, Puerto Ricans began moving to Connecticut, New Jersey, Pennsylvania, Illinois, Massachusetts, south Florida, and California.

Large Cuban immigration happened after Fidel Castro took power, and there have been continuing waves of Cuban immigrants, mostly into south Florida, New York, California, and New Jersey. Cubans account for one-third of Miami's population, and many of the top Hispanic businesses are Cuban-owned. Major Cuban communities can also be found in Chicago, New Orleans, and Atlanta.

Other than Mexico, the largest source of immigrants in the past two decades has been Central America. About a tenth of the population of El Salvador is estimated to have entered the United States beginning in the 1970s following internal strife and a major earthquake. Large numbers of Salvadorans live in Los Angeles, the San Francisco Bay area, New York City, and Washington, DC. Guatemalans followed the same pattern. Nicaraguans

July 26, 2011. http://pewsocialtrends.org/2011/07/26/wealth-gaps-rise-to-record-highs-between-whites-blacks-hispanics/.

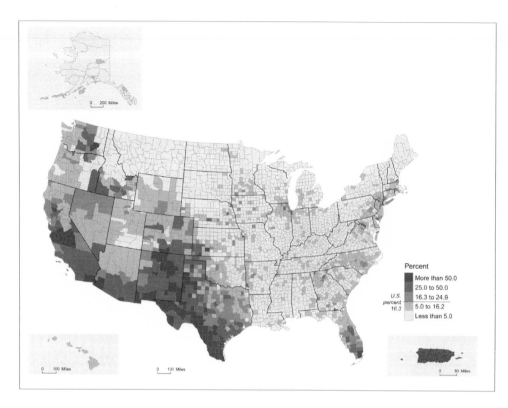

FIGURE 1-13. Hispanic or Latino Population as a Percent of Total Population by County, 2010

Source: US Census Bureau, May 2011. *The Hispanic Population: 2010.* http://www.census.gov/prod/cen2010/briefs/c2010br-04.pdf.

settled in Miami. Dominicans account for the single largest group of recent immigrants to New York City. Of South American immigrants, Colombians have also established a major presence in New York City and Miami.

Mexico continues to be the largest source of unauthorized immigrants, numbering 6.5 million of the total estimated 11.2 million in 2010 (down from a peak of 12 million in 2007). Other Latin American countries account for 23% (2.6 million) of unauthorized immigrants. Asia accounts for 11%, or 1.3 million. Europe, Canada, and Africa all account for fewer than 500,000 unauthorized immigrants. According to the Pew Hispanic Center, unauthorized immigrants made up 3.7% of the US population and 5.2% of its work force in 2010. Most of these workers have arrived since 1990 and provide crucial worker requirements in several sectors, including half the agricultural workforce and one-quarter of meat and poultry workers. The number of unauthorized workers declined in 2008 due to the recession and lack of work in the United States. Births to unauthorized immigrants (4% of the US population) accounted for 8% of all US newborns in 2009.[41]

41 J. Passel and D. Cohn, "Unauthorized Immigrant Population: National and State Trends, 2010." Pew Research Center, February 1, 2011. http://pewhispanic.org/files/reports/133.pdf.

Geographics

Like other minorities, the Hispanic population is concentrated in certain regions as depicted in Figure 1-13. About half of all Hispanics live in two states: California (31%) and Texas (19%). If New York, Florida, Illinois, Arizona, and New Jersey were added, the seven states would account for 77% of the US Hispanic population. With regard to subgroups, Mexicans are concentrated in California, Texas, Illinois, and Arizona; Puerto Ricans are in New York, Florida, New Jersey, and Pennsylvania; and the majority of Cubans are in Florida.

Facts contradict the stereotype of the Hispanic as a Spanish-speaking, rural laborer. Over 90% of Hispanics live in urban areas. The largest cities in the United States generally have the largest Hispanic populations. Their influence is particularly felt in Los Angeles, San Antonio, and El Paso, where they represent a large portion of these cities' populations.

The importance of the Hispanic vote gained special attention in 2004, when Hispanics were credited with swinging the presidential election. At least 12.2 million Hispanic voters are expected in the 2012 election, an increase of 26%, and they are expected to be 8.7% of US voters. Hispanic voters are 35% of New Mexico's

TABLE 1-5. Percent of Eligible Voters by Race/Ethnicity

	White	Hispanic	Black	Asian
Voting eligible	77.7%	42.7%	67.2%	52.8%
Noncitizen	1.4%	22.4%	4%	24%
Under 18	20.9%	34.9%	28.9%	23.3%

Source: M. Lopez, "The Latino Electorate in 2010: More Voters, More Non-Voters."
Pew Hispanic Center, 2011

TABLE 1-6. Hispanic Language Prevalence by Generation

	Language Prevalence		
	Spanish-Dominant	Bilingual	English-Dominant
First	72%	24%	4%
Second	7%	47%	46%
Third	0%	22%	78%

Source: Pew Hispanic Center, *Assimilation and Language*. http://pewhispanic.org/files/factsheets/11.pdf

voters, 26% of California's, 21% of Texas's, and 18% of Florida's.[42]

Hispanics have increasingly been involved in politics. According to the National Association of Latino Elected and Appointed Officials, there are more than 6,000 Hispanic elected officials, a 53% increase over the 15 years prior to 2011.[43] The bulk of these are local officials, with the largest number in Texas, California, and New Mexico. As of 2010, there were 21 Hispanic members of Congress and 3 senators. However, despite all these gains, Hispanic voters have the lowest proportion of eligible voters relative to population, due mainly to their youth and US citizenship status.[44]

Other Factors

Of all the racial and ethnic minority groups in the United States, Hispanics tend to have the largest families. Strong family values play an important role in the culture. For groups from Latin America, the Spanish conquest of some of their countries brought a colonial influence in religion (Roman Catholicism) and language. However, the indigenous Indian cultures (Maya, Inca, etc.) continue to permeate folk art, customs, and food.

According to the Pew Hispanic Center, the length of time Hispanics and their families have been in the United States is a key factor in their attitudes and behavior. About 40% of Hispanics are first generation or immigrants. Children of immigrants make up 29% of all Hispanics. The third generation is 31% of Hispanics. By 2020, demographers project that the second generation will be the largest segment at 36%. This second generation will fuel the workforce by adding 12.6 million workers by

2020, while the non-Hispanic labor force will increase by 11.6 million.[45]

Although recent immigrants and older people prefer to speak Spanish, most second- and third-generation Hispanics favor English. However, the proportion of second- and third-generation Hispanics who know Spanish is still high, as shown in Table 1-6. Marketers must also account for cultural differences in the Spanish language among the subgroups. For example, Hispanic food manufacturers promoting beans refer to "habichuelas" for Puerto Ricans and "frijoles" for Mexicans.

Second-generation Hispanics will drive population change in many ways. With increased English proficiency and acculturation, they will create more opportunities for themselves and the communities in which they live and work. Their educational attainment has increased compared to their first-generation counterparts as they attend college in greater numbers. Hispanic income levels have also risen, with the second generation earning more than the first generation. Like many other second-generation immigrants, 32% of second-generation Hispanics marry outside of their ethnicity, compared to 57% of the third generation and 7% of the first generation. Greater cultural fusion is on the horizon for the US population based on the sheer growth in numbers of second- and third-generation Hispanics.

Even with the acculturation of second- and third-generation Hispanics into the US population, Hispanics report that racial discrimination is a problem in their community. Although the proportion of Hispanics who experience personal discrimination is lower than for blacks, they experience discrimination at a significantly

42 National Association of Latino Elected Officials, "The 2012 Latino Vote: Turning Numbers into Clout." Retrieved 12/20/11 from http://www.naleo.org/latinovote.html.

43 National Association of Latino Elected Officials. Retrieved 12/20/11 from http://www.naleo.org/aboutnaleo.html

44 M. Lopez, "The Latino Electorate in 2010: More Voters, More Non-Voters." Pew Hispanic Center, April 26, 2011. http://pewhispanic.org/files/reports/141.pdf.

45 R. Suro and J. Passel, "The Rise of the Second Generation: Changing Patterns in Hispanic Population Growth." Pew Hispanic Center, October 14, 2003. http://pewhispanic.org/files/reports/22.pdf.

TABLE 1-7. Comparative Hispanic Consumer Spending

Item	All Consumer Units	Hispanic or Latino	All Consumer Units, Percent of Total	Hispanic or Latino, Percent of Total	Difference
Number of consumer units (in thousands)	120,847	14,295			
Average Annual Expenditures	$49,067	$41,981			
Food at home	$3,753	$3,784	7.6	9.0	**1.4%**
Food away from home	$2,619	$2,310	5.3	5.5	0.2%
Alcoholic beverages	$435	$267	0.9	0.6	-0.3%
Housing	$16,895	$15,983	34.4	38.1	**3.6%**
Shelter	$10,075	$10,043	20.5	23.9	**3.4%**
Utilities, fuels, and public services	$3,645	$3,532	7.4	8.4	**1.0%**
Household operations	$1,011	$714	2.1	1.7	-0.4%
Housekeeping supplies	$659	$517	1.3	1.2	-0.1%
Household furnishings and equipment	$1,506	$1,177	3.1	2.8	-0.3%
Apparel and services	$1,725	$2,002	3.5	4.8	**1.3%**
Transportation	$7,658	$7,156	15.6	17.0	**1.4%**
Health care	$3,126	$1,568	6.4	3.7	-2.6%
Entertainment	$2,693	$1,664	5.5	4.0	-1.5%
Personal care products and services	$596	$532	1.2	1.3	0.1%
Reading	$110	$36	0.2	0.1	-0.1%
Education	$1,068	$707	2.2	1.7	-0.5%
Tobacco products and smoking supplies	$380	$182	0.8	0.4	-0.3%
Miscellaneous	$816	$544	1.7	1.3	-0.4%
Cash contributions	$1,723	$1,015	3.5	2.4	-1.1%
Personal insurance and pensions	$5,471	$4,230	11.2	10.1	-1.1%

Source: Consumer Expenditure Survey, 2009. http://www.bls.gov/cex/csxann09.pdf
Note: Bold figures are larger expenditures as compared to general consumer.

higher rate than whites.[46] Hispanics who are less proficient in English also experience more discrimination.[47]

With respect to religious affiliation, according to the American Religious Identification Survey 2008, 59% of Hispanics identified as Catholic, down from 66% in 1990. Other Christian denominations totaled 21%.[48]

Purchasing Power

Purchasing power of Hispanics was estimated at over $1 trillion in 2010 by the Selig Center for Economic Growth.[49] Barring the lingering effects of the 2008 recession, as the proportion of households in middle and higher income groups increases, Hispanic purchasing power is projected to increase at a higher rate than the population as a whole, reaching $1.5 trillion by 2015, a 43% increase as compared to a 27% increase in total US buying power.

Even with lower incomes, Hispanics spend proportionately more on groceries, phone services, furniture, apparel, and footwear than the population as a whole. They spend less on alcohol, tobacco, health care, entertainment, education, and personal insurance than the population as a whole. A smaller proportion of Hispanics own their own homes (46.6%) as compared to 73.7% for non-Hispanic whites.[50]

Media

In 2009, there were 1,323 Spanish-language radio stations in the United States, up from 1,224 in 2008. Radio

46 Washington Post/Henry J. Kaiser Family Foundation/Harvard University, "National Survey on Latinos in America," conducted July–August 1999. www.kff.org/kaiserpolls/3023-index.cfm.
47 Ibid.
48 B. Kosmin and A. Keysar, *American Religious Identification Survey 2008*. Summary Report, March 2009. Hartford, CT: Trinity College.
49 Selig Center for Economic Growth, *The Multicultural Economy, 2010*. Athens, GA: Selig Center for Economic Growth.
50 US Census Bureau. "Housing." Retrieved 12/20/11 from http://www.census.gov/hhes/www/housing/hvs/historic/index.html.

has the strongest reach of all media, touching 95% of Spanish-dominant Hispanics and 93% of English-dominant Hispanics.[51] Hispanic men between 45 and 54 years of age spend the most time listening to radio at 18.34 hours per week. Hispanic men between 55 and 64 (18.26 hours) and those between 35 and 44 years of age (17.18 hours) are close behind. Hispanic women between 45 and 54 years of age spend 15.49 hours per week listening to radio. Top-ranked radio stations in Los Angeles and New York have over 2 million listeners.[52] Four in ten Hispanics who mostly speak English also listen to Spanish-language radio. A nationwide poll showed that they did so for sports, entertainment, a cultural connection, and because of the belief that English-speaking media outlets portray Hispanics in a negative light. Univision is a major media outlet with the largest number of Spanish-language viewers in the US according to 2012 Nielsen ratings. Other significant outlets include Bustos Media (28 stations), Entravision (48 stations), Liberman Broadcasting, Spanish Broadcasting System, LA Public Media, and LA> Forward.

According to Nielsen, Hispanic households comprised 40% of new TV households in the 2010–11 season. Television advertising to Hispanic households accounted for $4.3 billion in 2010, and it grew 10% from the previous year. Univision is a dominant force in Spanish-language television, reaching 95% of Hispanic television households. About a third of its programming is provided by the large Mexican company Televisa. The network's platforms include Univision, TeleFutura, Galavision Networks, Univision.com, Univision Movil, and Univision on Demand. Its top show has a rating of as high as 29.0 and helped Univision beat ABC, NBC, and CW in the 2010–11 season opening week. Univision was ranked the number three network for adults 18–34 years old.

Telemundo, a division of NBC Universal Media, LLC, reaches 94% of US Hispanic households. Telemundo is in 210 markets with 14 stations, 46 affiliates, and 1,000 cable affiliates. It also offers content through mobile platforms. Five years ago it began making its own tele-

novelas, or Spanish soap operas, and has grown to the second-largest producer of Spanish-language content behind the large Mexican company Televisa. The company has moved to multiplatform, and its telenovas can be accessed through mobile phones. Telemundo has entered into partnerships to distribute its telenovelas in Mexico and Asia. Telemundo also owns Mun2, which directly targets young Spanish- and English-speaking viewers. It has created a new format called the dramela, a drama in novella style about Hispanics who move comfortably in the Spanish and English worlds. Other television includes Azteca America (owned by Mexican broadcaster TV Grupo Azteca), Extrella TV, and LATV and V-me (a bilingual music and entertainment network).

At the end of 2010, there were 26 Hispanic daily newspapers,[53] down from 33 in 2007 and 38 in 2006 (circulation 1.02 million). There were 428 weekly Hispanic newspapers (circulation 11.08 million), up from 417 in 2007. The number of biweekly or monthly newspapers in 2010 was 378 (circulation 4.92 million), down from 381 in 2008. Only 40% of Hispanics read a Spanish-language newspaper, while 60% read an English-language newspaper. About 33% read Spanish-language magazines, and 56% read English-language magazines, varying with acculturation. There is still a high level of engagement with Hispanic publications among Hispanics of all ages. The largest US Hispanic magazine is *People en Español*. Most magazines are aimed toward women or entertainment.

Hispanic media is moving to multiplatform, which encompasses online and mobile to reach Hispanic consumers. Growth rates of Hispanics online are three times that of non-Hispanic whites. Higher rates are experienced for native-born, English-proficient, and younger Hispanics. Hispanics are more likely to engage in music and video streaming. Their number one activity is shopping online, and they are more likely to shop online than non-Hispanic whites. Facebook is the fourth-ranked website among Hispanics; they are more likely to have an online social network profile than non-Hispanic whites or blacks. Hispanics are four times more likely to have a Twitter account than non-Hispanic whites.

51 Center for Spanish Language Media, *The State of Spanish Language Media, 2010*. Denton: University of North Texas. http://spanish media.unt.edu/english/pages/researchresources.html.

52 *Advertising Age*, 2011, Hispanic Fact Pack 2011 Edition. http:// www.adagewhitepapers.com/adage/hispanicfactpack2011#pg1.

53 State of the Media, 2011, "Hispanic Media: Faring Better Than the Mainstream Media." Retrieved 12/20/11 from stateofthemedia .org/2011.

TABLE 1-8. Asian Population in the United States by Country of Origin

2004 Population	Population	Percent of Asian Alone Population
Chinese, except Taiwanese	2,829,627	23.4
Taiwanese	70,771	0.6
Asian Indian	2,245,239	18.6
Filipino	2,148,227	17.8
Vietnamese	1,267,510	10.5
Korean	1,251,092	10.3
Japanese	832,039	6.9
Other Asian	391,237	3.3
Laotian	226,661	1.9
Pakistani	208,852	1.7
Cambodian	195,208	1.6
Hmong	163,733	1.4
Thai	130,548	1.1
Indonesian	52,267	0.4
Bangladeshi	50,473	0.4
Sri Lankan	22,339	0.2
Malaysian	11,458	0.1

Source: US Census Bureau. *The American Community—Asians 2004* http://www.census.gov/prod/2007pubs/acs-05.pdf

ASIAN AMERICANS

Demographics

Asian Americans alone or in combination with another race numbered 17.3 million in 2010. This group experienced the fastest rate of growth of any demographic group between 2000 and 2010 at 43% and in 2010 accounted for 5.6% of the population. Asian Americans are projected to grow to 33.4 million, or 8% of the population, by 2050, a 413% increase as compared to 49% for the population as a whole. With regard to market size, consider also the adjacent Asian Canadian population of close to 4 million in 2006.[54] The largest segment of this group includes 1.3 million Chinese.

This is the most diverse of all racial/ethnic categories. Significant numbers of Asians immigrated from over 20 countries, with the Chinese ethnicity being the largest. Each group has a different history and cultural heritage. Unlike Hispanics, the groups do not even share a com-

mon language. Often their countries of origins experienced strained relations with or outright hostility toward one another in the past.

The median age of Asians in 2008 was 35.8, more than five years younger than the median age for non-Hispanic whites. Different from all the other groups, Asians are more likely to be married (62%) than non-Hispanic whites (57.3%). Birth rates for Asian women are much higher than non-Hispanic white women, with a high of 74 out of 1,000 versus 50 per 1,000 for non-Hispanic whites. More than one-third of Asian households do not speak English at home; Vietnamese households have the highest proportion of non-English speakers at 55.1%.[55]

The population has continued to put value on education, and their educational levels outpace the rest of the population, as shown in Figure 1-14.

Note that educational attainment varies across groups, with 68% of Indians and over 50% of Chinese and Koreans having bachelor's degrees or higher, but only 23.5% of Vietnamese, a rate that is lower than for non-Hispanic whites.[56]

Similarly, income levels are higher than those of non-Hispanic whites. Concentration of Asians in professional occupations accounts for their high incomes. In 2010, 20% of medical school graduates were Asian as compared to 6.7% black and 7.4% Hispanic.[57] Asians are 17% of scientists and engineers, or three times their proportion in the population.[58] For the most part, these individuals were first and second generation and part of the brain drain from places like Taiwan and India. Of the Asian American labor force in 2010, 49% of men and 46% of women were in managerial and professional occupations.[59]

Higher income levels are not consistent across all Asian groups. On the other end of the spectrum, Southeast Asian refugees from Vietnam, Cambodia, and Laos, without the endowment that East Asians have, struggle

54 Statistics Canada, 2009, "Visible Minority Population, by Age Group (2006 Census)." Retrieved 12/20/11 from http://www40.statcan.ca/l01/cst01/DEMO50A-eng.htm.

55 US Census Bureau, *The American Community—Asians 2004.* American Community Survey Report. February 2007.

56 Ibid.

57 Kaiser Family Foundation, "Distribution of Medical School Graduates by Race/Ethnicity, 2010." Retrieved 12/20/11 from http://www.statehealthfacts.org/comparetable.jsp?ind=454&cat=9.

58 National Science Foundation, "Women, Minorities, and Persons with Disabilities in Science and Engineering: 2011." Retrieved 12/20/11 from http://www.nsf.gov/statistics/wmpd.

59 US Census Bureau, "Race Data 2010." Retrieved 12/20/11 from http://www.census.gov/population/www/socdemo/race/ppl-aa10.html.

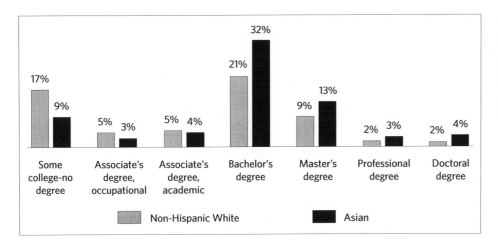

FIGURE 1-14. Asian American Educational Attainment

Source: US Census Bureau http://www.census.gov/hhes/socdemo/education/data/cps/2010/tables.html EducationbyRace2010.xlsx

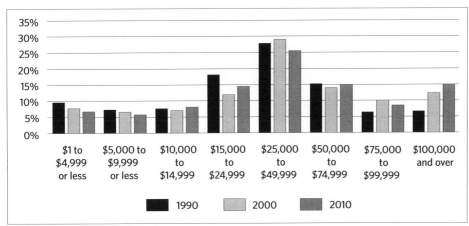

FIGURE 1-15. Asian American Household Income Levels

Source: US Census Bureau, 2010 http://www.census.gov/hhes/www/income/data/historical/household/index.html HouseholdIncomebyRace.xlsx

with adapting to the United States. Asian poverty rates are higher than whites for all age classes and particularly for those over 65, where the Asian poverty rate is 15% compared to 6% for non-Hispanic whites.

Immigration

The first Asian-American settlers were recorded in the 1700s. Workers from China were brought over in the 1800s to build railroads. Racist sentiment brought about exclusion laws that prohibited the immigration of Chinese people and gradually other Asians until after World War II. Even after exclusion laws were lifted, quotas continued to be levied on Asians, while there were no such quotas for immigrants from European countries. Immigration and the rejoining of families continue to be issues for most first-generation Asian Americans. Most Asian Americans are first generation. Only 24% of Asian Americans were born in the United States.

The Spanish-American war made the Philippines a colony/protectorate of the United States in 1898. Filipinos joined the American military and became workers for US military bases. Japanese workers were brought over in

the early 1900s, and immigration has been relatively small since then. Some Japanese women immigrated with their US military husbands after World War II. The Korean War brought a wave of immigrants from that country in the 1960s and 1970s, including children who were adopted by white families. The Chinese communist takeover sparked Chinese immigration from the 1960s onward, with another wave coming from Hong Kong in the 1970s. The Vietnam War brought Eurasian children of American military and created refugees from the war, particularly supporters of the US military who found it difficult, if not impossible, to live under communist rule. Economic, social, and political hardship prompted other groups to seek a better life in America, including South Asians from India and Pakistan. Their reasons for emigrating to the United States varied depending on the circumstances that they faced in their country of origin.

The earlier waves of Asian immigrants were low-wage workers who sought to escape war and economic hardship. In the 1970s, highly educated people who had the means to escape political turmoil immigrated to the

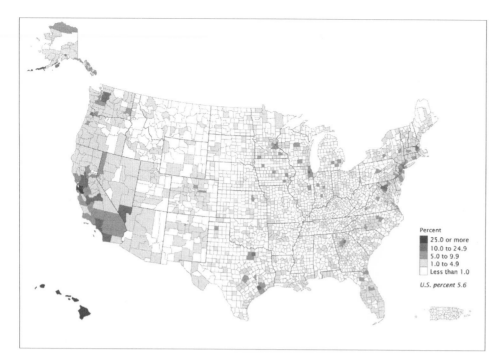

FIGURE 1-16. Asian as a Percentage of County Population, 2010

Source: US Census Bureau
http://www.census.gov/population/www/socdemo/race/Asian-slide-presentation.html

Percent
■ 25.0 or more
■ 10.0 to 24.9
■ 5.0 to 9.9
□ 1.0 to 4.9
□ Less than 1.0

U.S. percent 5.6

United States. Often they were college educated, owned businesses, or had wealth. The flight of these individuals from Asia was referred to as the "brain drain" as their emigration caused their home countries to lose highly educated human resources. Significant brain drain occurred, particularly with the immigration of Taiwanese and Indians. In 2007, approximately 69% of Indian Americans held four-year degrees as compared to 51% for East Asians and 30% for non-Hispanic whites. They were 3% of US engineers, 7% of IT workers, and 8% of doctors while accounting for only 1% of the population.[60]

Despite the long history of immigration, 38.2% of foreign-born Asians entered the United States on or after 2000.[61] In 2010, 61.6% of Asians were foreign born and 28.4% were not citizens.[62]

Geographics

Asian immigrants settled mainly on the west coast, in Hawaii, and in pockets in the Northeast (New York and New Jersey) and Midwest. Hawaii has the highest concentration, with 58% of the population being of Asian

descent, followed by California with 12%. California has attracted nearly one-third of Asian immigrants since 1980.

Of all the larger racial/ethnic groups, Asians are the least politically involved, perhaps because of the relatively larger proportion of noncitizens. There are 489 elected officials in the Asian Pacific American Political Database.[63] California has the largest number with 187. Hawaii is next with 97. On the national level, there were one senator and eight representatives in the 111th Congress.

Other Factors

Many of the countries from which Asian immigrants hail have histories and cultures significantly older than US history and culture. India is the birthplace of two world religions: Buddhism and Hinduism. Prior to the 1600s, China had preeminence over Europe and the rest of the world in science and government and consistently had the largest gross domestic product (GDP) for most years before 1800. It promises to regain that spot in the next decade. Many Asian countries were subject to European military and economic conquest in the 1800s. The United States was engaged in several conflicts of major dimensions, including World War II against the Japanese, the Korean War, the Vietnam War, which included Cambodia and Laos, and hostilities toward

60 J. Richwine, "Indian Americans: The New Model Minority," *Forbes Commentary*, February 24, 2009. Retrieved 12/20/11 from http://www.forbes.com/2009/02/24/bobby-jindal-indian-americans-opinions-contributors_immigrants_minority.html.

61 US Census Bureau, "Race Data 2010." Retrieved 12/20/11 from http://www.census.gov/population/www/socdemo/race/ppl-aa10.html.

62 Ibid.

63 Asian Pacific American Institute for Congressional Studies, "Asian Pacific American Political Database." Retrieved 12/20/11 from http://www.apaics.org/index.php/resources/database.

Communist China. These conflicts figure in mainstream attitudes toward Asian Americans and contribute to the stereotype of the perpetual foreigner. They also figure into the sensibilities and current circumstances of Asian Americans.

Internment of Japanese Americans during World War II significantly interrupted the growth of their businesses. Internment meant being relocated to camps where they could take and keep only what they could carry with them. Recent expressions of Cold War attitudes led the US government to falsely accuse Wen Ho Lee of spying for China in 1999. In 2006 the charges were found to be false. The government, as well as several large media outlets, paid his legal fees and provided compensation for damages.[64] But the stereotyping and projecting of his alleged conduct affected other Asian American scientists in high-security posts. Aside from understanding what these various groups have experienced, lessons learned from this information should be that the negative effects of pervasive racial bias and discrimination sometimes extend over many generations.

First-generation immigrants identify mainly with their country of origin and take great pains to preserve their culture with their families and communities. Immigrants from China number 2.8 million and, next to Mexico, China is the leading country of US foreign-born residents. Chinese, Japanese, Korean, Vietnamese, and Indian American communities preserve religions, language, and traditions within their own homes. In the past 20 years, Asian communities have increasingly created their own religious institutions, language schools, and commercial centers in highly concentrated areas. First-generation Asian Americans continue to partake in their home country's culture by watching Asian-language television, enjoying films and television shows from their home country via an extensive distribution system of videos, DVDs, or satellite, reading Asian-language newspapers that report on home country events, and listening to music from their home countries.

In all these cultures, the family continues to be the most important influence. Second-generation Asian Americans are discouraged from behaving like their white counterparts in terms of dating or experimenting with drugs. They are encouraged to value education, work hard, and respect their elders. The range of second-generation response has varied from outright rebellion to strict compliance.[65]

Asian Americans, particularly Japanese Americans, provide the best picture of cultural fusion among immigrants. As Japanese move into their third and fourth generations with limited immigration, the effects of acculturation are apparent. Multiple-race Asians account for 15.3% of the population of any Asian descent. The highest proportion occurs with Japanese and Filipino Americans. Despite this, there is a return to Japanese culture by third-generation and multiple-race Japanese Americans. Some want their children to learn the language. Others are very interested in learning music and cultural activities such as taiko drumming, while others have an interest in Japan itself.

With regard to religion, Asians constitute 20% of Muslims in the United States, 32% of Buddhists, and 88% of Hindus.[66] According to the American Religious Identification Survey 2008,[67] 17% of Asians are Catholics, and this constitutes the largest religious group in the Asian population. Protestant denominations total 21%.

Purchasing Power

Purchasing power of Asians is estimated at $544 billion in 2010 (a 98% gain from 2000) by the Selig Center for Economic Growth. This growth was second only to Hispanics at 108%. High education attainment and larger households explain more disposable income per capita for the group. During the 2008 recession, Asians were better able to retain their jobs and were therefore less impacted financially than other minority groups.

Asians tend to spend more on food, housing, clothing, education, and personal insurance compared to other ethnic or racial groups; they spend less on utilities, vehicles, alcohol and tobacco, health care, and entertainment.

Media

In 2007, Chinese was spoken in the home by 2.5 million Asian Americans (87% increase over 1990), Tagalog by 1.4 million (76% increase), Vietnamese by 1.2 million (138% increase), Korean by 1 million (70% increase),

---

64 P. Farhi, "US, Media Settle with Wen Ho Lee," *Washington Post*, A01, June 3, 2006.

65 Wesley Yang, "Paper Tigers: What Happens to All the Asian-American Overachievers When the Test-Taking Ends." *New York Magazine*, May 8, 2011.

66 Pew Forum on Religion and Public Life. "US Religious Landscape Survey." Retrieved 12/20/11 from http://religions.pewforum.org.

67 B. Kosmin and A. Keysar, *American Religious Identification Survey 2008, Summary Report*. March 2009. Hartford, CT: Trinity College.

TABLE 1-9. Asian Expenditures

Item	All Consumer Units	Asian	All Consumer Units, Percent of Total	Asian, Percent of Total	Difference
Number of consumer units (in thousands)	120,847	4,584			
Average Annual Expenditures	$49,067	$56,308			
Food at home	$3,753	$3,905	7.6	6.9	-0.7%
Food away from home	$2,619	$3,660	5.3	6.5	**1.2%**
Alcoholic beverages	$435	$350	0.9	0.6	-0.3%
Housing	$16,895	$20,395	34.4	36.2	1.8%
Shelter	$10,075	$13,571	20.5	24.1	**3.6%**
Utilities, fuels, and public services	$3,645	$3,270	7.4	5.8	-1.6%
Household operations	$1,011	$1,347	2.1	2.4	0.3%
Housekeeping supplies	$659	$536	1.3	1.0	-0.4%
Household furnishings and equipment	$1,506	$1,671	3.1	3.0	-0.1%
Apparel and services	$1,725	$2,150	3.5	3.8	0.3%
Transportation	$7,658	$8,784	15.6	15.6	0.0%
Health care	$3,126	$2,498	6.4	4.4	-1.9%
Entertainment	$2,693	$2,270	5.5	4.0	-1.5%
Personal care products and services	$596	$557	1.2	1.0	-0.2%
Reading	$110	$111	0.2	0.2	0.0%
Education	$1,068	$2,327	2.2	4.1	**2.0%**
Tobacco products and smoking supplies	$380	$122	0.8	0.2	-0.6%
Miscellaneous	$816	$611	1.7	1.1	-0.6%
Cash contributions	$1,723	$1,452	3.5	2.6	-0.9%
Personal insurance and pensions	$5,471	$7,117	11.2	12.6	**1.5%**

Source: *Average Annual Expenditures and Characteristics*. Consumer Expenditure Survey, 2009. http://www.bls.gov/cex/tables.htm 9/24/11

Note: Bold figures are larger expenditures as compared to general consumer.

and Japanese by 459,000 (7% increase). Chinese is the third most spoken language in the United States after English and Spanish. (Chinese is the most spoken language in the world[68] and is fast catching up to English as the number one language on the Internet. Spanish holds second place in terms of languages spoken in the world.)

New America Media lists 597 Asian media in its directory.[69] There are more than 139 entities that cover the Chinese community, 61 Filipino, 147 Korean, 50 Japanese, 97 Vietnamese, and 29 pan-Asian. Similar to mainstream print media, Asian media faced strong challenges to sustainability in 2009. *AsianWeek*, the only national pan-Asian, English-language newsweekly, was able to survive by moving to online only.

Major media survive because of large Asian parent companies. Two examples are the major Chinese-language newspapers *World Journal*, published by United Daily News in Taiwan with an unaudited circulation of 280,000, and *Sing Tao Daily*, headquartered in Hong Kong and serving mainly the San Francisco area with a circulation of 30,000. Relative larger local print media include the *Korean Journal*, headquartered in Houston, a Korean-language monthly with 97,000 circulation. Other print publications have much smaller circulations of 20,000 to 30,000.

Most Asian households have access to Asian-language television through cable or satellite connections. These may broadcast content produced in Asia.

68 Ethnologue, "Summary of Language Size." Retrieved 12/20/11 from http://www.ethnologue.org/ethno_docs/distribution.asp?by=size#2.

69 New America Media, *NAM National Ethnic Media Directory*. Retrieved 12/20/11 from http://news.newamericamedia.org/directory/sub_category.html?id=05622e11c9568c1aadc093ae9da75c07.

A Study of the Complexity of Cultural Markets

English-Language Media, Activism, and the Pan-Asian Community
(from *Northwest Asian Weekly*)

In 1982, Assunta Ng was volunteering for a Chinese radio station when she realized that the Asian community lacked access to information. At the time, there were no Chinese newspapers in the Pacific Northwest. Chinese immigrants were relying on San Francisco–based papers for news. Ng decided to create a Chinese-language newspaper for the Chinese community: the *Seattle Chinese Post*. Her first inclination was to set up the newspaper as a nonprofit. But she quickly learned that was a nonstarter as a basis for revenue generation or making a profit. So with just $20 for a business license, Ng launched a for-profit newspaper business. Within three months, the first issue was printed.

Other Asian groups (Japanese, Filipino, Vietnamese, Cambodian, Korean, and more) wanted a weekly paper that addressed the broader Asian community. In response, Ng established the *Northwest Asian Weekly*; it remains the only weekly English-edition newspaper serving Washington's Asian community. The two newspapers emphasize different content. After six years, Ng transitioned operations to a family-run business.

Similar to other small business owners, Ng faced many challenges as a woman entrepreneur. Although Ng was college educated and highly motivated, she did not have many strong community connections. However, through perseverance and dedication to serving the community, she began to establish herself as a leader in the Asian community. She also proved to be a savvy business owner. Within the first few years of operation, Ng had to make the decision to continue printing in black and white or convert to color. Because color printing was significantly more expensive, she opted for black and white. Instead she invested in her building, which is nestled in

the heart of Seattle's Chinatown/International District. Ng wanted to create a comfortable work environment and a place of which the community could be proud. After about ten years in business, Ng added red print to the newspaper. In the Asian culture, red symbolizes good luck. She eventually converted to full color in 2002.

Ng continues to support the local community. In 1994, she founded the Northwest Asian Weekly Foundation, which provides a summer youth leadership program and diversity scholarships for high school students. In addition to her foundation, Ng hosts about eight events each year to honor women and others who have broken the glass ceiling. She is passionate about connecting people; she strives to meet three new people at each event. The newspaper has enabled her to build many bridges in the community.

After 30 years, Ng has built sufficient community support to sustain both newspapers. She still finds each day challenging but "takes every hurdle as an opportunity." Ng empowers her employees: "Everyone is a generalist, not a specialist." She brainstorms with her team to solve problems, and employees are not limited by their title or role. The *Northwest Asian Weekly* has earned a reputation for being fair, and it often runs stories not covered in mainstream papers, including political stories and issues related to the Asian community, with one simple goal: to empower the Asian community.

US-based Asian-language television concentrates in the California, New York, and Hawaii (mainly Honolulu) markets.

According to the 2009 New America Media survey,[70] only 15% of Asian Americans listen to Asian-language radio. A high proportion of Asians (67.8%) have access to the Internet, and they tend to go to overseas sites to look at Asian content. China Gateway, Sina, and Sohu are three online portals with social networking, news, videos, and entertainment. Hip young Asian Americans like the group Wong Fu have been able to develop a young, English-language following on YouTube.

AMERICAN INDIANS AND ALASKA NATIVES

When Columbus "discovered" the Americas, it was estimated that there were several million (ranging from 2 to 7 million) indigenous people in North America. Since Europeans started settling in the Americas, American Indians have faced military violence, subjugation, epidemics (many brought by the European settlers, including smallpox, which decimated tribes), and governmental policies aimed at terminating their way of life. At the beginning of the twentieth century, American Indians numbered a few hundred thousand and were predicted to vanish by 1935.

The American Indian tribes are sovereign entities. This is inherent within the tribes and was recognized by the European colonists and later by the US government in the Constitution. Indian tribes have their own lands, cultures, languages, and governments. Tribes fought for decades to regain their right of self-governance as sovereign nations. For the most part, the federal government (principally the Bureau of Indian Affairs [BIA]) has been the primary decision maker for the tribes and for their land and resources. As a result of treaties signed with the Indian tribes, the US government held the lands of the tribes in trust. Over the past 200 years, much of the land has been lost by federal government policies and practices. In particular, until its repeal in 1934, the 1887 Indian General Allotment Act resulted in 90 million acres of the best lands in the 134 million acres held in trust for American Indians to be passed on to non-Indian owners.[71]

Seizures of their lands and other Indian assets brought about economic deprivation among American Indians. Mismanagement of the assets held in trust and outright fraud by the government and other parties has led to a ruling and court order for the government to properly account for the estimated $5 billion in payments due individual Indians for the use of their land held in trust by the US government.[72] It is not just the economic value of the land that is at stake. The crucial role that tribal lands play in the core of a tribe's identity is demonstrated by the dispute over the Black Hills of North Dakota. The Lakota tribes turned down money that now totals more than $400 million for the wrongful alienation of their lands, instead holding out for the return of their sacred Black Hills. This is especially telling when it is pointed out that the Lakota tribes live on the Pine Ridge Reservation, which sits in one of the poorest counties in the United States.

Racism has taken its toll on American Indians in a variety of ways. Genocide in the form of forced relocation under inhumane conditions occurred in the 1800s. Prohibiting the use of tribal languages in American Indian schools and expunging many other forms of their culture were common policies in the 1900s. For example, in the 1950s the US government adopted a policy of termination in which Indian children were forcibly removed from their families to "assimilate" them. These children were beaten if they spoke their own language and were put in Christian schools where they were not allowed to practice their own religions. Indians were encouraged to marry outside of their race, and incidents of sterilization were documented. The policy of termination resulted in the loss of 100 tribes. Additionally, federal programs deprived the tribes of sufficient funding for education and crime prevention while cultivating a culture of dependency.[73]

Since the mid-1960s, in response to the civil rights movement in which American Indians fought with other

---

70 New America Media, *National Study on the Penetration of Ethnic Media in America,* 2009. Downloaded 9/24/11 from http://media .namx.org/polls/2009/06/National_Study_of_the_Penetration_ of_Ethnic_Media_June_5_2009_Presentation.pdf.

71 Harvard Project on American Indian Economic Development, *The State of the Native Nations: Conditions under U.S. Policies of Self-Determination.* New York: Oxford University Press, 2008.

72 *Cobell v. Salazar Settlement.* Retrieved 12/20/11 from indiantrust .com.

73 Harvard Project on American Indian Economic Development, *The State of the Native Nations: Conditions under U.S. Policies of Self-Determination.* New York: Oxford University Press, 2008.

TABLE 1-10. American Indian Population by Tribe and Groups of Tribes

	Percent of Group
Cherokee	15.4
Navajo	10.7
Chippewa	4.3
Pueblo	3.2
Apache	3.1
Sioux	3.1
Lumbee	2.8
Choctaw	2.6
Iroquois	2.4
Pima	2.3
Alaska Native	5.2

Source: US Census Bureau. *The American Community—American Indians and Alaska Natives 2004*

minorities for their rights, the government has adopted a policy of self-determination and self-governance. After more than a century of broken treaties and ineffective government policies plunged the tribes into poverty, destroyed their culture and identity, put their communities into disarray, disrupted their families, and dismantled their governments, many American Indian tribes are rebuilding their nations. Hundreds of distinct Indian nations continue to survive and grow in Indian Country.

In the 21st century efforts have increased to gain formal recognition of the racism and injustices imposed on American Indians. But a formal apology by the head of the BIA in 2000 is about as far as the government has gone to make amends for centuries of racism practiced against them.

As of the 2010 census, there were 5.2 million American Indians and Alaska Natives alone or in combination with other races and 2.9 million declaring American Indian and Alaska Native alone. Many tribes cross the Canadian border, and adjacent Canada's aboriginal population of 1.17 million enlarges the market.[74]

Demographics

The American Indian population consists of more than 565 federally recognized tribes and a number of other tribes yet to get official recognition.[75] Tribal membership ranges from 330,000 to a few members. American Indians identify strongly with their tribes, and there are major differences in culture, language, and governing structures across tribes. The ten largest tribal groupings as of 2004 are shown in Table 1-10.

The population has shown rapid growth, due in part to persons acknowledging their American Indian heritage. The inclusion of one or more race on the 2000 census also allowed individuals to fully disclose their heritage. American Indian and Alaska Natives report the highest proportion (43%) of multiple race.

In 2004, the median age of American Indian and Alaska Natives was 31.9 years, about eight years younger than non-Hispanic whites. About 30% of American Indians and Alaska Natives were under 18 in 2004 compared to 22% of non-Hispanic whites They were less likely to be married or ever married (42%) as compared to non-Hispanic whites (57.3%) and more likely to be divorced or separated than whites. Native women have higher birth rates compared to non-Hispanic whites; 46% of women who gave birth were unmarried as compared to 20% of non-Hispanic whites. There were more than twice as many single-parent households and more women heads of household than non-Hispanic whites. Three times as many households had grandparents living with grandchildren, and 58% of grandparents were responsible for their care, compared to 45% of non-Hispanic whites.

American Indians and Alaska Natives (AIANs) have half the proportion of population with a bachelor's degree as compared to non-Hispanic whites. Educational attainment lags that of the general population mainly because federal educational spending has lagged that of the general population. Without a tax base and increased dependence on federal government funding, tribes have been allocated half the funding typically necessary for educational needs. Additionally, educational institutions do not understand the needs of American Indian students, causing low retention rates. About a third of American Indians drop out before attaining a high school education, a rate one and a half times higher than other minorities. Indian children are more likely to be in single-parent families, and Indian youth are 17 times more likely to suffer alcohol-related deaths. The suicide rate is 130% of the national rate. Teen pregnancies are 180% of the national rate.[76]

74 Statistics Canada, "Aboriginal Identity Population." Retrieved 12/20/11 from http://www40.statcan.ca/l01/cst01/DEMO60A-eng.htm.
75 Bureau of Indian Affairs. Retrieved 12/20/11 from www.bia.gov.

76 Harvard Project on American Indian Economic Development, *The State of the Native Nations: Conditions under U.S. Policies of Self-Determination*. New York: Oxford University Press, 2008.

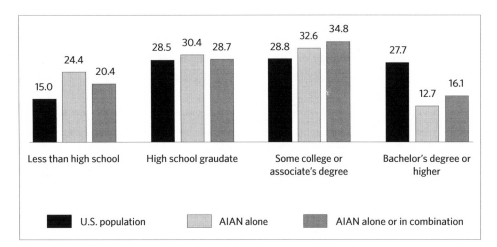

FIGURE 1-17. American
Indian and Alaskan Native
Educational Attainment
Source: American Community Survey.

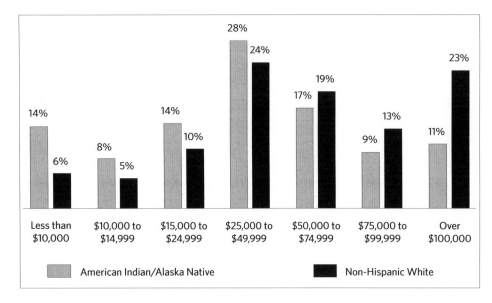

FIGURE 1-18. American
Indian Household Income
Source: *American Community Survey
2005–2009*, Table B19001C http://
factfinder.census.gov/servlet/DTSubject
ShowTablesServlet?_lang=en&_ts=
335587740064 AIANIncome.xlsx

With more self-government, the tribes have taken control of half the BIA schools. Initial results show better performance and retention with the culturally sensitive curriculum and high-quality education. Enrollment in higher education doubled between 1976 and 2006.[77] In 2006, 26% of college-aged AIANs were enrolled in college versus 41% for non-Hispanic whites. More AIANs received bachelor's degrees (45.7%) than two-year degrees (35.7%) in 2006. American Indians have increased the rate of college graduation from 9% of the population in 1990 to over 14% in 2010. The gender gap is 21 percentage points among AIANs with 61% female and 39% male, second only to blacks with 30%.

In response to the high college dropout rates for American Indians, tribally operated colleges were created. There are now 32 tribal colleges with about 17,000 students in 2006 or 79% of total enrollment, up from 2,100 students in 1982.[78] The bulk of tribal colleges are two-year institutions with seven four-year institutions. They offer two-year degrees in over 200 disciplines and 200 vocational certificate programs. Evidence shows that tribal colleges are increasing employment rates and success in four-year institutions for American Indian students.

Native household income is lower than that of the US population. American Indian median household income in 2010 was $30,693 as compared to $41,994 for the US population. American Indians suffer poverty rates of 23.2%, which is equivalent to the rate for African Americans and more than twice that for white Americans

77 National Center for Education Statistics, *Status and Trends in Education of American Indian and Alaska Natives: 2008*. Washington, DC: NCES. http://nces.ed.gov/pubs2005/2005108.pdf.

78 American Indian Higher Education Consortium. Retrieved 12/20/11 from http://www.aihec.org/colleges/TCUroster.cfm.

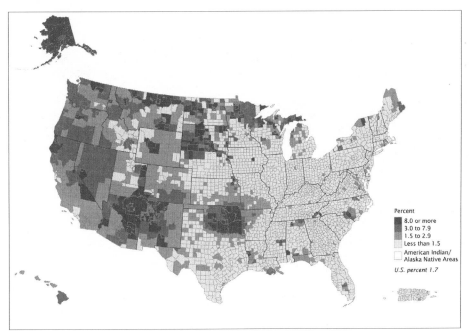

FIGURE 1-19. American Indian and Alaska Native as a Percentage of County Population, 2010

Source: US Census Bureau
http://www.census.gov/population/www/socdemo/race/AIAN-slide-presentation.html

(10%). Poverty rates are particularly high for the population under 18. Median income and poverty levels can vary tremendously among tribes. The small number of tribes with gaming compacts near major metropolitan areas has met economic success, while those far from population centers continue to seek other means to escape poverty.

It is estimated that of the 100 most populous tribes, about one-third of the people have knowledge of their native language. There are roughly 150 languages currently spoken or that could still be revived. Of the American Indian and Alaska Native tribes, the Navajo, Pueblo, Apache, and Eskimo are least likely to speak English at home.

Geographics

About 36% of individuals who identify themselves as American Indians or Alaska Natives live on reservations or trust lands. Historically, reservations have higher rates of unemployment, poverty, health problems, and crime than other communities. This disparity can be attributed to a lack of resources. American Indian reservations are typically allocated half or substantially less than half of the health dollars, law enforcement, etc. than the general population and less than amounts guaranteed in treaties signed with the federal government.

The highest concentrations of non-reservation American Indians are in the central and western United States. California ranks first as the state with the most American Indians. Half of all American Indians live in California, Oklahoma, Arizona, New Mexico, and Washington, as shown in Figure 1-19.

The sovereignty of the tribes necessitates American Indian involvement in many levels of politics. Many tribes are governed by tribal councils, which are evolving with the integration of traditional tribal governing structures. Some traditional tribal structures are close to the US political structure (with a central constitution), while others are not. The Harvard American Indian Project[79] found that when the governing structure emulates a more traditional structure, governance tends to be more successful.

Other Factors

The tribes continue to fight the effects of the policies and actions against them. According to the Centers for Disease Control and Prevention, Office of Minority Health, Native people have the highest rate of Sudden Infant Death Syndrome, twice that of all other groups. They have the second highest diabetes death rate after African Americans. They have twice the death rate from chronic liver disease and cirrhosis of all other populations. The Office of Minority Health cites cultural barriers, geographic isolation, inadequate sewage disposal,

---

79 Harvard Project on American Indian Economic Development, *The State of the Native Nations: Conditions under U.S. Policies of Self-Determination.* New York: Oxford University Press, 2008.

and low income as issues with which AIANs must contend.[80]

Purchasing Power

American Indian buying power is estimated at $67.7 billion in 2010, a 69% growth rate since 2000. Ten states account for most of the purchasing power: California ($9.7 billion), Oklahoma ($6.5 billion), Texas ($4.9 billion), Arizona ($4.2 billion), New Mexico ($2.9 billion), Washington ($2.6 billion), Florida ($2.6 billion), North Carolina ($2.5 billion), Alaska ($2.5 billion), and New York ($2.4 billion).

Media

Six hundred tribal newspapers and nearly 40 tribal radio stations comprise the media within the American Indian population. There are two national newspapers. They provide an important function in giving voice to American Indian values, concerns, and lives. Native radio stations often broadcast in English and in the native language of the tribe. Given the portrayal of American Indians in mainstream media, they are essential to providing a balanced picture.

NATIVE HAWAIIANS AND PACIFIC ISLANDERS

Similar to American Indians, Native Hawaiian people faced decimation by the influx of white settlers. In 1778 when Captain Cook arrived in Hawaii, it was estimated that between 400,000 and 800,000 people inhabited the islands. The Hawaiian monarchy was overthrown by US naval forces in 1893 and was annexed in 1898 mainly due to its attractiveness in producing sugar. By 1900, the pure Native Hawaiian population had declined to 29,800, with 7,800 of mixed heritage, due to the introduction of cholera, measles, whooping cough, influenza, leprosy, and tuberculosis—diseases for which the Native Hawaiians had no immunity. Although historical wrongs have been meted to the Native Hawaiians, unlike American Indians they do not have recognition as a sovereign people.[81] In fact, a 2000 court ruling questioned the status, rights, and protection of Native Hawaiians. The issue of one-half blood quantum to define native Hawaiians as defined by the Hawaiian Homes Commission Act of 1921 has undermined Hawaiian sovereignty.[82]

As of 2008, Pacific Islanders alone, or in combination with other races, numbered 1.1 million. Polynesians, which are composed of Native Hawaiians, Samoans, and Tongans, form the largest group, followed by Micronesians (largely from Guam). According to 2008 National Population Estimates, the population is projected to grow to 2.38 million in 2050.[83]

In 2008, Pacific Islanders had a median age of 29.1 (in combination with other races, the median age was 27.7), about 11 years younger than non-Hispanic whites. They are less likely than non-Hispanic whites to marry, and they are more likely to be divorced or separated. Pacific Islander women have a higher fertility rate and are also less likely to be married than non-Hispanic whites. Pacific Islanders are more likely to be in family and single-parent households than non-Hispanic whites. They are four times more likely to have grandchildren in the household.[84]

Pacific Islanders are more likely to be native US-born simply because those born in Guam, American Samoa, and the Commonwealth of the Northern Mariana Islands are considered native-born Americans. About 42% speak a language other than English at home as compared to 6% for non-Hispanic whites. For Pacific Islanders, 15.4% have bachelor's degrees, about half the rate of 29.7% for non-Hispanic whites. They are less likely to be in management and professional occupations than non-Hispanic whites. In 2008, the Pacific Islander median income for employed full-time, year-round workers 16 and older was $38,762 as compared to the median income of $45,556 for the US population.[85] The poverty rate (18.1% for Pacific Islanders) was twice that of non-Hispanic whites (8.8%) in 2008. Only 46.4% owned their own homes as compared to 73.9% for non-Hispanic whites. About 39% of inmates in Hawaiian jails are Native Hawaiians, which is disproportionate to their 24% proportion of the state pop-

80 Office of Minority Health, "American Indian/Alaska Native Profile." Retrieved 12/20/11 from http://minorityhealth.hhs.gov/templates/browse.aspx?lvl=2&lvlID=52.

81 Office of Hawaiian Affairs, *Hawaiian History Timeline*. Retrieved 12/20/11 from http://www.oha.org/pdf/HwnHistoryTimeline.pdf.

82 J. Kehaulani Kauanui, *Hawaiian Blood: Colonialism and the Politics of Sovereignty and Indigeneity*. Durham, NC: Duke University Press, 2008.

83 US Census Bureau, 2007, *The Native Hawaiian and Other Pacific Island Population in the US*. Retrieved 12/20/11 from http://www.census.gov/population/www/socdemo/race/NHPI-slide-presentation.html8.

84 US Census Bureau, 2007, *The American Community—Pacific Islanders: 2004*. American Community Survey Report.

85 US Census Bureau, 2007, *The Native Hawaiian and Other Pacific Island Population in the US*. Retrieved 12/20/11 from http://www.census.gov/population/www/socdemo/race/NHPI-slide-presentation.html8.

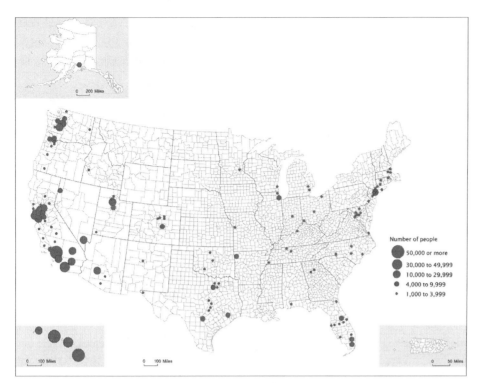

FIGURE 1-20. Native Hawaiian and Other Pacific Islander Alone or in Combination by County, 2010

Source: US Census Bureau
http://www.census.gov/population/www/socdemo/race/NHPI-slide-presentation.html

ulation. Controlling for other factors, Native Hawaiians are much more likely to get a prison sentence than almost all other groups except for Native Americans.[86]

In comparison to other groups, Native Hawaiians/Pacific Islanders have higher rates of smoking, alcohol consumption, and obesity. They have little access to cancer prevention and control programs. Some leading causes of death include cancer, heart disease, unintentional injuries (accidents), stroke, and diabetes. Other health conditions prevalent among Native Hawaiians and Pacific Islanders are hepatitis B, HIV/AIDS, and tuberculosis, which occur at a rate 21 times higher than for non-Hispanic whites.[87]

There has been a net migration of native Hawaiians outside of Hawaii. Most have settled on the West Coast, with high concentrations in California, Washington, and Texas (see Figure 1-20).

MULTIPLE RACE

Multiple race group identity only recently received official recognition. Yet this group provides substantial diversity,

TABLE 1-11. Percent of Groups in the Multiple Race Population

White	3
Black	7
American Indian Alaska Native	44
Asian	15
Native Hawaiian Pacific Islander	56
Some Other Race	12

Source: US Census Bureau.

richness, and numbers of multiple heritage people in the US population. Interracial marriage (illegal in some states until 1967) has resulted in the explosive growth of a multiple-race population. The 2010 census, the first to allow the complexity of multiple races, counted 9 million people who self-identify as more than one race. Multiracial individuals account for more than 3% of the population but 5.9% of people under the age of 18. As previously stated, it is estimated that over one-third of blacks are of multiple-race heritage, and US history shows documentation of accepted interracial marriages going back as far as the 1600s.[88]

86 Justice Policy Institute, "The Disparate Treatment of Native Hawaiians in the Criminal Justice System." September 28, 2010. http://www.oha.org/images/stories/files/pdf/reports/es_final_web.pdf.

87 Office of Minority Health, "Native Hawaiians and Pacific Islanders Profile." Retrieved 12/20/11 from http://minorityhealth.hhs.gov/templates/browse.aspx?lvl=2&lvlID=71.

88 Audrey Smedley, "The History of the Idea of Race . . . and Why It Matters." Paper presented at the conference "Race, Human Variation, and Disease: Consensus and Frontiers," American Anthropological Association, Warrenton, Virginia, March 14–17, 2007.

Native Americans, Alaska Natives, and Native Hawaiians show a particularly high proportion of mixed race, which may be due to policies such as termination, which encouraged American Indians to marry outside of their race. Among American Indians, 44% of the population consists of multiple races, with white in combination with American Indian being the largest group. Hawaiians show an even higher proportion, with 56% of the population reporting multiple-race heritage. The states of Hawaii and California, both minority-majority states (only 27% of Hawaii's population is white, while 25% of California's population is non-Hispanic white), provide a glimpse of the multiracial future. Native Hawaiians have intermarried with Asians and whites. The term *hapa*, used to describe individuals of multiple race or ethnicity, was first coined in Hawaii.

Inter-ethnic marriages and pairings are increasing and create more complexity in the cultural landscape. The Pew Research Center estimates that 14.5% of marriages were between spouses of different races or ethnicity in 2008.[89] There are gender differences, with more black males and Asian females marrying outside of their race. First-generation immigrants are less likely to marry outside of their race as compared to second and third generations. The trend is expected to continue with more accepting attitudes toward race, the upward mobility of many minorities, and increased opportunity for social contact. The Pew study shows that acceptance of interracial marriages is 81% for whites, 75% for Asians, 73% for Hispanics, and 66% for blacks.

This breadth, magnitude, and speed of cultural fusion is likely unprecedented in any other country and society. Previously interracial marriage with the dominant white culture was seen as a measure of assimilation. By marrying into the majority culture the minority adopted its norms. More interracial marriages signaled greater assimilation. Increasing evidence points to a different phenomenon in the United States with the fading of the dominant culture. Increasingly it is recognized that acculturation or the mutual influence of cultures upon each other exists. Minority cultures are not subsumed by the majority. This has borne itself out in multiple-race individuals seeking to be connected to all their heritages,

not just their white heritage. It is also evidenced by trans-racially adopted children seeking their (often Asian) roots. It is manifest in third-generation immigrants wanting to retain their native languages or cultures.

Psychological studies have also shown that mixed-race children are better adjusted and suffer less stress when they accept all their heritages.[90]

According to the Selig Center for Economic Growth, 2010 purchasing power for the multiracial population was $115 billion, and it grew 94% in the previous decade. It is expected to grow to $164.6 billion in 2015. New York, California, and Florida have the largest multiracial populations.

CULTURE AND MARKETS

The influence of culture on interactions between businesses and customers is an important consideration as marketplaces continue to diversify.[91] Since ethnicity is a broad dimension of culture (including national origin, language, cultural heritage, and religion), it poses many challenges for business owners that are not attuned to diverse customer needs. Ethnic customers may respond differently to marketing campaigns compared to non-ethnic customers; businesses should have the cultural competence and resources to address ethnic customers' needs. A key component of this competence is to understand how ethnic customers commonly identify with and respond to individuals who are from their ethnic group and with whom they have a shared ethnicity.

Montoya and Briggs[92] conducted research with a sample of Asians, Hispanics, and Caucasians to understand how shared ethnicity affects marketplace exchanges between businesses and ethnic customers. When studying culture, researchers often classify groups based on the individualism-collectivism dimension (discussed in Module 3). For example, people of Western cultures, such as US Caucasians, are considered to be more *individualist,* with an emphasis on individual differentiation. On the other hand, Hispanics and Asians are typically considered *collectivists.* Collectivists define themselves

89 J. Passel, W. Wang, and P. Taylor, "Marrying Out: One-in-Seven New U.S. Marriages Is Interracial or Interethnic," June 4, 2010. Pew Research Center. http://pewresearch.org/pubs/1616/american-marriage-interracial-interethnic.

90 D. Bowles, "Bi-racial Identity: Children Born to African-American and White Couples," *Clinical Social Work Journal*, vol. 21, no. 4 (1993): 417–28.

91 Detra Y. Montoya and Elten Briggs, "Shared Ethnicity Effects on Service Encounters: A Study across Three U.S. Subcultures," *Journal of Business Research,* forthcoming.

92 Ibid.

based on the groups to which they belong and emphasize their connectedness to others. The studies conducted showed that this important cultural distinction can influence ethnic customer expectations and actual service encounter experiences under conditions of shared ethnicity.

Montoya and Briggs's results provide preliminary evidence of important patterns of ethnic customer responses in their studies. They report that:

1. Respondents representing collectivist groups (e.g., Asians and Hispanics) often expected more favorable service experiences when they shared ethnicity with a contact employee, compared to customers from individualist groups (e.g., Caucasian).
2. Asian and Hispanic respondents reported feelings of comfort and fondness during service exchanges when they shared ethnicity with a customer contact employee more often than Caucasian respondents.

3. Asian and Hispanic respondents reported receiving tangible benefits such as discounts and free products when they shared ethnicity with a customer contact employee more often than Caucasian respondents.
4. Regardless of ethnic group membership, respondents expressed loyalty to a business after having a service encounter involving an employee of the same ethnicity.

These results provide evidence that shared ethnicity is an important factor in a diverse marketplace. Business owners should be aware of cultural norms of behavior, especially related to the individualism-collectivism dimension. Businesses should consider hiring employees from the ethnic groups they are targeting and offering cultural training for their employees. Effectively addressing the needs of ethnic customers can be beneficial to both the business (increased loyalty) and customer (enhanced experience).

REFERENCES

General Sources

New America Media. *NAM National Ethnic Media Directory.* http://news.newamericamedia.org/directory/sub_category.html?id=05622e11c9568c1aadc093ae9da75c0.

Office of Minority Health. http://minorityhealth.hhs.gov/.

Selig Center for Economic Growth. 2010. *The Multicultural Economy, 2010.* Athens, GA: Selig Center for Economic Growth.

US Census Bureau. *Race Data 2010.* http://www.census.gov/population/www/socdemo/race/ppl-aa10.html.

Yearbook of Immigration Statistics. 2003. http://www.dhs.gov/files/statistics/publications/YrBk03Im.shtm, downloaded 9/24/11.

Yearbook of Immigration Statistics. 2010. http://www.dhs.gov/files/statistics/publications/LPR10.shtm, downloaded 9/24/11.

Black

National Conference of Black Mayors. http://ncbm.org/2009/04/our-mission.

US Census Bureau. *The American Community—Blacks: 2004.*

White House Initiative on Historically Black Colleges and Universities. http://www2.ed.gov/about/inits/list/whhbcu/edlite-index.html.

Hispanic

Center for Spanish Language Media. 2010. *The State of Spanish Language Media 2010.* Denton: University of North Texas. http://spanishmedia.unt.edu/english/pages/researchresources.html.

Humes, K. R., N. A. Jones, and R. R. Ramirez. 2011. *Overview of Race and Hispanic Origin: 2010.* 2010 Census Briefs. March. http://www.census.gov/prod/cen2010/briefs/c2010br-02.pdf.

National Association of Latino Elected Officials. 2012. *The 2012 Latino Vote: Turning Numbers into Clout.* http://www.naleo.org/latinovote.html.

US Census Bureau. *The American Community—Hispanics: 2004.*

Pew Hispanic Center

Fry, Richard, "24 Percent Growth from 2009 to 2010: Hispanic College Enrollment Spikes, Narrowing Gaps with Other Groups." Pew Hispanic Center. August 25, 2011. http://pewhispanic.org/files/reports/146.pdf.

Lopez, Mark Hugo, "The Latino Electorate in 2010: More Voters, More Non-Voters." Pew Hispanic Center. April 26, 2011. http://pewhispanic.org/files/reports/141.pdf.

Passel, Jeffrey, and D'Vera Cohn, "Unauthorized Immigrant Population: National and State Trends, 2010."

Pew Research Center. February 1, 2011. http://pew
hispanic.org/files/reports/133.pdf.

Pew Hispanic Center and Kaiser Family Foundation, *2002
National Survey of Latinos.*

Suro, Roberto, and Jeffrey Passel, "The Rise of the Second
Generation: Changing Patterns in Hispanic Population
Growth." Pew Hispanic Center. October 14, 2003.
http://pewhispanic.org/files/reports/22.pdf.

Taylor, Paul, Richard Fry, and Rakesh Kochhar, "Wealth
Gaps Rise to Record Highs between Whites, Blacks,
Hispanics." Pew Research Center. July 26, 2011.
http://pewsocialtrends.org/2011/07/26/wealth-
gaps-rise-to-record-highs-between-whites-blacks-
hispanics/.

Washington Post/Henry J. Kaiser Family Foundation/
Harvard University. *National Survey on Latinos in America.* Conducted in July and August 1999. www.kff.org/
kaiserpolls/3023-index.cfm.

Asian

Lai, Eric, and Dennis Arguelles, eds. *The New Face of Asian
Pacific America. AsianWeek,* with UCLA Asian American Studies Center Press, 2003.

US Census Bureau. *The American Community—Asians
2004.*

American Indian—Alaska Native

Bureau of Indian Affairs. http://bia.gov.

Harvard Project on American Indian Economic Develop-
ment. *The State of the Native Nations: Conditions under
U.S. Policies of Self-Determination.* New York: Oxford
University Press, 2008.

National Center for Education Statistics. *Status and Trends
in Education of American Indian and Alaska Natives:
2008.* Washington, DC: NCES. http://nces.ed.gov/
pubs2005/2005108.pdf.

Native Hawaiian Pacific Islander

Office of Hawaiian Affairs. www.oha.org/.

US Census Bureau. *The American Community—Pacific
Islanders: 2004.* American Community Survey Report.
February.

US Census Bureau. *The Native Hawaiian and Other Pacific
Island Population in the US.* http://www.census.gov/
population/www/socdemo/race/NHPI-slide-pre
sentation.html8.

Multiple Race

A compendium of mixed-race studies is available at
www.mixedracestudies.org

DISCUSSION

1. Select demographic information on the census tract
   or zip code that includes the client business. How
   does it differ from the demographics of the city,
   county, or state? Identify some of the main social, cultural, or other characteristics of the community where
   the client business is located. Visit the community in
   which your client business is located. Based on your
   data analysis and your visit, describe how your results
   could be used by your client business.

2. Select two groups and compare them on a variety of
   demographic and other factors. Summarize their main
   multicultural characteristics. What are the main differences in reaching each of the groups? Which socio-
   cultural factors would need to be considered? How
   will this change in ten years?

3. In order to make sure that you fully understand some
   of the terms introduced in this module, find some
   examples that illustrate the idea that people of color
   have been subject to racism, racial discrimination,
   or some kind of challenge or barrier associated with
   their race, cultural attributes, ethnicity, or national
   origin.

4. Pertaining to the cultural aspects of this course, how
   would you describe or define your own awareness of,
   exposure to, and tolerance of differences? Consider this
   with respect to race and ethnicity, disability, sexual orientation, or any other cultural distinction with which
   you have had limited exposure or experience. How
   do you react to stereotyping or expressions of bias
   against these characteristics?

5. Based upon your own ethnicity and experiences in service businesses, how do your judgments compare with those reported in the research in markets and culture?

6. What potential advantages or challenges should business owners from your ethnic group have in attracting and serving customers with whom they share ethnicity? What cautions would you suggest to your team regarding attempts to define expected relationships based on shared ethnicity.

2. Multicultural Entrepreneurship

ABOUT THIS MODULE

Most business knowledge and theory focuses on the administration of large enterprises with thousands of employees and billions in revenues. These long-lived enterprises are not representative of the majority of businesses in America, which are significantly smaller.

In fact, small enterprises account for half the GDP and, according to studies by the Small Business Administration (SBA) and the Kauffman Foundation, are responsible for almost all net job growth in the United States. Recent data are starting to call this into question, as these previous studies do not account for job destruction when small businesses fail. Small businesses are also a major source of innovation.[1] Some evidence suggests that they play an important role in moderating the troughs in the economic cycle. They also contribute to increasing productivity of all enterprises. The Kauffman Foundation makes the case that entrepreneurship is central to sustaining American competitiveness and, unless there continues to be a high rate of business start-ups, the country faces decline.

In the last decade, the majority of business growth has come from groups that previously showed lower proportions of entrepreneurship relative to their populations. Minority business enterprises (MBEs), immigrant-owned businesses, and women-owned business enterprises (WBEs) have shown growth rates that exceed those of non-Hispanic white male businesses. Additionally, high unemployment rates have driven more individuals to self-employment. The return of military veterans in 2012 and

beyond will create another pool of human capital that offers potential for growth in entrepreneurship.

Despite the need for entrepreneurship, for a variety of reasons the survival rates of small businesses remain dismally low. The positive side is that data collection has improved substantially, and there are a number of excellent centers that are driving research that identifies the attributes of high-impact businesses. This section attempts to summarize this dynamic area in which more data continue to emerge.

After Studying This Module

Reviewing the material in this module will provide theory and knowledge about how businesses evolve. Not all student teams will consult with MBEs. Some will work with WBEs or businesses in economically distressed areas. Much of the knowledge provided can be applied to all emerging enterprises. Understanding how businesses evolve will allow the consulting team to place the client business in a framework and devise a strategy that will propel the business to critical mass and survival.

This section also provides information specific to minority business enterprises. Data are presented on the number and characteristics of these businesses. Comparisons are made to non-Hispanic white businesses so that key factors that may hinder the success of the client firms can be discerned. In addition to having to beat the odds of survival for emerging businesses, MBEs face additional obstacles that often require substantial additional effort to overcome. The support and understanding of the consulting team can do much to assist the business in overcoming these obstacles.

---

1   Steven J. Davis, John Haltiwanger, and Ron Jarmin, *Turmoil and Growth: Young Businesses, Economic Churning, and Productivity Gains.* Kansas City, MO: Kauffman Foundation, June 2008.

After studying this module the student will be able to:

- Distinguish between employer and nonemployer firms and cite factors that may contribute to businesses becoming employer firms.
- Describe business and owner attributes that are more conducive to business survival and the development of a high-impact firm.
- Differentiate between multicultural population groups as to the type of businesses started and challenges faced.
- Determine sources of capital and their characteristics in relation to business start-ups.

MINORITY AND OTHER SMALL ENTERPRISES

It is generally agreed that multicultural markets will play an increasingly important role in the US economy. The first tremors of the cultural and ethnic shifts in the American population were felt throughout the 1990s, confirmed by the 2000 census, and evidenced in the explosive growth of multicultural groups in the 2010 census. As these populations grow, the corollary growth in related business activity is having its impact on local economies. The effect of these businesses is much more complex than a simple increase in revenues. Economists have come to realize that these small enterprises stabilize economies. Minority business enterprises (MBEs) were a major factor in the revitalization of inner-city Los Angeles after the 1992 race riots. They played a major role in the recovery of Houston after the drop in its oil industry. Minority-owned businesses, for a time, were the only bright spot in New York City's economy, where over 30,000 financial service workers left the city in the three years after 9/11. The factors that enhance the success of minority business enterprises are the same ones that enhance other small businesses. This module, in its knowledge and theory, addresses immigrants, women, veterans, businesses in economically depressed areas, and, indeed, all small businesses.

In periods of downturn and austerity, local governments are realizing the importance of these businesses in providing a stable backing for the economy. These businesses have ties to the community and are unlikely to pick up their operations and move out of state to reduce costs. They are unlikely to merge with larger firms and eliminate jobs. Minority businesses, being for the most part small businesses, are more likely to generate jobs and, because of their ties to their own communities, are more likely to hire minority workers who consistently have higher unemployment rates than non-Hispanic whites. In fact, it is overwhelmingly the dynamic cycle of the creation of new businesses that, in turn, creates net jobs in the United States, according to the Kauffman Foundation.[2] From its analysis, the foundation finds that roughly two-thirds of job creation since 1980 has occurred in firms less than five years old and with fewer than 250 employees.

Multicultural marketing is inextricably tied to multicultural entrepreneurship, and thus both are the focus of this book. Many unique relationships exist between multicultural aspects of the marketplace and businesses owned by persons of color. It is commonplace for such businesses to predominantly serve customers of particular racial and ethnic backgrounds. Obviously, this is not true of all such businesses. Some have locations that serve mainstream customers. Some are positioned by strategies and operations to cross over into the larger or mainstream marketplace.

Crossover market opportunities are increasingly prevalent in cities with large ethnic populations where gentrification and revitalization are occurring. Such developments mean that communities are changing in ways that usually bring higher-income residents, increased property values, and other improvements that expand business opportunities.

Mirroring growth trends in multicultural populations in the past two decades, the number of minority businesses increased at a much faster rate than all firms in the United States. As can be seen in Table 2-1, black-owned businesses achieved 61% growth in number of firms and 53% growth in revenues as compared to white firms, which increased 14% in total number while revenues increased 24%. All MBE categories grew faster than white firms.

Women-owned businesses continued to grow at rates higher than male-owned businesses. For the first time, veteran-owned firms were added to the 2007 US Census.

Although minority businesses are showing large

---

2 D. Stangler and R. Litan, *Where Will The Jobs Come From?* November 2009. Kauffman Foundation Research Series: Firm Formation and Economic Growth. http://www.kauffman.org/uploadedFiles/where_will_the_jobs_come_from.pdf.

TABLE 2-1. Firm Growth in Number and Revenues

Group	All Firms, 2007 (Number)	All Firms, 2002 (Number)	Percent Change	Receipts, 2007 ($1,000)	Receipts, 2002 ($1,000)	Percent Change
All firms	27,092,908	22,974,655	17.9	30,031,519,910	22,603,658,904	32.9
White	22,595,146	19,899,839	13.5	10,240,990,714	8,277,812,084	23.7
Black or African American	1,921,864	1,197,567	**60.5**	135,739,834	88,641,608	53.1
American Indian and Alaska Native	236,691	201,387	17.5	34,353,842	26,872,947	27.8
Asian	1,549,559	1,103,587	**40.4**	506,047,751	326,663,445	54.9
Native Hawaiian and Other Pacific Islander	37,687	28,948	**30.2**	6,319,357	4,279,591	47.7
Hispanic	2,260,309	1,573,464	**43.7**	345,183,070	221,927,425	55.5
Female-owned	7,793,364	6,489,259	**20.1**	1,190,057,451	939,538,208	26.7
Male-owned	13,909,064	13,184,033	5.5	8,507,846,994	7,061,026,736	20.5
Veteran-owned	2,447,608			1,219,551,078		

Source: US Census Bureau 2007 Survey of Business Owners
Note: Bold figures represent the larger than average changes.

growth rates, as a group, they face some notable limitations on the basis of their general characteristics in comparison to nonminority firms. They tend to be smaller than nonminority firms. With the exception of Asian firms, minority firms have a larger proportion of microbusinesses (businesses with $10,000 or less in sales). Conversely, with the exception of Asian firms, a smaller percentage of minority firms have over $1 million in sales.

According to the Kauffman Index of Entrepreneurial Activity, in 2010, 340 businesses per 100,000 were started in the United States. Entrepreneurial rates range from 240 per 100,000 for blacks, 310 per 100,000 for whites, 370 per 100,000 for Asians, and 560 per 100,000 for Hispanics. The intensity of activity by state is shown on the map in Figure 2-2, with the heaviest regions in the west and south. Entrepreneurial activity did not decrease after the 2008 recession. In fact, it increased, a phenomenon Kauffman attributes to divergent trends: a general increase in entrepreneurial rates and unemployed individuals looking for ways to earn money. Table 2-2 shows that new entrepreneurs are

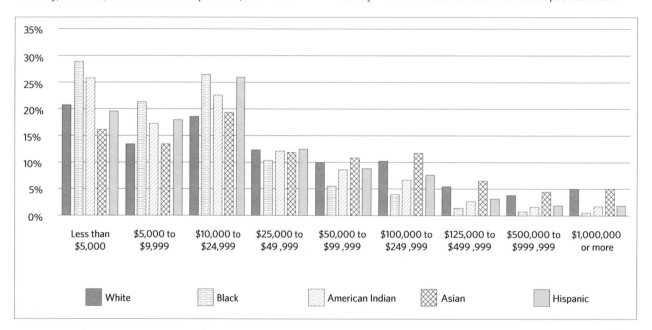

FIGURE 2-1. Comparative Percent of Firms by Revenues
Source: 2007 Survey of Business Owners. factfinder.census.gov. Release Date: 6/28/2011 Firms_SurveyofBusiness2007.xlsx

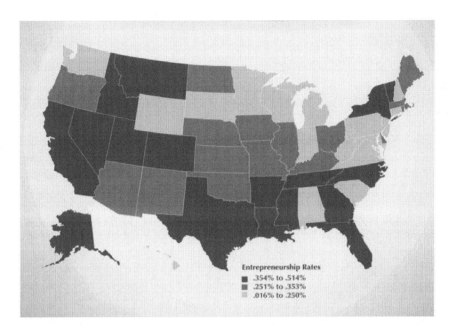

FIGURE 2-2. Composition and Location of New Entrepreneurs by State, 2010

Source: Robert W. Fairlie, University of California, Santa Cruz, using the Current Population Survey

Entrepreneurship Rates
- .354% to .514%
- .251% to .353%
- .016% to .250%

TABLE 2-2. Attributes of New Entrepreneurs

	1996	2010
Race		
White	76%	60%
Black	8%	9%
Latino	11%	23%
Asian	4%	6%
Other	1%	2%
Age		
Ages 20–34	35%	26%
Ages 35–44	27%	26%
Ages 45–54	24%	25%
Ages 55–64	14%	23%
Nativity		
Native-born	86%	71%
Immigrant	14%	29%

Source: Robert W. Fairlie, University of California, Santa Cruz, using the Current Population Survey.

increasingly diverse, immigrant, and older, mirroring changes in the US population.

The Kauffman Foundation postulates that the churning (birth and death) of firms is a ubiquitous and necessary feature of the US economy. New firms create the most jobs. At the same time, they drive productivity gains for all firms by competition with other small and large firms.[3] Firm termination is also necessary in the entrepreneurial ecosystem.

Despite healthy birth rates for businesses, survival rates are daunting. According to the Kauffman Foundation, 80% of businesses (both employer and nonemployer) will survive the first year, 33% will survive five years, 12% will survive to year 25, and only 8% will survive to year 40.[4] SBA research shows that 50% of businesses survive four years. To begin the analysis of success factors, businesses have been divided into groupings on key characteristics that seem relevant to the evolution of businesses. Figure 2-3 and Table 2-3 divide the universe of 30 million businesses into groups that are relevant to the evolution of businesses.

Of all businesses, the great majority involve self-employment with no employees. The balance, about a quarter of the total, is employer firms that have people on their payrolls. Of the employer firms, there are about 350,000 *gazelles*, according to David Birch,[5] who coined the term. Gazelles represent the holy grail of business in that they grow very quickly (over 20% per year) and generate employment as a result of their growth. Unlike the "mice" or microbusinesses that do not survive, or the "elephants" or large firms that shed jobs, gazelles typify the best in entrepre-

3   S. Davis, J. Haltiwanger, and R. Jarmin, *Turmoil and Growth: Young Businesses, Economic Churning, and Productivity Gains*. June 2008. Kansas City, MO: Kauffman Foundation.

4   D. Stangler and P. Kedrosky. *Neutralism and Entrepreneurship: The Structural Dynamics of Startups, Young Firms, and Job Creation*. September 2010. Kauffman Foundation Research Series: Firm Foundation and Economic Growth. http://www.kauffman.org/uploaded Files/firm-formation-neutralism.pdf.

5   Z. Acs, W. Parsons, and S. Tracy, *High-Impact Firms: Gazelles Revisited*. June 2008. SBA Office of Advocacy. http://archive.sba.gov/advo/research/rs328tot.pdf.

30 million firms

6 million employer firms

350,000 gazelles

17,000 long-lived firms

FIGURE 2-3. How Businesses Evolve

neurship in America. Gazelles may evolve into long-lived businesses. Long-lived businesses command the most attention. They constitute the largest 17,000 firms, of which about 7,000 are listed on the public stock exchanges. Much of the business literature is focused on this small segment of business enterprises.

How Small Businesses Can Reach Escape Velocity

While not all small businesses have the goal of becoming large enterprises, it is important that promising small businesses be given the full set of strategies and tools to survive, as it is critical to wealth creation in multicultural and underserved communities. Small businesses are more likely to survive and thrive by using the concepts and characteristics outlined below to determine their current stage and the key factors that are important to reaching escape velocity into the next stage. Boundaries between these groupings are often fuzzy, and businesses can migrate between groupings or be part of two groupings at the same time. A self-employed sole proprietor can hire employees, or an employer firm can downsize to self-employment. Gazelles can both have high growth and have more than 500 employees.

Firms with No Employees

The great majority of small firms have no employees or are self-employed firms. Although they comprise 79% of businesses, they account for only 3%–4% of the revenues. The number of self-employed firms has grown 65% for blacks, 47% for Asians, 33% for Native Hawaiians, and 20% for American Indians, as compared to 18% for white firms. This growth is consistent with previous studies that showed growth across all groups, with more growth in minority groups.[6]

In sheer numbers, the self-employed tend to be mostly male and mostly white. About 58% are home-based businesses compared to 22% that are employer firms. Studies of the self-employed show that these individuals often start businesses as an income-generating hobby or to supplement their income. The self-employed tend to be concentrated in industries that have low capital requirements; services (29%), construction (16%), and retail trade (11%) dominate. The ranks of the self-employed include a broad spectrum of occupations, from construction workers to doctors and lawyers. Most of these individuals have no desire to grow their businesses past self-employment. About 3% of the nonemployers became employers within three years of operation, and nearly 2% of employers migrate to nonemployer status.[7]

Of all nonemployer firms, 26% claim they do not need start-up capital as compared to 10% of employer businesses. About 36% of the nonemployer firms start their businesses with $5,000 or less (see Figure 2-5). More than 80% start with $10,000 or less in capital. Although a small percentage of these businesses can generate significant revenues and profit, 80% generate less than $50,000 in revenues, as shown in Figure 2-5. Some evidence suggests that the low revenue generation may be a result of the number of hours put into the business. The birth rate (34.3% in 2003–2004) and death rate (29.6%) for the self-employed are almost three times higher than for businesses with employees (12.6% and 10.8%).

About 43% of these businesses rely on business income for the owners' primary income, as compared to 69% of employer firms. Previous studies have suggested that when self-employment becomes the primary source of income, the business is more likely to evolve to an employer firm. Other factors may stimulate the growth of self-employment yet inhibit the growth of these types of businesses. The US Black Chamber of Commerce explains the self-employment growth among blacks as a consequence of higher black unemployment (see Figure 2-6) and claims the lack of growth of these businesses is due to lack of access to capital and opportunity.[8] It

---

6   R. Fairlie, *Self-Employed Business Ownership Rates in the United States: 1979–2003.* http://archive.sba.gov/advo/research/rs243tot.pdf.

7   Z. Acs, B. Headd, and H. Agwara, "Nonemployer Start-up Puzzle," December 2009. SBA Advocacy. http://archive.sba.gov/advo/research/rs354tot.pdf.

8   Tri-State Defender, "Self-Employment Rises as Survival Option for More African Americans," March 17, 2011. http://tri-statedefenderonline.com/articlelive/articles/5905/1/Self-employment-rises-as-survival-option-for-more-African-Americans/Page1.html.

TABLE 2-3. Reaching Escape Velocity

	Self-Employed	Employer Firms	Gazelles	Long-Lived Firms
Definition	Firms with one owner/employee	Firms that have employees	High-impact businesses that typify the best in US entrepreneurship.	Established large enterprises characterized by publicly listed companies.
Number	25 million	5 to 6 million	About 350,000	About 17,000
Characteristics	Most self-employed start businesses to accommodate lifestyle choice	Most are small marginal businesses and continue to be small.	Growth rates of over 20% per year.	S&P 500 growth rates.
Capital	Low capital requirements: 75% start with less than $5,000. More than 90% start with less than $25,000.	Low capital requirements: About 75% start with less than $25,000. More than 50% required less than $5,000.	Do not differ much from employer firms. Two-thirds use less than $50,000 to start their businesses. More capital seems to accelerate process, though it does not increase profitability. Key is that the entrepreneur knows how to bootstrap. Only 4% use venture capital.	Large banks and financial markets.
Industries	Professional and other services, retail, and construction.	Most are low capital and low barrier industries.	"Fuzzy" market opportunities not completely defined. No major competitors.	S&P 500 classifications.
Owner or manager characteristics	Wants to be own boss, control over number of hours worked, and family reasons.	Risk-averse	Strong tolerance for ambiguity. Strong self-confidence. Sales skills. Problem solving in a fuzzy environment. Open to learning from mistakes. Previous experience in industry. 80% have college degrees.	Leadership. Audacious goals. Strategic outlook. Coherence of goals.
Business characteristics	Marginal businesses with low-risk incremental opportunities.	Most popular are restaurants, beauty salons, and construction firms.	Few substitutes for products/services. Not an original idea.	Portfolio of businesses.
Revenue generation	Most generate less than $50,000, and one-third operate at loss.	Most do not grow. Majority have less than $100,000 in sales	High revenue growth of over 20% a year.	Averages to GDP growth rate.
Job generation	None.	Only 24% of employer firms tracked over ten years show any growth in employment.	Estimated that these generate 60% of the new jobs.	Dispute as to how many net jobs are generated. Some estimate one-third of net jobs.
Cycle	Self-employment increases during economic downturns.	Growing at 1% to 2% a year. Follows business cycle with more starts during expansions and more deaths during downturns.	Downturns do not seems to impact the growth of these firms.	Business cycle specific to industry.

TABLE 2-3 (continued)

	Self-Employed	Employer Firms	Gazelles	Long-Lived Firms
Survival	One study showed 51% survive five years as compared to 82% of businesses with employees.	About 500,000 started every year and about 500,000 terminated. One SBA study shows lack of capital is a major source of business dissolution.	Survival may be subject to industry life cycle.	Survival rate is very high.
What causes it to move to the next phase	If self-employment becomes primary source of income then move to become employer firm. 41% contribute less than 10% of family income.	Choosing a market without major competitors. Information about the market is imperfect and evolving. Previous experience in that industry. Strong sales skills. Bootstrapping and making do with little at the fledgling stages.	Ability of management to transition from entrepreneur to manager. Vision to set audacious goals. Moving from single business to portfolio of businesses. Ability to motivate teamwork. Coherence of vision.	

Source: Modified from Amar Bhide, *The Origin and Evolution of New Businesses*. New York: Oxford University Press, 2000.

TABLE 2-4. Employer and Nonemployer Firms by Race/Ethnicity/Gender

	Businesses		Nonemployer Firms		Nonemployer Firms as Percent of All Businesses	
2007	Number (1000)	Revenue ($ million)	Number (1000)	Revenue ($ million)	Number	Revenue
All firms	27,093	30,031,520	21,357	972,691	79%	3%
White	22,595	10,240,991	17,955	834,441	79%	8%
Black or African American	1,922	135,740	1,815	38,595	**94%**	28%
American Indian and Alaska Native	237	34,354	213	6,860	**90%**	20%
Asian	1,550	506,048	1,152	52,474	74%	10%
Native Hawaiian and Pacific Islander	38	6,319	34	1,069	**89%**	17%
Hispanic	2,260	350,661	2,011	70,741	**89%**	20%
Women	27,110	30,176,155	21,357	972,694	79%	3%

Source: 2007 Survey of Business Owners
NOTE: Bold figures represent larger than average changes.

is noted that populations with higher unemployment rates such as American Indians, Native Alaskans, Native Hawaiians, Pacific Islanders, and Hispanics have a higher proportion of nonemployer businesses.

Employer Firms

Employer firms numbered about 5.9 million in 2007 and have been growing at a rate of 1% to 2% a year. About 670,000 businesses were started in 2007 and about 600,000 were terminated.[9] Business termination is not always because the business failed. About 25,000 to 65,000 business bankruptcies are filed every year. They

9   SBA, "Employer Firm Births and Deaths by Employment Size of Firm, 1989–2007." Retrieved 12/20/11 from http://archive.sba.gov/advo/research/dyn_us_tot.pdf.

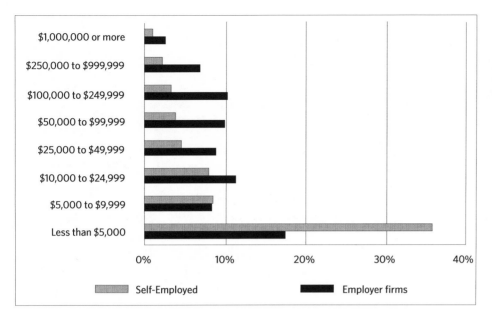

FIGURE 2-4. Start-up
Capital
Source: *Statistics for All US Firms by Total
Amount of Capital Used to Start or Acquire
the Business.* 2007 Survey of Business
Owners Survey_Business_2007.xlsx

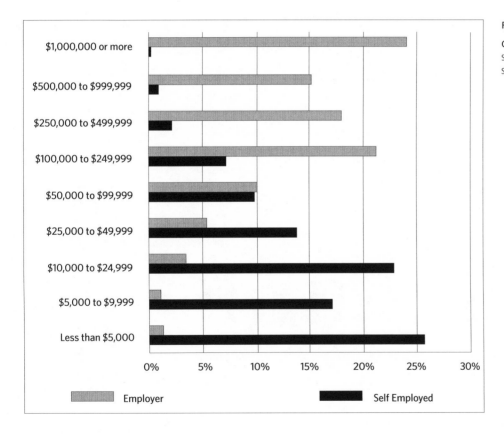

FIGURE 2-5. Firms by Size
of Revenues
Source: 2007 Survey of Business Owners
Survey_Business_2007.xlsx

trend upward during downturns and downward during expansions.[10]

The bulk of these enterprises do not grow. Only 32% of employer firms tracked over five years reported expansion.[11] Amar Bhide, a professor and business author, has theorized that these firms stay small because typically the business owners select marginal industries that have

10 US Courts, "Bankruptcy Statistics." Retrieved 12/20/11 from
http://www.uscourts.gov/Statistics/BankruptcyStatistics.aspx.

11 Y. Lowrey, "Dynamics of Employer Establishments, 2002–2003,"
December 2009. SBA Advocacy. http://www.sba.gov/sites/
default/files/rs356tot.pdf.

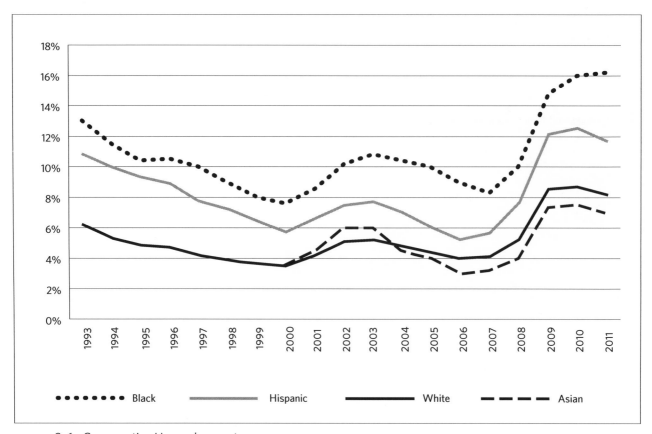

FIGURE 2-6. Comparative Unemployment

Source: US Bureau of Labor Statistics http://www.bls.gov/cps/demographics.htm#raceUnemployment.xlsx

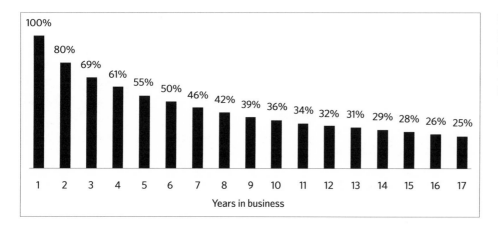

FIGURE 2-7. Survival Rates
by Year in Operation

Source: *Establishment Age and Survival Data,*
US Bureau of Labor Statistics http://www
.bls.gov/bdm/bdmage.htm#TOTAL Survey_
Business_2007_02.xlsx

dim prospects of high growth. Contrary to the popular entrepreneurial myth, most business owners are risk averse when selecting their businesses. They choose businesses with low capital requirements and, as such, low barriers to entry.

Table 2-5 shows that WBEs and MBEs tend to be younger (a smaller proportion were started prior to 1990 and a larger proportion have started in recent years) as compared to all employer firms.

In 2007, more than two-thirds of business owners reported completing at least some college education at the time that they started or acquired their business, as can be seen in Table 2-6. More than one-quarter (27.8%) had bachelor's degrees, and 20.4% had earned a master's, doctorate, or professional degree before starting or acquiring their business. These proportions were generally 2% to 3% higher than for nonemployer firms.

The proportion of women with a bachelor's degree

TABLE 2-5. Proportion of Group by Year Business Started

	All Firms	Female	Hispanic	Black	AIAN	Asian	NHPI
Before 1980	21%	15%	9%	10%	15%	8%	15%
1980 to 1989	18%	16%	13%	14%	17%	12%	15%
1990 to 1999	25%	27%	26%	26%	26%	25%	23%
2000 to 2002	11%	13%	16%	15%	13%	15%	12%
2003	4%	5%	6%	6%	4%	6%	0%
2004	5%	6%	7%	8%	6%	7%	5%
2005	5%	6%	8%	8%	6%	9%	11%
2006	5%	6%	8%	7%	6%	8%	5%
2007	3%	4%	5%	5%	5%	6%	4%

Source: 2007 Survey of Business Owners Survey_Business_2007_02.xlsx

TABLE 2-6. Highest Educational Attainment of Employer Firm Owners

	White	Female	Hispanic	Black	AIAN	Asian	NHPI
Less than high school graduate	3%	9%	12%	5%	7%	6%	4%
High school graduate: diploma or GED	21%	26%	25%	16%	22%	17%	21%
Technical, trade, or vocational school	6%	6%	6%	6%	7%	3%	9%
Some college, but no degree	17%	19%	17%	17%	22%	12%	21%
Associate degree	6%	8%	6%	6%	7%	5%	8%
Bachelor's degree	28%	19%	18%	24%	21%	31%	24%
Master's, doctorate, or professional degree	20%	14%	16%	27%	16%	27%	14%

Source: 2007 Survey of Business Owners Survey_Business_2007_02.xlsx

was 1.3% lower than that of men, while the proportion of women with a master's, doctorate, or professional degree was 3.7% lower than that of men. The 2007 Survey of Business Owners shows that both black and Asian business owners are highly educated, while Hispanic, AIAN, and NHPI business owners lag behind by 10% to 13% compared to white firms. The increase in the number of educated blacks should have a positive impact on black entrepreneurship. In the past, education was noted as a factor in the success of Asian businesses. For all businesses, education is found to be correlated with increased rates of survival, more employees, increased sales, and profits.[12] Owners with bachelor's degrees have 25% higher sales than high school dropouts, and owners with master's degrees have 40% higher sales than holders of bachelor's degrees.[13] Other factors that portend success include family-business background and having worked in a family business.[14]

Sources of capital. The 2007 Survey of Business Owners showed that the overwhelming source of capital for businesses was from the owner's personal savings, personal borrowing, or home equity. For women-owned and MBEs, there was more reliance on personal sources and less on bank loans. Studies have documented large disparities in access to financial capital. MBEs are less likely to receive loans or they receive loans of lower amounts, and they are more likely to be denied loans and pay higher interest rates,[15] despite the fact that MBEs outpace the growth in white firms and garner similar returns. There is evidence that MBEs produce healthy returns equal to, if not slightly higher than, traditional investments in venture capital.[16]

12 R. Fairlie and A. Robb, *Race and Entrepreneurial Success, 2008.* Cambridge, MA: MIT Press, 2008.

13 Ibid., 91.

14 Ibid., 92.

15 R. Fairlie and A. Robb, "Disparities in Capital Access between Minority and Non-Minority-Owned Businesses: The Troubling Reality of Capital Limitations Faced by MBEs," January 2010. Minority Business Development Agency. http://people.ucsc.edu/~rfairlie/presentations/Disparities%20in%20Capital%20Access%20Report%202010.pdf.

16 T. Bates and W. Bradford, *Minorities and Venture Capital: A New Wave in American Business.* October. Kansas City, MO: Kauffman Foundation, 2007.

TABLE 2-7. Source of Capital

	All Firms	Female	Hispanic	Black	AIAN	Asian	NHPI
Owner personal savings	62%	65%	67%	68%	64%	69%	67%
Family savings	10%	10%	9%	10%	13%	10%	9%
Personal home equity loan	8%	10%	10%	10%	9%	11%	13%
Personal credit card	11%	14%	14%	16%	15%	11%	19%
Government loan	1%	1%	1%	2%	1%	1%	2%
Government-guaranteed loan	2%	2%	1%	2%	3%	2%	2%
Bank loan	19%	17%	14%	16%	18%	18%	17%
Family/friends loan	5%	5%	4%	4%	5%	6%	5%
Venture capital	1%	0%	0%	1%		0%	
Grants	1%	0%	0%		0%	0%	1%
Other	4%	3%	3%	4%	4%	3%	5%
Don't know	6%	4%	4%	4%	4%	6%	5%
None needed	11%	11%	8%	9%	10%	6%	8%

Source: 2007 Survey of Business Owners Survey_Business_2007_02.xlsx

The Small Business Administration (SBA) was charged by federal legislators to enhance small business success. The 7(a) program for up to $5 million in general purpose loans was implemented on the premise that it would help businesses that have difficulty obtaining loans from other sources. SBA 504 loans of more than $10 million can be used to acquire physical assets such as real estate or equipment. There is some controversy as to how successful these programs have been. As an example, following the recession in 2007 and 2008 when credit froze for all businesses, the SBA program contracted instead of increasing these two programs and created more duress for small businesses.

Additionally, it appears that the number of black and Hispanic businesses benefiting from these loans has decreased over the past five years. The black share of SBA loans dropped from 4% to 2% of loans, while Hispanic businesses fell from 8% to 4% of loans between 2006 and 2011.This has occurred despite the fact that these groups require the most assistance because of much lower family net worth. In 2009, the median wealth of white households ($113,149) was 20 times that of black households ($5,677) and 18 times that of Hispanic households ($6,353).[17] The low net worth figures prominently in the ability of black and Hispanic business owners to

17 P. Taylor, R. Kochar, and R. Fry, "Wealth Gaps Rise to Records Highs between Whites, Blacks, and Hispanics," July 26, 2011. Washington, DC: Pew Research Center's Social and Demographic Trends.

tap personal savings or home equity or to otherwise provide collateral for bank loans.

The general proportion of loans to minorities has fallen from 34% in 2007 to 25% in 2011 despite the much larger growth rate of MBEs.

Federal contracting. Federal contracting dollars were $442.3 billion in fiscal year 2009, and small businesses accounted for 21.9% of the total. Prior to 2000, the SBA had a program where they certified small and disadvantaged businesses, and these businesses could compete for federal contracts that were set aside for this group. Disadvantaged businesses, which include MBEs, accounted for 7.6% of federal contracting dollars in 2009. These programs were discontinued in the mid-2000s because the SBA found that they were not cost effective; that is, costs outweighed benefits. Also, small businesses were not making inroads in obtaining more federal contracts. However, women-owned small businesses continued to be part of the SBA's goals. In 2009 small WBEs accounted for 3.68% of federal contracting.

Diversity programs. Despite the federal government's commitment to helping minority businesses, major increases in MBE revenues have come from the private sector, where there has been an almost six-fold increase (565%) since 1990.

The National Minority Supplier Development Council, with its regional branches, advocates for large corpora-

TABLE 2-8. Total SBA Loans

	2006	2007	2008	2009	2010	2011
7(A) & ARC Volume	$14.5 B	$14.3 B	$12.7 B	$9.2 B	$12.6 B	19.6 B
Black	4%	6%	7%	5%	2%	2%
Hispanic	8%	7%	5%	4%	5%	4%
Asian	21%	20%	19%	15%	16%	18%
Native American	1%	1%	1%	0%	1%	1%
Other minority	1%	0%	0%	0%	0%	0%
Women	18%	18%	18%	15%	14%	12%
Veterans	7%	7%	7%	7%	7%	6%
504 Loans Volume	$5.7 B	$6.3 B	$5.3 B	$3.8 B	$4.4 B	$4.8 B
Black	2%	3%	3%	2%	2%	2%
Hispanic	7%	7%	6%	6%	6%	5%
Asian	21%	22%	21%	18%	16%	16%
Native American	0%	0%	0%	0%	0%	0%
Other minority	1%	0%	0%	0%	0%	0%
Women	14%	15%	16%	14%	14%	13%
Veterans	5%	5%	5%	4%	8%	9%

Source: US Small Business Association

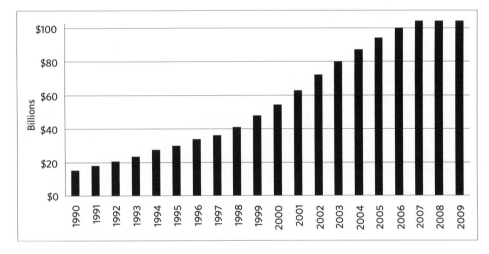

FIGURE 2-8. Minority Suppliers to Large Enterprises (Dollar Value)

Source: National Minority Supplier Development Council http://www.nmsdc.org/nmsdc/app/template/contentMgmt%2CContentPage.vm/contentid/1831 Finance.xlsx

tions to create opportunities for MBEs to compete for corporate purchasing dollars. It provides certification and forums for MBEs to improve their chances of becoming suppliers to major corporations. One of the main motivators for the corporations is fast-growing multicultural purchasing power. In recent years, the growth rate in diversity supplier dollars has also flattened.

Venture capital. Venture capital has been romanticized in the start-up stories of many Silicon Valley companies, including EBay, Google, and Facebook. Contrary to popular misconception, venture capital is a factor in only a small number of start-ups. Figure 2-9 shows that the

peak of venture capital investing occurred during the late 1990s dot.com period. In the 12-month period ending June 2011, approximately 3,500 deals for $24.7 billion were completed.

According to the 2007 Survey of Business Owners, 1% of businesses use venture capital for financing. Among MBEs, 1% of black businesses use venture capital. Only particular kinds of businesses lend themselves to venture capital funding. Venture capital firms typically look for proprietary products and managers who are highly qualified or experienced in the industry. Ventures need to be first or second to market, and there is an urgency to scale up quickly and become the market

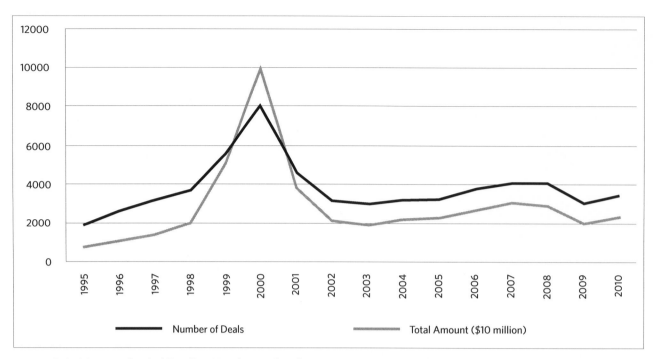

FIGURE 2-9. Venture Capital Funding Number and Dollars

Source: Price Waterhouse National Venture Capital Association Money Tree Report pwcmoneytree.comFinancing.xlsx

leader. Businesses must have the potential for hundreds of millions in revenues. The National Venture Capital Association[18] estimates that 40% of venture-backed companies fail, 40% have moderate returns, and 20% or less have high returns. The Cambridge Venture Capital Fund Index shows that for the 15 years ending March 2011, returns were 34.3% for all venture capital and 45.3% for early stage. The 25-year return was 19% for all venture capital index and 20.7% for early stage index.[19]

Venture capital firms also become intimately involved in the management of the enterprise using their contacts and resources to assist the firm in getting to scale. The investment is premised on an exit strategy into an initial public offering (IPO) in about five years; therefore venture funding is highly dependent on a "hot" IPO market. The large majority of companies make public offerings without going through venture capitalists; examples include Oracle, Walmart, and Dell.

Venture capitalists expect a major "win" in only about one-quarter of their portfolio. Experienced venture capitalists typically will give a "haircut" or reduction of up to two-thirds on financial projections. According to William Sahlman and colleagues,[20] the most important factor is the people involved. Venture capitalists look for individuals who have succeeded in bringing an innovative product to market. These individuals have the right experience, skills, and will power to bring the venture to fruition. The role of the venture capitalist is to accelerate the process and profit handsomely along the way.

Angel financing. The term angel was coined to describe wealthy businesspeople who invested in Broadway productions. It now refers to private individuals, typically successful entrepreneurs, who contribute their skills and money to start-up companies. Angel investors are typically hands-on people who bring industry expertise and contacts. Entrepreneurs often state that the value of an angel's expertise often exceeds the money put into the company.

The University of New Hampshire's Center for Ven-

18 Venture Capital Industry Overview. Retrieved from http://www. nvca.org/index.php?option=com_content&view=article&id=141 <emid=589.

19 Cambridge Associates, "Venture Capital Index, 2011." Retrieved 12/20/11 from http://www.cambridgeassociates.com/pdf/ Venture%20Capital%20Index.pdf.

20 William Sahlman et al.,*The Entrepreneurial Venture.* Boston, MA: Harvard Business School Press, 1999.

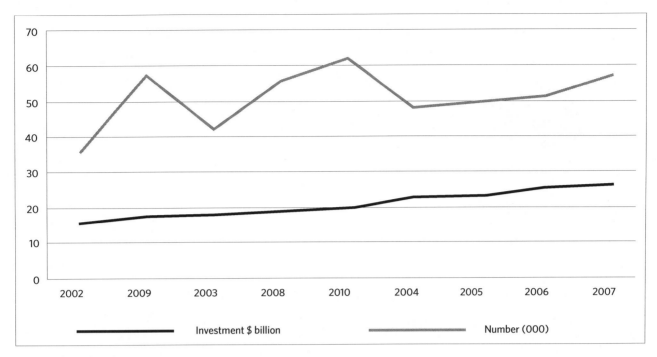

FIGURE 2-10. Angel Investments
Source: Center for Venture Research.

ture Research estimates that about 265,400 angel investors invested $20.1 billion in 61,900 ventures in 2010. Like venture capital, active angel investors peaked in 2000 at 400,000. About half of all angel exits were with yields of between 24% and 36%. The typical yield rate or the percent of proposals accepted is 18.4%, which is down from a peak of 23% in 2005. The Center for Venture Research estimates that the yield rate will revert to the historical average of 10% to 15%.

In 2010, 13% of angels were women. Women-owned ventures accounted for 21% of the entrepreneurs seeking angel capital, and 13% received angel investment in 2010, a yield rate 5% less than the average. Jeffrey Sohl of the Center for Venture Research suggests that increasing women's representation in angel investor groups would enhance investment decision making.[21] Minority angels were 2% of the angel population, and minority-owned firms represented 6% of the entrepreneurs seeking funding. The yield rate for these minority-owned firms was 19%, which is consistent with the average. Venture forums and personal networks are the most common

types of organization for angels, providing evidence of the importance of personal connections, which are not typically available to MBEs. The small proportion of MBEs seeking angel capital continues to be a concern in the marketplace, given the market yields on angel investments in these businesses.

Gazelles

Research on high-impact firms shows that they consistently number approximately 350,000 and represent about 6% of firms. They are younger and more productive than all other firms and can be found equally across all industries, even declining ones. Some researchers claim that they generate all net jobs, and their job creation appears to be immune to expansions and contractions of the business cycle. The greatest share (94%) of high-impact firms is in the 1–19 employee-size segment of all firms. The remaining 5.5% was in the 20–499 employee-size segment. Very few high-impact firms exist in firms with over 500 employees. They are characterized by high productivity per employee.[22]

21 J. Sohl, *Women Angel Investors Hampered by Gender Stereotypes.* Durham, NH: University of New Hampshire Center for Venture Research, 2011.

22 Spencer Tracy, "Accelerating Job Creation in America: The Promise of High-Impact Companies." July 2011. SBA Office of Advocacy. http://www.sba.gov/sites/default/files/rs381tot.pdf.

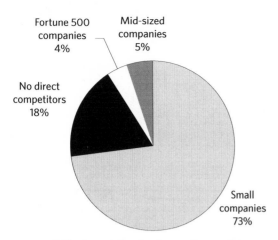

FIGURE 2-11. Promising Business Competition

Most high-impact entrepreneurs do not select original ideas for their businesses. The single biggest source of opportunity is previous employment. The entrepreneur copies, adapts, and modifies an idea from an industry he or she is familiar with. Prior work experience in the same type of business appears to be very useful in starting and running successful businesses.[23]

Gazelle entrepreneurs are adept at picking niche markets not being served by major competitors. As can be seen from Figure 2-11,[24] most promising businesses compete with other small businesses. This is an important factor in the idea search process because major enterprises have the deepest pockets and spend the largest amount of money on new products and service development. Successful entrepreneurs also compete in markets where there are few substitutes. The most promising businesses start in unsettled markets; either the markets are too new to be clearly defined or a significant transformation is changing the dynamics. The uncertainty of these types of markets allows the entrepreneur opportunity to develop a relationship with the customer whose needs are "fuzzy" or as yet undefined. Under these circumstances, large players have no informational advantages over the small start-up.[25]

Beyond demographics, there have been many attempts to create a profile of the successful entrepreneur. These attempts have largely been unsuccessful. It appears that entrepreneurs are characterized more by their actions, such as their tactical agility, than by their demographics. Adaptability is key. For new opportunities or uncertain markets, entrepreneurs must be able to change business concepts to adapt to customer needs that are being defined or redefined. Successful entrepreneurs cannot afford to make the same mistake twice. They must be able to ferret out the relevant information from the noise or make judgments from incomplete information. The level of self-confidence and self-control is high.

Entrepreneurs serve as the firm's main salespeople in its initial years, so having strong sales skills is important. Almost 90% of a fledgling enterprise's early sales are from direct sales, and the founder is the main salesperson in 82% of such ventures.[26]

Minority businesses face different handicaps in moving from marginal to promising businesses. They often lack access to capital because of smaller personal net worth. Some minority groups have lower levels of education because they only recently came to the United States. Some groups lack business experience during their formative years because they may have been prohibited from starting businesses. Immigrant entrepreneurs lack experience in US companies and face constraints in building business networks and developing sales skills and self-confidence. Even though they may have the education, they may not be successful because they do not fit the typical model or they speak accented English. African Americans and Native Americans face barriers in getting the education required for these jobs in industry. However, all these factors are changing in the dynamic environment. As more minority groups become better educated and gain more business experience and as more MBEs start and grow, it is expected that more MBEs will join the ranks of the gazelles.

AFRICAN AMERICAN BUSINESSES

African American firms totaled 1.9 million in 2007 (double that of 1997), or 7.1% of US firms. This was an increase of 61% in the number of firms and 53% in firm revenues over 2002, accelerating growth rates of 45% for the previous five years. Black firms employed 921,032

23 R. Fairlie and A. Robb, *Race and Entrepreneurial Success*. Cambridge, MA: MIT Press, 2008.
24 Ibid.
25 A. Bhide, *The Origin and Evolution of New Businesses*. New York: Oxford University Press, 2000.

26 Ibid.

Retail Lockbox

The Gazelle

Each day thousands of people submit payments for county taxes, medical bills, or credit card bills. Craig Dawson, co-founder and CEO of Retail Lockbox, makes it a priority to insure that these payments are processed quickly and accurately.

Dawson began his career selling mainframe computer systems. It was during this time that he realized there was a market opportunity for payment and remittance processing. In 1994, Dawson and co-founder Walt Townes launched Retail Lockbox, Inc. Within the first 30 days, and with equipment still sitting on the floor, Dawson was awarded a contract with a local city to process utility payments. The business grew to processing 100,000 payments in just six months.

Today, Retail Lockbox is the premier independent remittance processing, document imaging, and online payment processing company in the Pacific Northwest. It is entrusted with several billion client payment receivables each year as well as 60 million document images. Retail Lockbox has created unique and sophisticated processing services that save its clients valuable time, resources, and expenses associated with in-house processing.

Dawson believes in the importance of a strong brand identity. What do his customers associate with the brand Retail Lockbox? Outstanding quality, efficiency, and speed. The term *lockbox* originated in the 1940s. Retail stores provided "locked boxes," located on the wall, for customers to leave payments for bills. Today lockbox is a standard term for a secure payment portal.

Dawson described two keys to success: delegation and quality control. Many small business owners may excel at one particular skill but may not be experts in every needed skill to successfully manage operations. He believes that it is important to leverage the individual strengths in the organization. Dawson recruits, hires, and develops the brightest people. Quality is also an important ingredient in success. Dawson is fanatical about quality control while running a lean organization. His error rate is about 1 in 250,000 items processed.

After five years of courting a major health care provider, his persistence paid off. And it paid off for the client as well. Their data were consolidated into a more efficient digital format, providing easy payment inquiry and research capabilities and reducing the need for multiple file cabinets and storage space. Dawson and his team succeeded in reducing the client's transaction costs with a monthly savings of $50,000.

Retail Lockbox has reached more than $6.5 million in sales and continues to grow. Dawson predicts that the biggest growth will come from online merchant services, potentially doubling his business in the years to come.

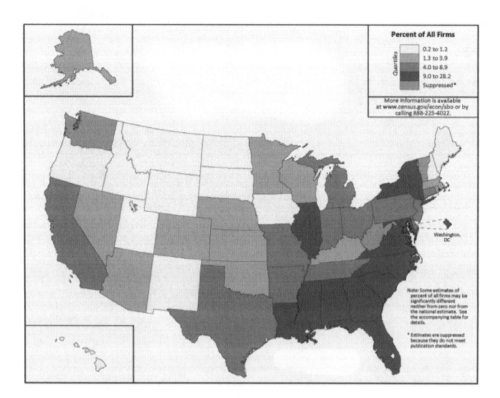

FIGURE 2-12. Black-Owned Firms by Location, 2007 (7.1% of all US firms)
Source: 2007 Survey of Business Owners

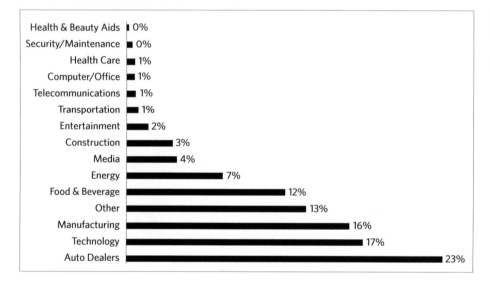

FIGURE 2-13. Black Enterprise 100 Distribution by Industry
Source: *Black Enterprise Magazine*

people and generated $137.5 billion in business revenues. Of these, 96% were nonemployer firms as compared to 79% of white firms. Black firms show evidence of increasing critical mass for enterprise success as a greater proportion of college degree holders are starting businesses.

New York topped the states with the most black-owned firms (10.6% of all-black firms), followed by Georgia (9.6% of all-black firms) and Florida (9.4% of all-black firms). Higher concentrations of African American businesses as a percent of all businesses are found along the East Coast, consistent with where the African American population is concentrated. The top metropolitan areas for black firms were the New York City metropolitan area, Los Angeles, Chicago, and Dallas (see Figure 2-12).

According to the 2007 Survey of Business Owners, the number one industry for African American business owners was health and social assistance (36% of all black firms), where they were 15% of all US businesses. Repair, maintenance, personal, and laundry services were the next common industries. Of all US firms in transportation and warehousing, 13.4% were black firms.

TABLE 2-9. Hispanic Firms by Ethnicity

Ethnicity	Number of Firms 2007	Percent of Hispanic Firms	Number of Firms 2002	Percent Change between 2002 and 2007	Receipts 2007 ($1,000)	Percent of Hispanic Firms	Receipts 2002 ($1,000)	Percent Change between 2002 and 2007
All Hispanic	2,260,309		1,573,464	44	345,183,070		221,927,425	56
Mexican (58.5% of Hispanics)	1,035,748	46%	701,078	48	155,534,140	45	96,735,081	61
Puerto Rican (9.6%)	156,546	7%	109,475	43	16,677,962	5	12,340,353	35
Cuban (3.5%)	251,070	11%	151,688	66	51,252,555	15	35,443,349	45
Other Hispanic (28.4%)	778,757	34%	596,125	31	113,892,563	33	74,219,213	54

Black Enterprise, the business publication for black-owned businesses, ranks the largest black-owned firms every year in its BE 100 list. In 2010, the BE 100 consisted of the industries shown in Figure 2-13.[27]

Inc. Magazine maintains its own list of 5,000 fast-growing companies. Of these, 86 (6%) were African American firms. The bulk of these fast-growing black firms were located in the New York City and the Washington, DC, corridor.

HISPANIC BUSINESSES

Hispanic Americans owned 2.3 million businesses in 2007, or 8.3% of all businesses, double that of 1997 and 43% compared to 2002. They employed 1.6 million in 2007 with $226 billion in revenues. Employer firms numbered 77,222 and employed 496,870 people.

As with Asian American business owners, the origins of Hispanic business owners are disparate. Mexicans and Cubans constitute the largest number of business owners. The number of Cuban businesses grew at the highest rate (65.5%), while Mexican business receipts grew the fastest (60%). Business owner education levels are lower than non-Hispanic whites, with one-third fewer bachelor's degrees and one-fifth fewer master's and higher. Cuban immigrants who came to America with more endowment in terms of education and wealth have the highest revenues per firm. They also represent the immigrants who have been in the United States the longest.

The prevalent industries for Hispanic-owned businesses are construction and repair, maintenance, and personal and laundry services, and they account for 10.4% of all firms in these sectors. Puerto Rican firms were involved in health care and social assistance.

California (36% of Mexican firms), Florida (74.5% of Cuban businesses), Texas (34% of Mexican businesses), and New York (22% of Puerto Rican businesses) all reported more than 100,000 Hispanic businesses. The highest concentrations were in New Mexico, Texas, and Florida. Top metropolitan areas include Los Angeles, Miami, New York, and Houston (see Figure 2-14).

With Hispanic firms, language, education, and access to capital are characteristics that frequently limit their operations and growth. At the same time, Spanish-speaking Hispanic firms have an advantage in serving a fast-growing market. More than one million businesses with $6.3 billion in revenues spoke Spanish to their customers. Of these, 447,065 were employer firms with $6.2 billion in revenue.

By industry, the *Hispanic Business* 500 showed a concentration in traditional service industries such as automotive, service, wholesale, and construction. The fastest-growing companies are in the service sector, followed by construction and wholesale. Of the *Hispanic Business* 500, 65 companies had revenues of more than $100 million. Table 2-10 includes a list of the top 20 companies on the 2011 *Hispanic Business* 500 list.

Inc. Magazine counted 195 Hispanic businesses, or 14%, among its fastest-growing businesses in the Inc 5000 list. The bulk of these businesses were in Florida and California.

27 "Re-thinking Business," *Black Enterprise*, vol. 41, no. 11 (2011): 110.

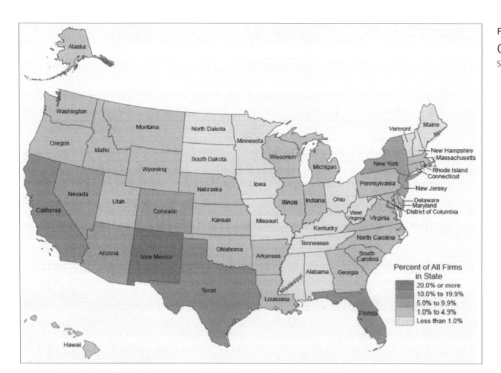

FIGURE 2-14. Hispanic-Owned Businesses, 2002
Source: Survey of Business 2002

Percent of All Firms in State

- 20.0% or more
- 10.0% to 19.9%
- 5.0% to 9.9%
- 1.0% to 4.9%
- Less than 1.0%

TABLE 2-10. Top 20 Businesses in 2011 Hispanic Business 500

		Industry	$ Million	Location
1	Brightstar Corp.	Global services delivering solutions including value-added distribution, supply chain services	4,600	Miami, FL
2	MasTec Inc.	Design, build, install, upgrade and maintain communications and utility/energy infrastructure	2,308	Coral Gables, FL
3	The Related Group of Florida	Developer of condominiums and rental buildings	NA	Miami, FL
4	International Bancshares Corp.	Full service financial institute	677	Laredo, TX
5	Quirch Foods Co.	Frozen food distribution	450	Miami, FL
6	Greenway Ford Inc.	Automotive sales & services	579	Orlando, FL
7	The Diez Group	Steel manufacturing, assembly	577	Dearborn, MI
8	Ruiz Foods Inc	Frozen hand-held food (El Monterey and Tornados)	525	Dinuba, CA
9	Group O Inc.	Packaging distribution, supply chain and marketing services, managed services, print management	515	Milan, IL
10	Genesis Networks Enterprises LLC	Network hardware, software & services; software development & testing; supply chain logistics; telecom	485	San Antonio, TX
11	Ancira Enterprises Inc.	Automotive sales & services	462	San Antonio, TX
12	Pan-American Life Insurance Group	Individual & group life, individual & group health, and worksite	455	New Orleans, LA
13	Fred Loya Insurance	Auto insurance	434	El Paso, TX
14	Crossland Construction Co. Inc.	General and heavy construction, construction management and design build	424	Columbus, KS
15	G&A Partners	Professional employment services	410	Houston, TX
16	OneSource Distributors Inc.	Electrical materials for maintenance, repair and operations construction, utility, automation & original equipment manufacturer applications	385	Oceanside, CA
17	Lopez Foods Inc.	Ground beef and pork products (hamburgers, sausage)	359	Oklahoma City, OK
18	MicroTech LLC	Technology services, systems engineering, products solutions, unified communication & collaboration	331	Vienna, VA
19	Navarro Discount Pharmacies	Retail drugstore chain with full service pharmacies	319.5	Medley, FL
20	Venoco Inc.	Crude oil and natural gas production	295.3	Denver, CO

Source: Hispanic Owners Magazine

TABLE 2-11. Asian Firms by Ethnicity

Ethnicity	2007 Number	% Asian	2002 Number	% change 2002–7	2007 Receipts ($000,000)	% of Asian	2002 Receipts ($000,000)	% change 2002–7	2007 Employer firms number	2002 Employer firms number	% change 2002–7
Asian	1,549,664		1,103,587	40	507,641		326,663	55	397,484	319,468	24
Asian Indian	308,514	20	223,212	38	152,468	30	88,128	73	109,196	82,422	33
Chinese	423,609	27	286,041	48	142,752	28	105,051	36	109,614	89,049	2
Filipino	163,217	11	125,146	30	20,217	4	14,155	43	21,071	19,888	6
Japanese	108,361	7	86,910	25	39,572	8	30,623	29	22,823	22,166	3
Korean	192,465	12	157,688	22	78,633	15	46,960	67	71,423	57,078	25
Vietnamese	229,149	15	147,036	56	28,800	6	15,512	86	29,782	25,591	16
Other Asian	153,565	10	89,118	72	45,142	9	24,275	86	37,367	24,835	51

Source: US Census Bureau 2007 Survey of Business Owners

ASIAN BUSINESSES

Asians owned approximately 1.5 million businesses, or 5.7% of all firms, in 2007 and represented growth of 40% over 2002. Asian firms employed 2.8 million people and generated $507.6 billion in revenues. Asian Indian, Chinese, Japanese, and Korean firms show a greater percent of employer firms than other Asian businesses. Chinese, Vietnamese, and other Asian groups showed the highest rate of growth in numbers, while Vietnamese, other Asian, and Asian Indian groups showed the highest growth in revenues (see Table 2-11).

The top industries for Asian firms were repair, maintenance, personal and laundry services (45%), professional, scientific and technical services, and retail trade. Of Asian Indian firms, 49% were in professional, scientific, and technical services, retail, and health and social assistance. For Chinese firms, 40% were in professional, scientific, and technical services, accommodation and food services, and repair, maintenance, and personal and laundry services. Korean firms were 40% in professional, scientific, and technical services and retail trade. Vietnamese firms were 67% in repair, maintenance, and personal and laundry services and the retail trade, consistent with lower educational attainment.

California had the most Asian businesses (33% of all Asian firms), with over half a million firms accounting for 15% of all firms in California. New York and Texas are second and third in the number of Asian businesses. High concentrations of Asian firms are found in the metropolitan areas around Los Angeles, San Francisco, and New York. Hawaii is the state with the largest concentration of Asian firms (47% of all firms in Hawaii).

Inc Magazine counted 195 Asian companies, or 27%, of its Inc 5000 fastest-growing list. Of these, 35 were located in California.

Immigrant Entrepreneurs

Asian immigrants number about 11 million, a more than ten-fold increase from 1970 to 2010, with the bulk of growth occurring from 1980 to 1990. Although the category of Asian includes more than 36 countries, the largest numbers came from China, India, Korea, the Philippines, and Vietnam. Among those who immigrated are entrepreneurs who owned and managed successful businesses in Asia. These individuals are able to start up businesses with their own capital and are successful in bringing the businesses up to scale. However, many of these entrepreneurs meet barriers in breaking out of their ethnic communities. The barriers include language and understanding of US marketing. Many of these owners have only recently emigrated from countries where cultural norms and business practices vary significantly from those in the United States.

Within Asian firms, there are marked differences in the size and number of firms. Chinese American firms have the largest number and sales. Of all minority firms, Chinese American firms have the largest sales, while Vietnamese firms have the smallest. Business owners also differ in endowments. Level of education can differ; Vietnamese business owners have the least education.

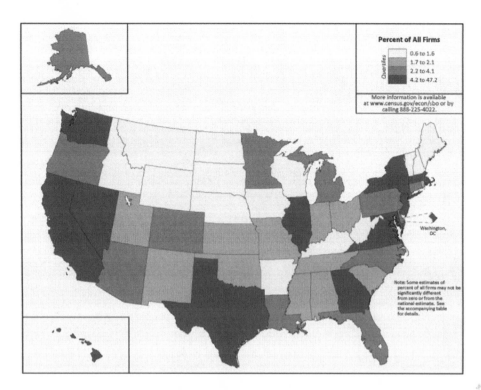

FIGURE 2-15. Asian-Owned Firms (5.7 percent of all firms in the United States)

Source: US Census Bureau 2007 Survey of Business Owners; released April 28, 2011

Japanese American business owners tend to draw the fewest number of customers from their ethnic markets, while Korean American and Vietnamese American business owners draw a large proportion from their ethnic markets.

Additionally, ethnic groups tend to cluster in business categories. For new Korean immigrants in the 1990s, the green-grocer business is popular in both Los Angeles and New York, while the dry cleaning business is popular in the Seattle area. Of the 50,000 independent donut shops in California, Cambodians and Chinese Cambodians operate as many as 90% of them. Indians dominate the independently owned low-end hotel business in the South. According to *Chinese Restaurant News*, as of 2009 there were 43,000 Chinese restaurants in the United States—more than the number of McDonald's, Wendy's, and Burger King combined. Within the Asian business community, the relatively short period of time these entrepreneurs have been in America might be a barrier to their expansion. Asian business owners tend to be less involved in community and civic affairs.

The impact of immigrant entrepreneurs is more prominent in technology companies. A 1999 study by Anne Lee Saxenian[28] found that Asian immigrants were at the helm of 24% of technology companies started from 1980 to 1998 in Silicon Valley. Another study, launched by the Kauffman Foundation, found that 52.4% of Silicon Valley start-ups between 1995 and 2005 had one or more immigrants as a key founder. The proportion of Chinese or Indian founders increased to 28% from 1999. Indians founded 15.5% of Silicon Valley start-ups, and Chinese immigrants (from both China and Taiwan) were key founders in 12.8%.

This study also found that 25.3% of engineering and technology companies in the United States had at least one key founder who was foreign born; Asian Indians are the largest proportion (26%). Almost 80% of immigrant-founded companies were in software and innovation/manufacturing services. The study estimates that foreign nationals were named as inventors or co-inventors of 24.2% of international patent applications filed in the United States in 2006, and the largest group was Chinese. In 2006, 16.8% of international patent applications from the United States had a Chinese-heritage name. Indian-heritage names constituted 14% of patent applications in the same year.[29]

These immigrants are highly educated, with 47% having a master's and 27% having a doctoral degree, with an

28 AnnaLee Saxenian, "Silicon Valley's New Immigrant Entrepreneurs." San Francisco: Public Policy Institute of California, 1999. http://www.ppic.org/content/pubs/report/R_699ASR.pdf.

29 V. Wadhwa et al., *America's New Immigrant Entrepreneurs*. Kansas City, MO: Kauffman Foundation, 2007.

emphasis on science and engineering. Most of the immigrants came to the United States to study. However, in recent years there has been a reverse brain drain, with many of these highly skilled workers returning to India and China to start companies. Estimates of these returning entrepreneurs are in the tens of thousands.[30] They cite better economic opportunities, access to local markets, and family ties as important considerations for their return. Many (72% of Indians and 81% of Chinese) believed there were better opportunities in their home countries, and they took pride in contributing to the economic development. These entrepreneurs continue to maintain ties with the United States, and there is speculation that a "brain circulation from Asia to the United States" is a better term for this phenomenon.

AMERICAN INDIAN AND ALASKA NATIVE BUSINESSES

American Indians and Alaska Natives (AIAN) owned 236,967 businesses in 2007, an 18% increase from 2002. They generated $34.4 billion in revenues and employed 184,416 people. About 30% of AIAN firms were in construction and repair, maintenance, and personal and laundry services. California, with 13% of AIAN firms, had the largest number of such firms, followed by Oklahoma and Texas. Los Angeles County had the largest number of AIAN firms. Similar to their population, AIAN business owners had lower educational attainment, start-up capital was more likely to be less than $5,000 or not used, and businesses tended to be younger than non-Hispanic white businesses.

Non-gaming Native businesses are concentrated in California, Texas, Oklahoma, and Florida (see Figure 2-16). The highest concentration is in Alaska, where they constitute 11% of businesses. With regard to metropolitan areas, Los Angeles ranks the highest, followed by Tulsa and Oklahoma. Non-gaming Native businesses tend to be in construction, services (amusement, business, and engineering/management) and retail (auto dealers/service stations).

Inc Magazine counted 19 American Indian businesses among its list of the 5,000 fastest-growing companies. The largest numbers were in Oklahoma.

US policies and actions have led to severe economic deprivation for many tribes. It was not until the past twenty-five years that the US government moved toward self-determination and self-governance for the tribes that have always been sovereign entities. It is now the task of each tribe to pick up the pieces and rebuild their economies.

---

30 V. Wadhwa et al., *The Grass Is Indeed Greener in India and China for Returnee Entrepreneurs*. Kansas City, MO: Kauffman Foundation, 2011.

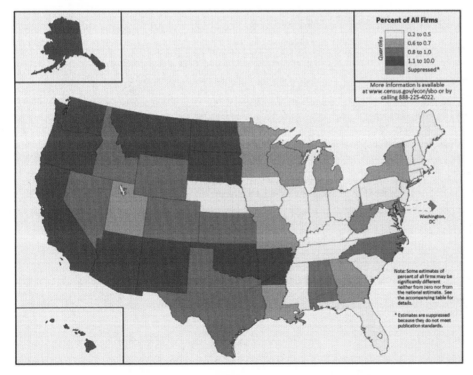

FIGURE 2-16. American Indian- and Alaska Native-Owned Firms, 2007 (0.9% of all firms in the US)

Source: US Census Bureau 2007 Survey of Business Owners; released March 11, 2011

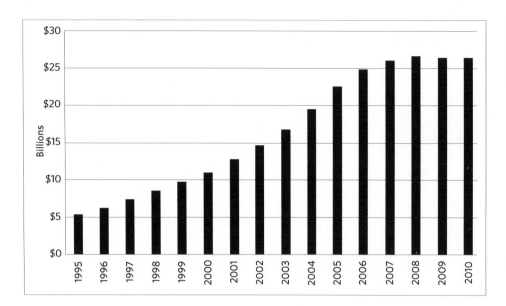

FIGURE 2-17. Tribal Gaming Revenues, 1995–2010

Source: National Tribal Gaming Commission http://www.nigc.gov/Gaming_Revenue_ Reports.aspxTribal.xls

Even as Indian Country has made amazing advances in economic development, each tribe must deal with economic development along with a host of challenges inherent in nation building. Although some tribes can adopt the constitutional model of the US government, many other tribes find this structure inconsistent with their traditional ways of governing. Additionally, economic development and thriving enterprises are dependent on a fair system of dispute resolution. Along with the creation of viable governance, the tribes must develop the equivalent of a court system to handle such matters. This they must do as they grapple with alcoholism, high suicide rates, health risks, and other social problems.

The Harvard Project on the American Indian states that it is easier to understand the economic development of American Indian tribes by comparing them to the communist economies of Eastern Europe and the former Soviet Union. Indian tribes are recovering from a century of a command-control economy imposed by the US government. On top of this, the government used economic development, job creation, and poverty relief as incentives for assimilation, with the rationale that American Indians needed to learn white ways in order to be economically successful. Besides having a false premise, these policies have nurtured a culture of dependency that distorted economic incentives.

American Indian reservations cover 55 million acres of land. Native villages and corporations account for an additional 44 million acres in Alaska. Excluding Alaska, this land contains 5,770 lakes; 765,706 acres of developed oil, gas, and mineral resources; 30% of the US coal reserve; 40% of US uranium deposits; and 4% of US oil

and natural gas deposits. Utilization of these natural resources varies among tribes and is sometimes dependent on culture and values. Even when tribes want to capitalize on their natural resources, inadequate funding and other factors such as commodity prices can play into the development of potential.

Tribal gaming has been a major factor in uplifting economic conditions in a few of the more than 500 tribes. It is a relatively new phenomenon that started in the 1970s with tribes using bingo games as a means of raising funds. This coincided with the efforts of a number of states developing gaming to generate state revenues. Conflict arose between tribal and state governments over whether the tribes could conduct gaming independent of state regulations. The 1987 Supreme Court ruling in *California v. Cabazon Band of Mission Indians* confirmed the authority of tribal governments to do so. Subsequently Congress grappled with the issue and passed the Indian Gaming Regulation Act of 1988, which was a compromise between state and tribal gaming interests. Tribal gaming has grown tremendously since the early 1990s, and growth stabilized in 2009.

Because of the many factors at play, the ease with which American Indians can start businesses on reservations will vary tremendously among the tribes. Tribes that have developed environments that are conducive to business start-ups (reduced bureaucracy, technical support, etc.) have been successful. Another important factor is the separation of political structure from enterprises. Tribes that separate tribal councils from business enterprises have a much higher success rate with their ventures.

In 2010, American Indian tribes operated 422 gaming

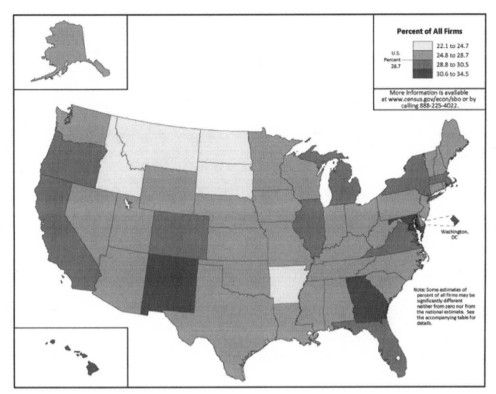

FIGURE 2-18. Women-Owned Businesses, 2007 (28.7% of all firms in the US)

Source: US Census Bureau 2007 Survey of Business Owners; released December 7, 2010

operations, which accounted for $26.5 billion in gaming revenues. Revenues of tribal gaming must be used to fund the tribal government, provide for the welfare of the tribe, promote economic development, donate to charitable organizations, or fund operations of local government agencies.

Although perceptions might be otherwise, only a few gaming operations generate high revenues. Seventy-four of the 422 gaming operations generate over $100 million in revenues because these enterprises have the advantage of being located near heavily populated areas.

Although objections have been brought against tribal gaming, evidence shows that gaming has had a beneficial effect, not just on the income of reservations but also on other social factors. According to a ten-year review of data conducted at the Harvard Project on American Indian Economic Development, in all but two categories gaming reservations showed a remarkable improvement over non-gaming reservations.

WOMEN-OWNED BUSINESS ENTERPRISES

In 2007, women accounted for 28.7% of businesses in the United States. They owned 7.8 million businesses, employed 7.6 million individuals, and generated $1.2 trillion in revenues. There is evidence that women-owned firms fared better in retaining employees in recent recessionary times. Despite their presence, women-owned business enterprises (WBEs) do not represent their proportion in the general population. WBEs are smaller and grow less quickly than male-owned businesses across all races and ethnicities.

With regard to entrepreneurial human capital, an SBA study shows that there are minimal differences between male and female business owners in education, experience, and preparedness. As more women are enrolled in college and obtain bachelor's degrees than men, it is expected that education will contribute less to the difference. Managerial experience contributes to entrepreneurial success, and a lower percentage of women hold managerial positions. Previous entrepreneurial experience, especially with a family business and particularly with a mother who was an entrepreneur, can affect the probability of success. Women also had less previous experience with entrepreneurship.[31] Women-owned firms start with less

---

31 D. Hackler, E. Harpel, and H. Mayer, *Human Capital and Women's Business Ownership.* Washington, DC: SBA Office of Advocacy, 2008.

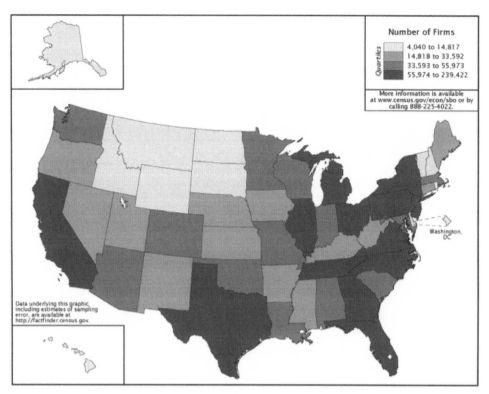

FIGURE 2-19. Veteran-Owned Businesses, 2007 (2,447,575 firms in the US)

Source: US Census Bureau 2007 Survey of Business Owners; released May 17, 2011

Number of Firms

Quartiles

- 4,040 to 14,817
- 14,818 to 33,592
- 33,593 to 55,973
- 55,974 to 239,422

More information is available at www.census.gov/econ/sbo or by calling 888-225-4022.

Data underlying this graphic, including estimates of sampling error, are available at http://factfinder.census.gov.

Washington, DC

capital, and a higher percentage have low credit scores.[32] On average, it took women four attempts to obtain debt capital and 22 attempts to obtain equity capital.[33]

Only 8% of active angel investors are women, which suggests that it is more difficult for female entrepreneurs to get angel financing and mentoring, and women angel investors are more likely to support other women than are men.[34] Women owners in high-tech firms are much less likely to use external equity, and this may affect their ability to grow as quickly as high-tech firms owned by men.[35]

Similar to MBEs, WBEs are concentrated in low-

capital, low-barrier-to-entry sectors. Women-owned businesses make up more than half (52.0%) of all businesses in health care and social assistance. The other top industries for women include educational services (45.9% of all such businesses are women-owned); administration and support; waste management; remediation services (37.0%); retail trade (34.4%); and arts, entertainment, and recreation (34.0%). WBEs are more likely to be home-based and less likely to have partners.

California had the largest number of WBEs (13% of all WBEs in the country), followed by Texas (7.8%) and New York (7.6%). Of US counties, Los Angeles, Cook, and Miami-Dade have the largest number of firms. New York City, Los Angeles, and Chicago were the cities that ranked the highest in the number of WBEs (see Figure 2-18).

Inc Magazine found that of its fastest-growing list of 5,000 companies, 52% were women owned. California and the New York City/Washington, DC, corridor had the largest number of fastest-growing women-owned businesses.

VETERAN-OWNED BUSINESSES

In 2010, 20.2 million men and 1.8 million women were veterans or individuals who served in the US military.

32 Kauffman Firm Survey, *Characteristics of New Firms: A Comparison by Gender.* Kansas City, MO: Kauffman Foundation, 2009.

33 National Women's Business Council, "Launching Women-Owned Businesses onto a High Growth Trajectory," 2010. Retrieved 12/20/11 from http://www.nwbc.gov/research/launching-women-owned-businesses-high-growth-trajectory.

34 Kauffman Foundation, *Women and Angel Investing: An Untapped Pool of Equity for Entrepreneurs.* Kansas City, MO: Kauffman Foundation, 2006. Retrieved 12/20/11 from http://www.phenomenelleangels.com/images/WhitePaper.pdf.

35 A. Robb and S. Coleman, "Sources of Financing for New Technology Firms: A Comparison by Gender." Kauffman Firm Survey, 2009. Retrieved 12/20/11 from http://www.kauffman.org/research-and-policy/sources-of-financing-for-new-technology-firms-a-comparison-by-gender.aspx.

Veterans who served in Korea or Vietnam number 11.0 million, and those who served in the Gulf Wars from 1990 onward number 5.9 million. A million veterans were unemployed as of the end of 2011, and another million are expected to leave military service by 2016. For veterans in their early twenties, 27% were unemployed in 2011. The Bureau of Labor Statistics claims that unemployment rates are consistent with those of the general population, with the exception of disabled veterans.[36] About one-third of younger veterans are employed in the public sector.

In 2007, veterans of the US military owned 2.4 million businesses, which accounted for 9% of all businesses. Employer firms (20%) were a larger proportion of all firms; they employed 5.8 million people and generated $1.2 trillion in revenues. A larger proportion of veteran firms were started prior to 1980, suggesting that more recent and younger veterans are less likely to start new firms. With regard to education, veteran business owners are more likely to have some college or advanced degrees

than nonveteran white business owners. The distribution of revenues is similar among all firms.

About one-third of veteran firms were in the professional, scientific, and technical services and construction sectors. Wholesale and retail trade accounted for 41.6% of veteran firms. California had the largest proportion of veteran firms (9%), followed by Texas and Florida. Los Angeles County had the largest number of all US counties. Among cities, New York, Los Angeles, and Houston had the largest number of firms (see Figure 2-19).

NATIVE HAWAIIAN PACIFIC ISLAND–OWNED BUSINESSES

Native Hawaiian and other Pacific Islanders (Guamanian and Samoans) owned 37,957 businesses, which accounts for a very small percentage of total businesses. They employed 38,750 people and generated $6.5 billion in revenues. Although spread more widely across sectors, construction, health care, and social assistance topped the list. Many of these businesses (30%) are located in Hawaii, while California is home to nearly 24% of NHPI businesses.

---

36 US Bureau of Labor Statistics, "Employment Situation of Veterans, 2010." Retrieved 12/20/11 from http://www.bls.gov/news.release/vet.nr0.htm.

REFERENCES

Acs, Zoltan, W. Parsons, and S. Tracy. *High-Impact Firms: Gazelles Revisited.* SBA Office of Advocacy, 2008.

Bhide, Amar. *The Origin and Evolution of New Businesses.* New York: Oxford University Press, 2000.

Fairlie, Robert, and A. Robb. *Race and Entrepreneurial Success.* Cambridge, MA: MIT Press, 2008.

Fairlie, Robert, and A. Robb. *Disparities in Capital Access between Minority and Non-Minority-Owned Businesses: The Troubling Reality of Capital Limitations Faced by MBEs 2008.* Minority Business Development Agency, January 2010.

Hackler, Darlene, et al. *Human Capital and Women's Business Ownership.* Washington, DC: SBA Office of Advocacy, 2008.

Kauffman Firm Survey. *Characteristics of New Firms: A Comparison by Gender.* Kansas City, MO: Kauffman Foundation, 2009.

Kauffman Foundation. Kauffman.org.

Lowrey, Ying. *Gender and Establishment Dynamics, 2002–2006.* Washington, DC: SBA Office of Advocacy, 2010.

Inc. Magazine. inc.com.

PricewaterhouseCoopers and National Venture Capital Association. *MoneyTree Report.* pwcmoneytree.com.

Robb, Alicia, and S. Coleman. "Sources of Financing for New Technology Firms: A Comparison by Gender." July 2009. Kauffman Firm Survey.

Sahlman, William, et al. *The Entrepreneurial Venture.* Boston: Harvard Business School Press, 1999.

SBA Office of Advocacy. Current: sba.gov/advocacy/7540. Archive: archive.sba.gov/advo/research.

Stangler, D., and P. Kedrosky. *Neutralism and Entrepreneurship: The Structural Dynamics of Startups, Young Firms, and Job Creation.* Kauffman Foundation Research Series: Firm Foundation and Economic Growth. September 2010. http://www.kauffman.org/uploaded-Files/firm-formation-neutralism.pdf.

Tracy, S. *Accelerating Job Creation in America: The Promise of High-Impact Companies.* Washington, DC: SBA Office of Advocacy, 2011. http://www.sba.gov/sites/default/files/rs381tot.pdf.

US Census Bureau, 2007. *Survey of Business Owners.* census.gov/econ/sbo.

Wadhwa, Viveck, et al. *America's New Immigrant Entrepreneurs.* Kansas City, MO: Kauffman Foundation, 2007.

Wadhwa, Viveck, et al. *The Grass Is Indeed Greener in India and China for Returnee Entrepreneurs.* Kansas City, MO: Kauffman Foundation, 2011.

Whitmore School of Business and Economics, University of New Hampshire, Center for Venture Research. wsbe.unh.edu/cvr.

DISCUSSION

1. List factors that contribute to firm survival and escape velocity for promising businesses. Consider your business and business owner's attributes. Analyze background information regarding work experience, reasons for starting the business, competitive environment, start-up capital, previous experiences with lending institutions, or other aspects of their experiences. Can this business reach escape velocity? What are the barriers, if any, for achieving this level of growth? How can you communicate needed changes?

2. The Survey of Business Owners has several categories for businesses. Are these categories sufficient for capturing, analyzing, and implementing business and economic development strategies? What other categories should be created to improve our analysis and understanding of small business and entrepreneurship?

3. Certification of minority businesses for federal contacts has been stopped at the SBA yet continues in the supplier diversity marketplace. Is your client business disadvantaged? Should initiatives in this area continue? Give your analysis of why or why not.

4. Tribal gaming often comes under attack for a variety of reasons. Analyze the need and future of tribal gaming. Give your conclusions on what its future should be. Should the United States attempt to stem the reverse brain drain? What should be the policy on immigrant entrepreneurs? How does immigration policy affect this?

3. Teaming and Project Management

ABOUT THIS MODULE

Most consulting projects are of such magnitude that they cannot be completed by any one individual. They require not just a group of people, but a team working collaboratively to complete the often complex tasks. Typically, consulting projects have tight deadlines, and the goal is to minimize costs and project a clear plan that identifies all the tasks. Attention must be paid to both plan and tasks in order for the project to be successful. Focusing on one to the exclusion of the other can hinder the level of accomplishment. This module discusses both the teaming process and the project management plan.

Consulting projects undertaken in an academic setting present challenges to the student team beyond what students typically face in a class and beyond what professional consultants face. Unlike other academic assignments, where the parameters are defined and presented in a classroom setting, these projects are open ended in a fluid environment. For students who are unfamiliar with working on such projects, this can be unsettling, and they may spend an inordinate amount of time honing in on goals and performing the work. The nature of the academic term requires that the project be substantially completed in the designated time frame. The student team must thus make full use of project management tools to keep the project on track. Student teams also tend to be diverse, and the team is often working with a business owner of a different culture.

With student consulting projects, the worst outcome is to consume the extremely valuable time of the students, advisors, mentors, faculty, and business owners to accomplish nothing of value for the business because of teaming issues. This is particularly harmful to a small business, which can scarcely afford the time and distraction. Student members suffer as well. An unpleasant team experience can foster dysfunctional team behavior that individuals may carry to the next team experience. Team conflict inhibits learning and development. A poorly executed project reflects badly on the school or other sponsoring organizations, as well as on all team members, including the faculty, advisors, and mentors who are guiding the students.

Good teams, however, have the chance to add value to a business and contribute to regional economic development. The majority of student consulting teams produce projects that are of great benefit to their businesses. The goal of teaming and project management is to make the teaming experience rewarding and project management effective. In order to accomplish this, team members have to spend as much time working and reflecting on teaming skills as on completing the tasks of the project.

After Studying This Module

The objective of this module is to prepare students for the teaming experience by presenting knowledge of theory and practice about the teaming process and project management. After reading this module, the student will be able to:

- Describe the attributes of high-performance teams.
- Identify and use techniques of divergent thinking.
- Articulate how culture can affect communication in a team.
- Explain the stages of teaming and describe what actions must be taken at each stage.
- Identify and use the concepts and tools of project management, including project planning, work structure breakdown, Gantt charts, critical path analysis, and project control systems.

TEAMING

Working with teams is the rule rather than the exception in any business environment. Throughout most business careers, the ability to rise in an enterprise will depend on the individual's ability to organize, manage, and participate in teams, committees, and communities. Sometimes teams are formed to accomplish long-term projects, such as new product development involving tasks ranging from concept, prototype, and testing to launching. The effort may pull together diverse people with many different skills. Other teams form around temporary issues and the life of the team is short. Still others may be virtual teams in which members are not in the same physical location. The ubiquitous use of teams makes teaming skills essential to any well-prepared business student.

Often college and university teams give students their first experience working with a diverse group of people. In the case of student teams working with client businesses, the students are required to deliver a quality result (product) that meets established professional standards. The product should be presentable to a client as well as to other stakeholders in the business community. Meeting these expectations presents opportunities to display or demonstrate important skills. But the process may also be a source of stress and turmoil for the team.

High-Performance Teams

High-performance teams produce extraordinary results often under great constraints. They are the appropriate model for student teams because the students are also being asked to perform against the odds to assist an underserved business in pursuing an opportunity. Projects must be completed under very tight timelines, with none of the resources available to employees of large corporations.

High-performance teams can produce results far above and beyond what prior teams have been able to accomplish. They solve the world's most difficult problems (e.g., low-cost and effective vaccination of children in underdeveloped countries) and often include experienced experts. Care and time should be taken in putting together such teams; choosing the right team members is crucial to success. It is also important to create the right context for the team to succeed. The process of a high-performance team was documented in a case study and

key attributes were identified.[1] Other characteristics and conditions associated with high-performance teams are also summarized briefly.

Commitment to excellence. It stands to reason that high-performance teams typically consist of high-performance individuals. In order to complete projects of extraordinary quality, all team members must have the highest expectations for success. They will not tolerate a substandard product from themselves or the team. Members will go to extraordinary lengths to achieve the best outcome. For student teams this is likely to happen when every student makes a commitment to excellence.

Mutual respect. With high expectations and short timelines, team members work under stressful conditions. Difficult situations and conflicts may occur. Emotions may run high, and team members may communicate in ways that they later regret. It is imperative that the team work in a context of mutual respect. Individuals understand that no matter how difficult the situation, they will emerge from the team experience with respect for each other and their contribution to the team effort.

Shared risk and reward. The leader of the team is not the only individual responsible for the performance and failings of the team. All team members feel accountable for all actions of the team. If an individual team member cannot complete a task, other team members will put forth the extra effort needed to assist so the project can continue moving toward on-time task completion.

Flexibility. Contrary to conventional wisdom, high-performance teams do not have plans that are created at the beginning of the project and followed religiously until the end. New information is generated and shared continuously. The usual linear model for completing projects gives way to the rapid generation of ideas that were exposed and evaluated while still in a relatively immature state. If they are deemed appropriate, the plan is changed to adapt to the new input. Experienced team leaders suggest that agile development techniques be used in which the team leader will check in every day with all team members, asking the following three ques-

---

1   Arvind Malhotra, A. Majchrzak, Robert Carman, and Vern Lott, "Radical Innovation without Collocation: A Case Study at Boeing-Rocketdyne," *MIS Quarterly*, vol. 25, no. 2 (2001).

TABLE 3-1. Team Task Behaviors

Task Behaviors	Behavior	Purpose
Initiating	Define task, goal, or process.	Helps team find direction when floundering.
Seeking information and opinions	Collect more data or ask for individual opinions or ideas.	Inadequate data gathering can lead to poor problem solving and decision making.
Giving information and opinions	Provide data, relevant information, opinions, and ideas.	Ensures the team has all the information it needs to accomplish the task.
Clarifying and elaborating	Ask for clarification, build on other's ideas, or clarify an idea.	Provides focus for team and builds on other's ideas.
Summarizing	Restate key points, decisions, action plans, or themes.	Focuses discussion and establishes closure.
Evaluating	Assess whether group is performing tasks or using procedures effectively.	Determines if team is functioning effectively.
Testing for consensus	Poll the group and determine if there is consensus. Open discussion on objections.	Determines if every team member supports decision.

Source: R. Blake and J. Mouton, *Spectacular Teamwork: How to Develop the Leadership Skills for Team Success.* New York: Wiley, 1987

tions: What did you do yesterday? What are you doing today? Do you need help?

Atmosphere of cooperation. As unfamiliar ideas and analyses are encountered in exploring solutions to problems, team members are likely to make mistakes. In the team environment, the mistakes are visible to everyone. Therefore, it is important to have an atmosphere of cooperation where team members understand that mistakes will be made and the team can learn from them and move on to successful results.

Acknowledged interdependence. Some students may assume that a few strong team members can complete the project, and this small group may break off from the team so that they can "more efficiently" get the job done. This is a mistake as it will lead to producing less work for the client. Acknowledging interdependence means that every team member is necessary to the success of the project. It is the combined efforts of all the team members that will come up with the best product.

Trust. Many teaming experts believe the success of the team depends on how quickly trust is established among the members. Most challenging projects involve an inordinate amount of work, willpower, and creativity. The more that you can count on your team members to meet project goals, the higher level of team trust you will reach. When first presented, innovative solutions may seem off the wall or even ludicrous. Trust is essential to

team members performing at the highest level of excellence.

Heroism. Team members on a high-performance team will do what it takes to get the job done regardless of position or title outside of the team. A difficult situation or conflict may arise that calls for someone to show courage. Often one or more members of the team will perform acts of heroism that will get the team through a rough spot.

Focus on shared performance outcomes. Each team member has a clear vision of the outcomes and a common commitment to achieve it. No time is spent on extraneous activities. Team time is used to accomplish team work. Meetings are not spent reviewing or summarizing the work of individual members. This review should be completed prior to the meeting. The team meeting is used to advance the project by completing other work. No distractions are tolerated.

Beyond these attributes, high-performance teams can be chaotic. They undergo large and small changes because team members are constantly experimenting and generating new ideas. A team may seemingly make no progress and then come through with a breakthrough in its eleventh hour. Often the process is the most disruptive just before such a breakthrough.

Task behaviors help the team stay focused on its task and accomplish its goals, as shown in Table 3-1.

Equally important are relationship behaviors. They help

TABLE 3-2. Team Relationship Behaviors

Relationship Behaviors	Behavior	Purpose
Gatekeeping	Ask individuals for their input and control individuals who wish to monopolize the discussion.	Balances communication and includes all team members.
Active listening	Paraphrase what was heard, indicate understanding, and ask clarifying questions.	Values contribution and ensures correct understanding.
Setting and maintaining standards	Set standards and define norms. Require that team members adhere to norms.	Defines how the team should work together and ensures they maintain their standards.
Harmonizing	Articulate common elements of conflicting viewpoints.	Promotes compromise and collaboration.
Encouraging	Give recognition and point out accomplishments.	Creates positive team environment.
Giving feedback	Give constructive feedback on behavior that is having a negative effect on the group.	Supports effective behavior and discourages dysfunctional behavior.
Receiving feedback	Actively listen without reacting or judging. Formulate a plan to change ineffective behavior.	Continuous feedback on team effectiveness.

Source: R. Blake and J. Mouton, *Spectacular Teamwork: How to Develop the Leadership Skills for Team Success.* New York: Wiley, 1987.

maintain a healthy environment for team members and keep communication open and flowing (see Table 3-2).

There is a third set of behaviors, self-oriented behaviors, that generally disrupt team functioning. They include depending on others instead of doing one's own work, resisting the direction chosen by the team, withdrawing from the group, pairing off, putting others down, getting off topic, complaining, moping, being silent, triangulating, and dominating the discussion. For novice teams, it is important for the team to name such behaviors so that team members understand that they are not acceptable.

Team Development

Researchers and practitioners have identified four stages through which a team progresses. These phases are commonly referred to by the terms *forming, storming, norming,* and *performing.*[2] (See Figure 3-1.)

Forming. Individuals meet and become acquainted with other team members. The purpose and direction of the team is made clear. They find out what the team can and cannot do. Team members begin to establish trust with each other.

Storming. The difficulty and complexity of the task may start to overwhelm some team members. Conflict arises, and team members begin to argue about what should be done. No progress is made toward task completion. Teams may backpedal on work done previously.

Norming. The team moves to develop ground rules (norms) by which the team will operate and communicate. Each team member adopts a role. Expectations and standards are defined. Relationships between team members are strengthened, and commitment to the team is fostered. The team will begin to make significant progress toward project goals.

Performing. Team members incorporate individual strengths and weaknesses and work together. The focus is on completing the project. Roles become flexible. Rela-

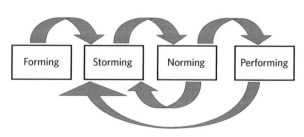

FIGURE 3-1. Teaming Phases

2   B. W. Tuckman and M. A. Jensen, "Stages of Small-Group Development Revisited," *Group and Organization Studies,* vol. 2, no. 4 (1977): 419–27.

tionships are strong. There is continuous improvement of the process.

Most depictions of these stages, however, assume that there is linear progression through each stage. In a real world environment, teams actually move both forward and backward through these stages. A move backward may be the result of the team having insufficiently addressed issues relevant to the previous stage of development or, often, disruptive events such as breakthroughs can trigger movement backward.

Forming Stage

The names of five students are called, and they are told they will be a student consulting team. With this unceremonious start, the forming stage begins. These five individuals must progress from knowing nothing about each other and the business with which they will work to being a team that will commit 400 to 500 hours (5 to 10 hours a week per person) to completing a challenging consulting project that will bring substantial value to a business. Although they will be successful in achieving this, at this early stage the students are full of insecurities.

Because they do not know each other, establishing an identity is a major concern with each of the team members at the forming stage. Individuals may want recognition from others on the team. They may seek status. In doing this, they ask themselves questions such as: What role will I play in this group? How do I want others to perceive me? What can I contribute? Who is the leader? What is supposed to happen?

Part of the sense of insecurity is brought about by unfamiliarity with the consulting process. Like professional consultants when they begin a new project, the students start with very little knowledge about their project. They may have the name of the business and a list of work areas, but there are many unknowns. They lack a sense of direction and are trying to get their bearings in this new situation. They feel self-conscious.

Being grouped with four other strangers only adds to the uncertainty. There may not be any shared history. Team members may be from different cultures and feel uncomfortable communicating in a group. Lack of trust prevents deep interaction between team members. Communication stays on a superficial level. Often the individuals look to faculty to provide leadership and direction. They will look to the mentor to guide them. At this initial phase, faculty will outline requirements and provide information. Experienced mentors will model leadership behavior, but both faculty and mentors will quickly turn the reins over to the team. In order to learn, the team must undergo the processing, planning, and executing of the project without too much intervention from faculty and mentors.

Each team member's goals in the forming stage are to get to know one another and to address questions about the process and the project. A team contract is usually drawn up once individuals have had a chance to interact with each other. The team contract includes a code of cooperation for the team and should establish team expectations, such as:

- Attend all meetings and be on time
- Listen to and show respect for the views of other members
- Critique ideas, not persons
- There are no stupid questions
- Avoid disruptive or distracting behavior
- Carry out assignments on schedule
- Resolve conflicts constructively, and always strive for win-win solutions
- All team members are responsible for the team's progress

Task issues may include:

- What is the best way to reach team members on a regular basis and in case of emergency?
- What are constraints on scheduling (include time away, other projects, or studying for exams)?
- How often, when, and where will the team meet?
- Is there a template for meeting agendas, minutes, and action items?
- How will data be collected, archived, and distributed?
- How will work be circulated for review?
- How will action items be followed up?
- What is the standard for team work?

Relationship issues may include:

- What is the protocol for communication and response to communication?
- What is each team member's role (leader, facilitator, knowledge manager, etc.)?

- How will the team deal with members missing or being late to meetings?
- What are the rules for discussion and decision-making during team meetings?
- How will team members' developmental needs be addressed?
- What mechanism will the team have for flagging problems?
- How will a team member signal for help?
- When will outside help be sought?
- How will team members be rewarded?
- How will the team experience be evaluated?

Even with the short time frame, it is important to take the time to bond and establish trust. Once team members know each other, a leader should be chosen. There are no set ways to choose a leader. Some teams allow individuals to volunteer; others vote for a leader. The question of who will be team leader is often a point of contention for novice teams. Be aware that natural leaders may emerge later in the teaming process.

Most student teams define the role of the team leader as supervising the rest of the team. They see the team leader as someone who will tell the team what to do. In actual fact, the most important function of the leader is to open lines of communication with all team members and remove obstacles so the team can complete its job. Each team member must establish a relationship with the team leader. It is the responsibility of the team leader to ensure that time is taken to communicate with all the individuals. It is also important to remember that, even though the team may have a titular leader, different leadership may emerge as needed. Leadership issues and leadership roles must be discussed and agreed upon.

Be aware that consensus is not the goal of the team because consensus does not always lead to a good product. All team members must be heard. Team members should restate to the speaker what was heard and confirm that it is correct. Even if team members did not vote for a team decision, they will be asked if they can buy into it. It is essential that team members make the distinction and act accordingly.

Each team member must clarify her or his perception of the project mission. When the team members have a clear vision of their goals, the rules and procedures with which they will operate, the standards with which they will perform, and their expectations of each team member, they will have moved to the next phase of teaming:

norming. Be aware that during the forming phase, little may be done to advance the project goals. However, time invested in establishing trust and eliminating uncertainty allows the team to be more productive in later phases.

Professional consultants often spend time in a planning retreat, where they discuss both the project and the team responsibilities and roles. While it is not necessary to spend an entire day in an off-site planning session, team members can discuss many of the same issues related to work styles and project goals. A candid discussion of each team member's strengths and weaknesses can go a long way toward establishing trust.

Novices often move through the forming stage in a superficial manner. This results from a lack of critical self-assessment and the desire to fit in with other team members. While it is commendable to try to fit in, honest communication is the best strategy. Without honest communication the team will never really form, and thus performance will be hindered later in the consulting process.

As the team moves toward developing its norms, cultural and personal differences will come into play. For example, team members for whom English is not their first language may be less vocal in expressing opinions. For some cultures, arriving on time means arriving no more than fifteen minutes late. For other cultures, arriving on time means arriving five minutes early. As team members commit to arriving on time to all meetings, it is important to clarify what "on time" means. It is equally important to iron out other matters of team protocol, keeping in mind that cultural perceptions may be different.

It is also important to recognize that, in a less diverse team, those who are in the minority might feel inhibited about offering opinions; likewise those in the majority might be tempted to bend over backward to accommodate what they perceive as differences. The keys to good team formation are honest self-assessment, open communication, appreciation of differences, and acknowledgment and full utilization of all of the skills and attributes of all team members.

Team formation culminates with the drafting and signing of a team contract. The purpose of the team contract is to document the rules and regulations under which the team will operate. Expectations of each team member are disclosed, task and work standards are defined, communication protocols are outlined, and scheduling conflicts are identified and resolved. Other

TABLE 3-3. Team Diagnostic Tool

	1 Low Evidence	2	3	4	5 High Evidence
Loss of production					
Grievances or complaints					
Conflicts or hostility					
Confusion about assignments or relationships					
Lack of clear goals or low commitment					
Apathy or lack of interest					
Lack of innovation, risk taking, imagination, or initiative					
Ineffective meetings					
Problems working with client					
Poor communication					
Lack of trust					
Decisions not understood or agreed with					
Good work is not recognized or rewarded					
People are not encouraged to work together					

Source: W. G. Dyer, *Team Building: Issues and Alternatives*. 2d ed. Reading, MA: Addison-Wesley, 1987.

conflict resolution procedures are specified and accepted by the team. For novice team members, the significance of the contract is that it facilitates complete discussion of these issues and should help in gaining compliance from all team members.

Storming Stage

The storming stage is necessary for groups if they seek to reach a high level of performance. During the forming stage, team members have become familiar with each other and some of the work has been done. Secondary research will likely have begun and the first fruits of teamwork begin to trickle in. At the same time, traces of discontent may surface. As tasks are undertaken, differences in perceived quality and standards will arise. Individual team members may feel that others are not producing to the standards or quality agreed to by the team. They may feel that some team members are digressing on tangents that are not pertinent to project goals. Expressing this dissatisfaction brings up defensiveness or counterattacks. A faction of team members may question the legitimacy of the team leader.

There may be duplication of effort because some team members choose to assume the roles assigned to others. Team members jockey for position and status. Frustration builds from perceived violation of boundaries. The storming phase is characterized by the lack of productive work; this results in additional consternation for the team.

As team members become more familiar with each other and develop their own views of where the project is going, disagreements often surface. The storming phase signals that team members are expressing their own viewpoints, and diversity in a team leads to superior results. The difficulty lies in teams not being able to move through this stage.

To move through the storming stage, the team must learn how to manage and resolve conflicts. The leader may play a key role in fostering a win-win resolution of disagreements. Faculty and advisors will redirect the team's focus to the project goals and successful completion rather than personal differences. At the same time, team members will be encouraged to express any ideas that advance project goals.

A diagnostic checklist to provide early detection of team conflicts can be extremely helpful. Teams are encouraged to use this checklist frequently enough so that solutions can be developed by the team in consultation with faculty and other mentors before team problems become serious and much more difficult to manage or resolve. The evaluation tool in Table 3-3 can be used by all team members to rate team interaction. For example, a score over 43 signals that the team requires more team building.

Frequently, persons in teams either misunderstand assignments or simply fail to follow through on what is requested. A feedback system (even a simple one such as the three questions: What did you do yesterday? What are you doing today? Do you need help?) can help to ensure that the project wheel keeps turning. If the team plans in advance how to handle members who do not meet their team obligations, there is less confusion about how to handle poor performance. Additionally, if a team member fails to perform, wasting time on recrimination is unproductive. Rather, time should be taken to work out a way to help the team member to succeed. This is not to say that all work should be taken away from the team member, nor should the team member be shut out of the process in any way. In these consulting teams and projects, a major goal is to develop businesses, students, and advisors so they can make value-added contributions to project task completion.

Punishments do not develop teaming skills. Often they insure that individuals who do not participate, never participate. If team members are unmotivated in the first place, punishment just excludes them completely. It is much more important to develop a system of reward. Business owners, mentors, advisors, and faculty can contribute to determining and offering an effective reward.

Norming Stage

When the team has worked through the storming stage, several things happen: (a) the original team contract is revised to reflect what was learned in the storming stage, (b) newly defined roles and responsibilities are assumed by team members, and (c) the focus shifts away from group dynamics to reaching the team goal.

The norming phase is characterized by the strengthening of relationships between team members. Team members begin to put team goals above personal goals. All team members have agreed on how they will work together, who will provide leadership in what areas of the project, and how they will handle future conflicts. Teams enter the norming stage by resolving conflicts, developing unwritten rules for team interaction, and developing trust in each other. Individual team members will become more comfortable with their role in the team. Each member relies less on the leader and takes more responsibility for completing tasks, solving problems, and resolving conflicts.

It is important to remember that there is no right way for the team to function. Experienced team members know that each team will develop its own communication protocol and operational process. Each team will have its own normative behaviors, which will be a combi-

nation and synthesis of those from its members. Norming happens when team members can contribute their unique perspectives and skills and when those perspectives and skills are embraced for the good of the project. The more time the team spends together, the more they should be able to collaborate and resolve these issues. It is also important to note that some teams may revert to the storming stage where issues need to again be addressed

Throughout the project, the team needs to be mindful that the project is focused on its overall mission and goals. This does not mean the goals cannot change. Every project will undergo some amount of adjustment or "tweaking" as more knowledge is gathered. When key information is uncovered, the project plan needs to be changed to reflect this. Another continuing question is whether the client is still committed to the mission of the project. If commitment wavers, the team needs to deal with this by communicating, clarifying, and perhaps even helping with client motivation. After all, client buy-in is critical to the acceptance and implementation of project results and team recommendations.

Team Roles

During the forming stage team members agreed to assume various team roles. When teams enter the norming stage it is advisable to revisit these roles, which can include the following:

Team leader. The leader is ultimately responsible for delivering the project on time and within budget. She generally shepherds team efforts and can serve as a coach and leader for the team. Her role is to provide expertise, guidance, clear direction, and leadership within the team. The leader must be supportive and foster commitment from all team members. She must create win-win resolutions out of conflicts. She must orchestrate exemplary performance. In novice project teams, the leader often must fill in to complete the day-to-day tasks in order to maintain the confidence and cooperation of the team members. Student teams tend to operate with little formal hierarchy so that trust and leadership needs to be earned.

Team facilitator. The facilitator may assist the leader in planning team meetings, leading meetings, and handling meeting logistics and administrative tasks. The facilitator creates awareness of the process and manages discussion flow and strategic moments. Additionally, the team

TABLE 3-4. Individualism and Collectivism as Perspectives in American Business Culture

Individualism	Group Collectivism
Independence and individual achievement. In American business press, business success is equated with individual entrepreneurial achievement (e.g., Michael Dell, Bill Gates, Sam Walton) rather than the collective efforts of a team of many individuals.	Interdependence and group success. Minority businesses often involve many people who support the venture.
Ideas and business activity out of social context. Maximizing profit is the ultimate goal. It is acceptable to push the envelope on the rules and violate relationships to achieve maximum profit.	Ideas and business activity in social context. Business is to enhance human relationships such as strengthen family or community.
Self-expression, individual thinking, and personal choice. American media and business myth often glorify the maverick or individual who goes against the grain to succeed.	Adherence to norms, respect for authority, and group consensus. Multiple members of the community may be consulted before a decision is made.
Private property. Ideas belong to the business and are protected by copyright and intellectual property laws. Time is private property and a resource to be allocated.	Shared property. Businesses may not understand that ideas cannot be copyrighted. They may not protect their own intellectual property.
Egalitarian relationships and flexible roles. It is acceptable for individuals to interrupt, assert their ideas, and assume the role of leader.	Stable, hierarchal roles. Rules of protocol apply to social and business interactions. Elders command respect.

facilitator may be the main contact person between the team the business owner, mentors, and advisors.

Team knowledge manager. The team knowledge manager documents the team process, captures key points, highlights decisions and action items, and distributes information. This role, previously called team recorder, has expanded with the complexity of teams and projects.

Devil's advocate. It is important that someone challenge the majority and present different points of view. This role may be rotated or assumed on an ad hoc basis. Often in the rush of completing the project, team members will opt for the easy route or succumb to groupthink. Having a team member who asks the hard questions is crucial to keeping the project on the right path.

Mentors. Industry mentors or advisors may be used in student consulting projects. As working professionals, these individuals have a high level of technical expertise and often can provide linkages to larger enterprises in the area. In challenging times, students may look to mentors to lead the effort. However, mentors are not the "responsible party" for the deliverables in the student projects. They provide guidance without taking leadership.

Cultural Considerations in Teaming

Frequently, during the data gathering process consultants must move away from a familiar cultural perspective toward an understanding of different cultural perspectives. In this context, different cultures can refer to racial/ethnic cultures, business/industry cultures, and corporate/organizational cultures. To be effective in creating change, the team needs to understand and respect the business owner's viewpoint. Much of the knowledge management in such businesses is not in databases or documents. Much of it comes out of the client's experiences, the skill set, and the environment in which the firm operates. In order to elicit this knowledge, the team must be sensitive to verbal and nonverbal communication. Often teams working with different cultures will engage culture coaches to understand what distinctions must be made. Table 3-4 highlights the differences between individualism, which is often characteristic of mainstream cultures, and group collectivism, which is often characteristic of minority cultures.

Although not entirely without controversy, Geert Hofstede of the Institute for Research in Intercultural Communication at Tilburg University identified five dimensions of cultures that are relevant to multicultural consulting engagements.[3] They are presented here for reference.

Power distance. Many cultures give high respect to authority and believe that rank and status are very important.

---

3 Geert Hofstede, *Culture's Consequences: Comparing Values, Behaviors, Institutions, and Organizations Across Nations.* 2d ed. Thousand Oaks, CA: Sage Publications, 2001.

TABLE 3-5. Intergenerational Differences

	Silent Born 1928–1945	Boomers Born 1946–1965	Generation X Born 1965–1980	Millennial Born after 1980
Perceived uniqueness	Shared WW II and depression	Work ethic	Technology	Technology
Technology (percent social networking)	6%	30%	50%	75%
Diversity	80% white	73% white	62% white	61% white
Education (percent with some college or more)	28% (21% for females)	38% (34% for females)	46% (52% for females)	49% (60% for females)
Loyalty (stay in job for rest of working life)		84%	62%	42%
Optimism (will earn enough in future)		46%	76%	88%
Values (people living together without getting married is bad for society)	58%	44%	31%	22%
Government should do more to solve problems	39%	43%	45%	53%

Source: Paul Taylor and Scott Keefer, eds., "Millennials," Pew Research Center.

Many Asian immigrant business owners have been very desirous of having university students assist their companies due to the respect they have for education. Conversely, some African American business owners have placed a higher value on prior business experience or knowledge of the African American consumer market. Consultants entering cross-cultural consulting relationships should determine the power-distance dimension that is most relevant and seek to build confidence with the client by having the appropriate team composition.

Masculinity/femininity. Masculine cultures tend to be more materialistic and value assertive, whereas feminine cultures value concern for others and relationships among people. In seeking to help a male-owned professional services firm, the consulting team successfully identified that the firm operated from a feminine-culture orientation when it came to approaching prospective new clients. Through early recognition of this orientation, the team was able to reorient its consulting contract to focus on building a more assertive approach to the firm's sales strategy rather than focusing on designing a broad marketing strategy.

Individualism and collectivism. Individualist-oriented cultures and businesses focus on taking care of the individual as compared to the collectivist-oriented cultures in which groups of people take care of each other. A number of African American business owners state that the reason they started their business was as a means of contributing to their community. They operate from a collectivist perspective. Other African American firms, and many firms owned by non-Hispanic whites, were launched as a means of creating economic well-being for the founder and thus come from an individualist approach. A team's effectiveness should be enhanced when there is some understanding of the client's value orientation.

Uncertainty avoidance. This dimension refers to the degree to which people feel threatened by and attempt to avoid ambiguous situations. Corporate cultures that desire to avoid uncertainty are resistant to change. Even for many bootstrapping entrepreneurs, change can be hard. They have built a business to a level of success and, though they may communicate a desire to change, consultants might find hesitancy to implement change.

Long-Term orientation. This dimension refers to the trade-offs that individuals and organizations make between focusing on long-term or short-term gain. Many fledgling companies are focused on making monthly payroll; they are fixated on increasing sales or decreasing costs immediately. More established firms can take a longer-term approach.

In addition to high and low context, consideration should be given to generational differences in team members. These differences affect the use of technology, value systems, and collaborative styles. If the differences are understood, there is less likelihood of conflict. Data and relationships in Table 3-5 help to explain some of these differences as disclosed by the Pew Research Center.[4] Thus, the Millennial student team is more educated, more diverse, less likely to value loyalty, more open to government solutions, and more likely to incorporate technology than earlier generations. They may be dealing with a business owner of an older generation. Misunderstandings can happen unless the team understands the differences that can occur across generations.

Divergent Thinking

Novice and experienced teams alike can fall prey to other constraints of effective analysis. It is essential at every phase of the project, from initial planning to conclusion, to encourage divergent thinking. Teaming literature provides many examples in which the opposite of divergent thinking, or groupthink, led to disastrous results.

The best solutions are likely to emerge outside the "box" in which teams routinely think. These solutions do not necessarily come from the people who are most likely to assert their thoughts. Therefore, it is important throughout the process to include all individuals who have a stake in the outcome and to keep all team members in the loop. Consultants use a number of techniques to encourage both divergent thinking in the generation of ideas and a refining of the abundance of ideas that might be generated for any one topic.

Brainstorming. Brainstorming is a technique familiar to most people who have worked in groups. The goal of brainstorming is to encourage a large number of ideas on the given issue or topic. The atmosphere should be freewheeling. Participants should be encouraged to come up with wild ideas. Nothing should be discounted. Participants are not allowed to evaluate or criticize ideas. This rule must be enforced in order for brainstorming to be effective. By brainstorming in a group, members are more likely to think of related ideas that in turn are built upon.

Ideas are improved as they are transformed into various combinations.

The process involves first generating the ideas, then clarifying and categorizing them, and finally narrowing the list. To avoid getting bogged down, set strict time limits for each of these steps. When clarifying or categorizing the ideas, avoid evaluation and criticism. When categorizing and narrowing ideas, make sure that everyone is in agreement.

The facilitator should ensure that everyone participates in the process and that participation is equal. Domineering individuals allowed to monopolize the time will stifle creativity. Setting a goal for the number of ideas can keep team members going.

Brainwriting. In diverse teams, it is important to keep in mind that some team members may come from cultures where open oral discussion is not commonplace. Additionally, some team members may think or express themselves better in writing. A variation of brainstorming is to have all participants write a few ideas on a sheet of paper. One team member writes an idea on the paper. It is then placed in the middle of the group, where another team member may take it and write at least one more idea on the same sheet. This process is repeated until all ideas are collected. Then ideas can be clarified, categorized, and narrowed.

Another writing variation is to have enough sheets for every member of the group. Each team member is given five minutes to write three ideas on the sheet. The sheet is then passed to the next team member, who also writes three ideas, and so on, until all team members have written three ideas on all the sheets.

Visualizing ideas is sometimes helpful in coming up with creative solutions. Each team member is given a sheet of paper. People are asked to draw the solution to the issue in question. Again, a time limit is given. When all team members are finished, they are asked to show their drawings and explain them to the group.

Mind mapping. Mind mapping involves putting ideas in the form of a web or network that shows the relationships among these ideas. Starting with a central idea or topic, branches representing different aspects of the main topic are added. This creates a "map" of the topic that can be used for further development. Often mind maps are used to develop project plans or organize notes, bringing the divergent thinking into convergent organization.

---

4   Paul Taylor and Scott Keeter, eds., "Millennials: Confident. Connected. Open to Change." February 24, 2010. Washington, DC: Pew Research Center.

In creating a mind map, individuals can use other divergent thinking tools such as reframing the problem or opportunity from a different perspective, focusing on the ultimate purpose, listing attributes, or creating other checklists of factors.

Performing Stage

Toward the middle of the project, the team moves into high gear. Team leadership has been strong and focused on accomplishing its goals. Even team members who were not completely in agreement with some decisions are feeling comfortable that their ideas were considered. Every team member knows that the final deadline looms and they must produce.

About 75% of the project is completed in the final few weeks of a typical student consulting project. Teams synthesize and summarize their secondary research, administer surveys, and compile the results. Data are collected and feedback is obtained from the client. Team members support each other. When a team member is unable to complete a task, others pitch in. There is no assignment of blame, although team members are held accountable for their work. Meetings are scheduled to come to a consensus about findings and recommendations. The discussion is spirited, but opinions and ideas are treated with respect. Feedback is solicited from all team members. Rough findings and recommendations are compiled. The team "sleeps" on the results and has one more meeting to reconsider and then prioritize their recommendations.

The number of hours spent on the project increases as the team moves into the rough draft of the final report and the presentation. Instead of relying on the strongest writers on the team to carry the load, the team has divided up the writing among all the team members so that each can work on improving writing skills. The draft report often exceeds 30 pages and up to an additional 50 pages of appendices. It is proofed and submitted for review by faculty.

The final presentation is drafted several days before the day of the presentation, and the team's mentors are asked to review evidence used. Revisions are made, and the day prior to the presentation is spent rehearsing in front of a mock audience. Final revisions are made, and team members spend the evening rehearsing their part of the presentation. Rehearsals often run several hours for a 20-minute presentation.

The final presentation goes smoothly. Team members know their material and speak with confidence. The client is thrilled with their commitment and work. The team's mentors are proud. However, as much as the team would like to rest on its laurels, it cannot. The reviewed draft of the final report has been returned to the team full of corrections and requests for clarification. It is tempting for the team to ignore the requests for clarification, but they collectively review and revise the report one last time. The final report is submitted on the due date.

Without exception, all team members are extremely proud of the work they completed. They understand that they have contributed to the success of a business and increased the vibrancy of the economy. A tremendous number of hours have been contributed to creating this original and unique work. Business owners express their appreciation and mentors give their nod to the professionalism with which the team conducted itself.

In this stage, teams perform efficiently. Team members understand and appreciate their roles and the roles of others. They operate at their highest level and support the work of others. In the final stages of the project, there is a tremendous amount of work to be completed. Pressure mounts as the deadline approaches, but a performing team will rise to the challenge. There will be unconditional commitment to getting the job done. Team members will motivate each other to keep the energy level high. They will coach and mentor each other. They will encourage new ideas and innovation because these will help maximize the achievement of goals.

Performing teams exhibit a variety of task and relationship behaviors. Modeling these behaviors can help set the team in the right direction. When a team is undergoing the storming phase, it is helpful to provide a list of these behaviors and ask all team members to monitor how often the behaviors are exhibited.

Teaming Postscript

Although all teams go through a storming phase, most teams succeed in fostering good team spirit for most of the process and deliver an excellent product to the client. Out of hundreds of projects, a handful undergo a particularly difficult time throughout the life of the project. Power struggles may ensue because it is not uncommon for ego to be an issue with novice teams. Jostling for personal status may take precedence over accomplishing project goals. Individuals may be assigned roles without their buy-in. This further alienates individual team members and communication breaks down. Team members violate their role boundaries, and some individual team

Week	1	2	3	4	5	6	7	8	9	10	11

Prepare for Kick-off Meeting
Assign teams
Team forming
    Review and execute consulting contract
    Interview and research business
    Draft, revise and execute team contact
        Draft and revise project management plan
        Start secondary research
            Draft and revise business case statement
            Analyze and organize secondary research
                Plan, draft and test primary research
                Conduct primary research
                    Analyze and organize primary research
                    Draft and revise preliminary recommendations
                      Draft final report
                        Draft, revise, rehearse presentation
                        Revise final report

FIGURE 3-2 Typical Project Timetable

members stop working altogether. Despite all this, the team must deliver a project to the client. In these cases, a few team members will assume the role of team hero and deliver the product. This outcome is absolutely essential. Failure to deliver a quality product is not an option.

PROJECT MANAGEMENT

The goal of a project is to fulfill the stated objectives for the client within the budgeted time and expenses. Once the objectives are achieved, the project ends. A project can be as simple as planning a party or as complex as building a defense system. Horror stories abound about how the government or private contracting entities spend millions or billions of dollars on projects for which the end product does not work as well as the previous model or, even worse, does not work at all. An effective team works to balance the project scope (what the project will and will not do) and the time and budget available.

Experience with more than 500 student projects has shown that student teams will commit 400 to 500 hours in performing the consulting engagement. Although the workload is higher than typical, students find it rewarding and satisfying. Working with a real business requires that more complex tasks be performed within a short timeline.

This section reviews all the phases of project planning, management, and control with respect to the stu-

dent consulting engagement. The project timetable in Figure 3-2 highlights the typical starting times for the tasks of the project using an 11-week schedule. The project timetable may differ, depending on how different institutions arrange the consulting engagements.

Project Mission

Discounting the amount of planning needed for a successful project is a mistake that novice teams often make. It is important to explore and define the scope of work needed prior to coming up with the project plan. If consulting with a company, the team should find out as much as possible about the company, its culture, resources, industry, and competitors, before defining the project. Typically, companies prefer to hire consultants who are experts in their field, so the consulting team has to attain "expert" status. Recognize that a business owner might be skeptical about how a group of student consultants can help solve real business problems. If a solution to the problem is to be found, the first order of business is not lining up solutions--it is ensuring that the right problem has been defined. The team cannot rely on the client business to be clear on the problems or opportunities. Businesses are not attempting to be deceptive, nor do they disrespect the consultant. More likely the business may be too preoccupied with the day-to-day operations to take a different perspective when approaching opportunities or problems. The business might be dealing

TABLE 3-6. Sample Goal and Objectives

Goal	Objectives
Capture the over 50–65 market in the city of Bellevue.	1. Conduct research and identify where the over-50 population is concentrated.
	2. Conduct research and identify activities in which the over-50 population may engage.
	3. Develop and administer a survey to a sample of 30 or more potential over-50 consumers to determine how to reach the over-50 market in Bellevue.
	4. Conduct competitive analysis of other businesses that serve the over-50 market in Bellevue.

with symptoms and not the root causes of the difficulties faced.

If trying to capitalize on an opportunity, the team should ensure that it is the right opportunity. Entrepreneurs are opportunistic and may be quick to capitalize on any attractive proposition. All businesses have limited resources, so they need to focus on the best opportunities. Conducting research and analysis will help determine the top alternatives.

Once the research is done and the team has a good understanding of the client company, the team will develop a project mission statement. The project mission defines the scope, objectives, and overall approach for the consulting engagement. It is the single point of reference between the team and the client as to what will be delivered. For example, the mission of the project might be to increase market share for the company by developing marketing strategies and programs. The mission statement is specific about what will be done, for whom, and how. All team members and the business should be included in coming up with this mission statement. It is essential to enlist the entire team's buy-in from the start. Otherwise, individuals may be confused about, disagree with, or knowingly or unknowingly work against the effort.

Although composing a project mission statement may seem redundant, it is an important step to ensuring that all team members are clear as to the direction of the project. The mission statement serves as a guidepost for the inevitable confusion that occurs early in any project. It keeps the team on track when the team is enticed with the many opportunities that arise when research begins. It allows mentors, advisors, faculty, or others who need to know, quickly understand what the project is about.

Project Goals and Objectives

A project mission provides broad direction for the work to be done. This is broken down into project goals that define what will be accomplished. The goals need to be attainable with the resources and within the time frame allocated. Project goals must also be measurable.

The goals are then broken down one more level to work objectives. Work objectives must tie directly to achieving project goals. As an example, a project team may have determined that the consumer market of adults 50–65 years old is an affluent and profitable local market to pursue. The project goal would be to capture a percentage of this demographic in the city of Bellevue. Specific goals would be to develop a potential customer survey to determine how best to capture this market. The goals and objectives factor into the evaluation of net costs and benefits of pursuing the goal.

For most student consulting projects, the project objectives comprise a list of deliverables for the client. (See Table 3-7.) Deliverables must be accompanied by end-item specifications. For instance, creating a website for a business is a deliverable. However, there is a difference between delivering a website that does or does not capture customers. A clearly defined deliverable might include the number of pages in the website, any graphic work, any copy that must be written, and how customers will be guided through the website. There might be a stipulation that the site has to be approved by key people in the business. It might be required that the website be tested successfully on customers and that it be compliant with any regulations. When the site is up, the number of hits and conversions to sales will be measured to determine if objectives were reached.

TABLE 3-7. Sample Deliverable and End-Item Specification

Deliverable	End-Item Specification
Business website	Website pages: Home page with mission statement, featured products, featured expert article, owner blog, customer quotes, top navigation to landing pages
	Landing pages, including product information and description
	Mock layout of all pages and navigation bars, including copy and graphics
	Results of usability test with three customers
	Search engine optimization: Suggested keywords, page title, meta tags
	Google page rank test. Website ranking

Project Scope

As the team goes through the process of determining what it will deliver, it must at the same time have a clear idea of what it *cannot* achieve. A project that tries to be all things to all people ends up achieving little. This is especially pertinent to resource-constrained small businesses. As the project evolves, the business owner often comes to realize how skilled the student consultants really are. He or she may also conceptualize additional, equally critical projects. Moving beyond the scope of the project is not limited to the business owner. It is also natural that the more the team learns about an area, the more ideas it will have about what to do. This enthusiasm on the part of both business owners and student consultants to take on more work than specified by the project mission is known as scope creep. It needs to be contained. One approach to containment is to delineate the relevance of options and their worth to the overall goal. Clearly stating and restating priorities is another way of responding to scope creep.

This does not mean that the scope of the project will never change. As the team and business gain more knowledge, there might be good reason to change the scope. For example, the team might find out that a market segment initially thought to be attractive is not viable. In this case,
it would not be effective to continue to put together a marketing plan for this segment. Rather, the team should choose another segment. However, there also needs to be a way of controlling the changes. It could be that the new ideas are more attractive than the old ones, but unless the team focuses on the project mission, it runs the risk of accomplishing nothing of value to the business.

Project Team

In student-consulting projects, students are generally preselected and industry advisors or mentors are preassigned. If advisors and mentors are used, the student team should give thought as to how they fit into the team. Having mentors or advisors who are experienced in the industry is beneficial, but they tend to be busy people with many other priorities. The best use of their time is often to call on them as needed or on a just-in-time basis. They may be consulted briefly by e-mail or telephone when a particularly difficult problem is encountered. They may be solicited to facilitate communication or add weight to decision making. The student team should learn how to use advisors and mentors selectively to get the most out of their expertise.

Following the initial period of research by the consulting team, a "kick-off" meeting or a required face-to-face meeting with core and extended team members is held. The goal of the meeting is to build trust with the business owner. Teams will need to have the full trust of the client. They can do this by informing the business owner of their credentials, outlining their role in the project and their working styles, and establishing personal rapport. More often it takes a personal bond between the business owner and individual team members to make the project successful. At the same time, the student team will build relationships with advisors or mentors. Contact with these individuals may be intermittent after the kick-off meeting, and it is important to have a basis for future interaction.

During the kick-off meeting, implicit agreements are reached and expectations are set on how often the team will meet and what communication protocols will be. This is especially important in a multicultural consulting environment where the business owner may be multilingual.

Considerations of culture must be incorporated ensuring that messages are conveyed correctly. Team members should differentiate between the social constructs of white individuals in large corporations and collectivists who are more often represented in minority businesses. Keep in mind that these constructs represent two opposing poles of a continuum, and businesses may fall anywhere in between.

Knowing what skills and knowledge people have is important. If long-term viability of the enterprise is a concern, the project can be used to build capacity within the organization. It can also be used to develop team members so they can lead other projects. All team members have to be committed to project goals. If they do not come with this commitment, the project leader must facilitate its development. Communicate the importance of achieving the goals. Create a connection between each team member and the goals.

Key stakeholders have to be involved in the project team. Unless they are involved, it is unlikely that the fruits of the project will have any staying power. For example, if the project is to improve sourcing for a company and the purchasing person is not involved, it is unlikely that the recommendations will be implemented. A project champion may be necessary to explain the project's role to the stakeholders. Often mentors and advisors have the clout to get this message across. Good project champions can make more resources available to the project. Effective teams are aware of this and use it to optimal advantage. Getting the right people on the team will also take excellent persuasion and negotiation skills.

Inexperienced consultants may find it difficult to stay focused on the project goals. Business owners can come up with many other tasks that seem just as important. Team members have differing opinions or are unable to focus on specific goals. Individuals may gravitate toward what is comfortable as opposed to what needs to be done. It is important to keep the project mission in clear focus. Distractions will be plenty, while time and resources are in short supply. Being unfocused during the planning process can cause the project to veer far off course by its conclusion. It is important to resist being discouraged or sidetracked by such an occurrence. Each problem is an opportunity to adapt to the situation and put the project back on schedule.

Knowledge Management

Knowledge management is an important concept that is not limited to data contained in digital media. It includes any relevant knowledge that can be mined to achieve the mission. With many businesses, especially small businesses, the knowledge within the enterprise often resides in people. For example, production workers might have their own method of troubleshooting a line breakdown that is never documented. This would be a crucial piece of information that is needed to understand operations. If enterprises could access all the knowledge their people possess, they could unlock a huge goldmine of resources. True knowledge management means that the team can get to the knowledge where it resides.

Within-team knowledge management can be enabled with digital file sharing. This is an effective way of managing large amounts of data that are common with most projects. If labeled properly, these files provide a chronology of data gathered and analysis completed. This is important because sometimes data gathered or analysis done, if not initially pursued, may gain prominence later. The project team needs to have access to this information. Good archiving of data when the project is completed also allows the business owner to reuse the knowledge. Rather than reinvent the wheel when a similar project is done, the business owner can draw on work previously done.

The project knowledge-manager role can be assigned to a team member to provide a focal point for archiving the material. The team should have templates for agendas, meeting summaries, and decision making to simplify the recording of repetitive tasks and ensure accountability for action items. If the team is geographically dispersed, consider using a web service such as Google Docs as a repository for files. For best results, the team will select collaborative tools that allow editing concurrently, measure team performance, and communicate regularly with each other.

Project Plan

A project plan is a detailed breakdown of milestones, tasks, interrelations, resources, and schedules. For unseasoned project managers, project planning may be seen as an "overhead" item. These managers think it important to pare this down to the smallest value possible. Carefully setting out what has to be done, how completion is to be measured, how one task might relate to another, and when each task is to be completed gives a blueprint for management.

The project plan is important for several reasons. It:

- Specifies how the team will meet its ultimate goal within the time frame allowed
- Shows that the team has access to the information it needs at the time that it needs it to remain on schedule
- Provides the team with a tool to manage the client's expectations
- Assigns resources to address the right issues at the right time
- Determines the communications mechanisms that are needed to maintain progress on the project
- Establishes team roles and responsibilities
- Identifies leaders for each area of the team's work
- Schedules deadlines and milestones
- Ensures that the scope of work satisfies the mission of the project.

As a general rule, all individuals who are part of the consulting project, its execution, or the subsequent implementation of its recommendations should be part of the planning. It follows that greater commitment to the change process will be fostered when all team members and other responsible parties are involved. Those who participate in planning a task have a stronger stake in its execution. Additionally, getting as much input in the initial stages contributes to a better solution.

Once the project mission and deliverables are set, the student team typically begins creating its work breakdown structure. In this stage of the planning, the team starts with the deliverables and identifies the milestones, tasks, assignments, and schedule.

Be aware that business owners, mentors, and advisors may not be able to meet deadlines for feedback or decision-making as determined by the team. Advisors and mentors in particular are likely to have other pressing tasks to draw their attention elsewhere. It is important for the team to seek out and solicit these team members when their feedback is required, while keeping feedback windows flexible so that their contribution can be included. At the same time, discretion should be used in drawing lines as to when project issues should be closed.

Work Breakdown Structure. With the project mission clearly in mind, break the project into objectives or deliverables. For each objective, determine the subtasks that must be accomplished. For example, under the objective "competitive analysis," one subtask might be to obtain a list of competitors. Another might be to review competitor price lists. Still another might be to survey customers for their assessment of competitors. Each of these subtasks may be broken down further. For example, the customer survey would be broken down into obtaining a list of customers, creating a survey, administering the survey, and analyzing the results.

Some tasks can be performed only if a predecessor task is completed. In the previous example of the customer interviews, the survey can be administered only once the customer list is available. Tasks that do not have linked predecessor tasks can be performed independently. This is important to document as it has an effect on resource scheduling. Independent tasks can be completed simultaneously by different team members, while linked tasks must be completed sequentially. If the customer list is outdated, incomplete, or otherwise unusable, the team cannot interview customers. If the team member charged with completing a task does not complete it on time, the scheduling of all subsequent tasks will be affected. Often project managers will identify critical paths or tasks that can delay the entire project; when they focus management efforts on these, they can reduce the risk of a project falling behind.

Along with the task, it is important to specify exactly what constitutes a standard for completion of the task. If specifications are not clearly spelled out at the beginning, team members may not complete what is required. For example, a survey of customers can be as simple as informally stopping ten customers when they shop or as extensive as completing 1,000 surveys using random telephone sampling. Unless the requirements are mapped out, team members may inadvertently miss the target, client expectations will not be met, and the final product will be of no value to the business.

Often within a team there are varying perceptions of what is acceptable. In order to keep the process smooth, take the time to be as specific as possible. This can enhance team functioning.

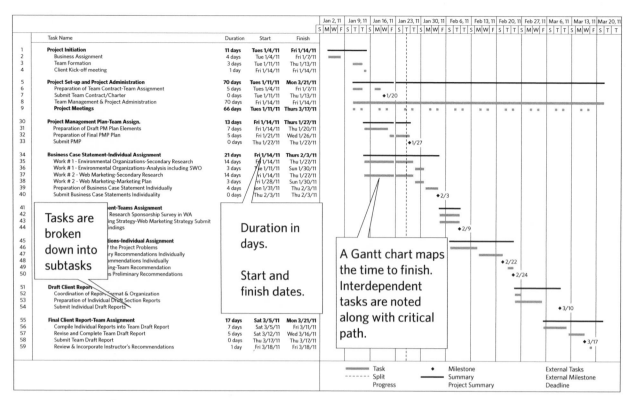

FIGURE 3-3. Sample Task and Gantt Chart for Student Project

Go and No-Go Review. When exploring new territory, the team may not have a clear concept of whether the finished product will be feasible. Instead of automatically completing all the tasks, project planning should include key points when the team reevaluates whether it should continue. For example, a project mission might be to develop a new product for a new market. There are several decision points at which the team can determine whether to go forward. After secondary research of the market, the team might decide that there is not enough potential to proceed.

Scheduling and Resource Allocation. Once all the tasks have been laid out in the project plan, time requirement or duration (number of hours and date) must be determined for each task. It follows that the more experienced the project planners are, the more accurate they will be in determining the amount of time each task requires. It also follows that the more experienced the team is, the less time it will take to complete the tasks. Conversely, in planning for a novice team, it is important to allow some slack time for everyone to complete their tasks effectively.

Once the time for completion has been determined, specific team members will be assigned to each task. For a team leader who knows the team well, it is relatively easy to match the individual with the task. Keep in mind that the most highly skilled individual for the task may not be selected. It may be in the team's best interest to develop these competencies in other individuals to increase skill depth.

In a consulting firm, each consultant will have a specific billing rate based on technical expertise and experience. Student team members may not have the expertise to command high billing fees. However, it is still important to assign market billing rates to each team member. Quantifying the cost of such endeavors will always be a part of the formula for determining beneficial gain. Likewise, all other expenses of the project should be quantified whether they are out of pocket or not. Formulating a budget that proves to be accurate is an important skill for all project managers. These budgets are a critical part of a request for proposal; the consulting firm stands to lose significant profit if budgeting is not done properly. Budgets also provide the basis for management and control as the project progresses.

Most project-management software packages easily handle the input of tasks, task dependencies, duration resource allocation, and budgeting. Baseline budgets are automatically tallied based on the information given. The software also provides graphics such as Gantt and critical path charts to show project status visually (see Figure 3-3). Even if a software package is not available, the student consulting project is of a complexity that can be handled easily on a spreadsheet program.

Review Project Plan for Risks. Each project has risks that jeopardize its successful completion. Good planning will anticipate these risks and develop contingency plans to mitigate the risks. For student consultants, one common risk is spending significant time on a task that turns out to be useless. For example, a team decided that it was important to conduct a survey of former customers to determine how a business could improve its marketing strategy. The business assured the team that it had a comprehensive list of former customers. The team obtained the list, uploaded it to a database, divided the list into sections, created a survey, and proceeded to contact the customers by e-mail and then by follow-up telephone calls. After a few days it was determined that e-mails were out of date and telephone numbers were disconnected. The project hit the halfway mark in its timeline, and the team had to start again with no other options for getting in contact with former customers.

This risk could have been mitigated if the team had spent some time testing the list prior to proceeding with the design of the survey. Additionally, once research surfaces that a task may lead to a dead end, it is important that the team have a means of changing the deliverable quickly to make it relevant. Is it necessary to survey former customers? Would a list of potential customers be just as effective for getting information?

Project Management and Control

Projects, once started, move quickly, and they need to continue to progress in order to be completed successfully. The team should establish weekly meetings (or daily feedback via e-mail or telephone) to review project status. Project status reports need to be given to all interested parties, including mentors and advisors, on a regular basis.

Often teams find it more efficient to transfer the tasks to a spreadsheet and track task completion and team member hours directly onto the spreadsheet. This information can be kept on the shared document file so that all team members can access the completion of tasks, milestones, and deliverables.

Dealing with Problems

Problems will arise in any project, no matter how well it is run. The team needs to establish a means of flagging problems. Catching the problem early can do much to counteract its impact. Often individual team members will not notice the start of a problem. They may be too involved in the details or too busy completing their own tasks to pick up the signals that something might be amiss. Team members need to be vigilant and aware of all aspects of the project to assist their colleagues in identifying the first signs of problems. Trust needs to be such that a team member will not be too polite, too embarrassed, or otherwise hesitant to call for help or point out issues.

Once problems have surfaced, there needs to be a process for dealing with them. If conflicts arise, rules for resolving them must already be in place. Determining rules of engagement in the heat of an argument rarely leads to resolution. Team members must be knowledgeable about the conflict-resolution procedures and must abide by them. Problems that are identified need to be monitored separately from normal project status to ensure that there is follow-through in resolving them satisfactorily.

From the outset, the team must set up a team culture that is conducive to having team heroes emerge. In the flurry of activities that characterize project work, it is not always the person with titular responsibility for a task who will be able to come through. Rather, it is the team member who steps up to the plate to perform the heroic task to save the day. Team culture should allow this type of courage to be expressed. It should reward team heroes who contribute in this manner.

There are instances in which the team is better served by shared leadership, and this must be accommodated. These issues should be explored with faculty, mentors, and advisors to arrive at a solution that best serves the project and client.

Project Close

Project close is signified by delivery of the finished product to the client. Along with the final report, the team should have complete documentation of the project process, including the actual budget to complete the project. The documentation also provides a base of knowledge that will be invaluable in future consulting projects. It can provide direction for research that will not have to be redone or a critical analysis framework that will expedite problem solving.

Although the tendency is to physically and psychologically exit the project when the product is delivered to the client, it is best to resist this tendency. Taking time to reflect at project close on what went well and what could be improved is an important part of the developmental process of every team member. Reflecting can provide valuable knowledge for future consulting, teaming, and project management. Additionally, it is important to acknowledge the achievements and contributions of each and every team member. This type of reflection and recognition is vital to team member development and, according to many teaming experts, will lead to effective high-performance teaming.

REFERENCES

Blake, R., and J. Mouton. *Spectacular Teamwork: How to Develop the Leadership Skills for Team Success*. New York: Wiley, 1987.

Paulus, Paul B., and Bernard A. Nijstad, eds. *Group Creativity: Innovation through Collaboration*. New York: Oxford University Press, 2003.

Project Management Institute. A *Guide to the Project Management Body of Knowledge*. 4th ed. Newton Square, PA: Project Management Institute, 2008.

Wysocki, Robert K. *Effective Project Management: Traditional, Agile, Extreme*. 5th ed. New York: Wiley, 2009.

DISCUSSION

1. As a team, make a list of behaviors that the team should engage in and a list of behaviors the team should not engage in. Listing and naming the behaviors can lead to better team functioning.

2. Discuss differences within the team backgrounds, such as high and low context or generational differences. What accommodations should be made to ensure that communication is open and clear?

3. Select two techniques for divergent thinking in coming up with project risks. Analyze and explain why one technique is more effective.

4. Have each team member compose the project mission or charter and discuss similarities and differences. Did all team members buy into the same mission?

5. Develop a team meeting agenda template, including communication protocols. Based on where you are in your project task completion, explain which task or phase has been the most challenging and why.

4. Marketing Analysis and Strategy

ABOUT THIS MODULE

Developing and implementing marketing strategies and programs are critically important activities in any business enterprise but are especially pertinent to all small businesses. The authors of this textbook have guided more than 500 student teams working with small businesses, and the most frequently cited need is assistance with marketing for emerging businesses. The success of the enterprise is ultimately measured in terms of how well the enterprise satisfies the needs and wants of its customers. That goal cannot be achieved effectively without defining a strategic direction and devising specific programs to execute that strategy. For emerging businesses, moving from a bootstrapping mode of operation to one where planning is important is a pivotal transition in survival. It can be particularly challenging for growing MBEs because growth may dictate movement into market segments outside familiar cultures, into other minority cultures, or into the white culture.

Consultants use the standard tools of the marketing trade to help enterprises grow. Segmentation, targeting, positioning, and branding all figure prominently in marketing analyses. Although commonplace in large enterprises, these concepts may be unfamiliar to small businesses. Often the business owner has come from a background or country where marketing may be approached differently or the business owner has grown her or his company by bootstrapping. It may be the consultant's role to develop a structure for the company's marketing efforts. Another frequent role for small business consultants is to develop a brand identity that can carry a business beyond its core customers.

Often emerging businesses build market share one customer at a time. The principles of customer relationship management are critical to success in acquiring new customers at a faster rate. Along with growing market share, small businesses must devise strategies to retain current, profitable customer share. They need to articulate a customer value proposition and work to retain the customer, culminating with the customer becoming a strong advocate for the business.

A web strategy and social media are important for small businesses because these media are doing much to level the playing field in competition between small and larger businesses. Use of the web is essential for small businesses that operate in the business-to-business sphere, as most large enterprises require the convenience and efficiency of the web. Often small businesses are not familiar with how to communicate using these channels.

The purpose of this section is to provide a compendium of marketing tools that could be used. Given the breadth of topics covered in this textbook, there is insufficient space to provide comprehensive details about each tool. Thus the authors assume that student teams will find more detailed information about each tool in other sources.

After Studying This Module

With the tools in this module, teams will be able to use marketing concepts, define strategies, gather the appropriate data, and apply the correct analysis. The interrelatedness of marketing, operations, and accounting requires that the tools presented in this module must be used in tandem with business and accounting process analysis described in Module 6, Emerging Business Consulting.

In reading this module the student will be able to:

- Describe effective segmentation, targeting, positioning, and branding strategies for a business to reach its target market(s).
- Articulate the customer value proposition and the stages of the customer life cycle, along with outlining appropriate marketing and customer service programs for each stage.
- Identify and apply the techniques of designing and operating a business website, achieving search engine optimization, and using social media.
- Describe and use all elements of the marketing mix to develop programs for a specific business.

SEGMENTATION, TARGETING, POSITIONING, AND BRANDING

Segmentation and Targeting

It is important to look at each market segment in its totality. The usual dimensions of demographics (age, gender, education, and income), geographics, psychographics, and behavior are inadequate when it comes to under-standing all potential market segments. This is especially true when looking at multicultural markets as a segment. For these market segments it is important to understand history, culture, sociological context, discrimination, and languages, among many other additional factors.

With regard to emerging businesses, especially those in the retail, hospitality, and personal service industries, their markets are often hyper-local and target a city or even a neighborhood. It is important for the team to take the time to conduct detailed research of these hyper-local economies and articulate a segment that is understand-able to the business owner. Defining the segment in terms of key characteristics and size can do much to help the business owner reach the market. Analyzing the potential revenues from the target market is also impor-tant. Newer business owners may have limited experi-ence with the idea of business cycles, migration patterns, or other factors that might affect their business. In pre-paring this analysis, the team needs to incorporate the dynamic nature of segments and what factors may affect the success of reaching each segment.

Business-to-business market segmentation uses the same principles as consumer market segmentation, but

TABLE 4-1. Segmentation, Targeting, Positioning, and Branding

Marketing Tool	Description	Opportunities
Segmentation	A process for identifying market niches that can be profitable to the enterprise. Typical segmentation identifies demo-graphic, geographic, behavioral, and psy-chographic groups that interact with a product or service in a similar manner.	Multicultural or targeted geographic markets can be small compared to segments pursued by large enterprises and provide opportunities for emerging businesses.
Targeting	Strategies and programs for capturing market segments.	The full breadth of current social, psychological, economic, and other factors must be assessed in targeting multicul-tural market segments. Cultural analysis (which includes history, art, music, etc., of the population and its home country) must be taken into consideration in targeting multicultural segments.
Positioning	Strategy for setting the enterprise apart from competitors on key attributes impor-tant to the customer value proposition. Could also include strategies for creating entry barriers for future competitors.	Small businesses seeking to expand beyond their initial market niche focus on building new value propositions that include benefits to a distinct market segment.
Branding	The creation of a consistent image of the enterprise that positions it strongly in the customer's mind. The brand will cause the customer to buy the product and pay a premium over others with similar functionality.	Small businesses often first focus on building a consistent brand image when they begin planning to reach multiple market segments. With many small businesses moving to adjacent or mainstream markets, brand imagery may have to be changed. The key is to find something that is memo-rable, valuable, and persuasive enough to build loyalty.

rather than focusing on issues such as demographics, segmentation is more typically focused on industry clusters, sales cycles, and the tier of contracting at which a small business will operate.

For all businesses, the highest growth potential exists within market segments that are growing. New markets do not have clearly defined requirements, and information is evolving. The emerging business may have advantages over larger enterprises in that it may be more flexible in responding to quickly changing market conditions. Additionally, it is important to recognize that an emerging business usually lacks the resources to compete head-on with large, well-endowed enterprises. For the emerging business, business-to-business marketing relies heavily on expensive one-on-one sales efforts. Often, segments are defined as the business owner encounters success with sales calls. In this fluid environment, constant assessment must be made of the profitability and cash flow generation of each opportunity.

Branding

A brand is the image the customer has of the product or company. It conveys the nature of the user, a personality, core values, a culture, product benefits, and product attributes. Attributes may include price, safety, quality, and performance. Benefits are what the customer gets from the product, which may include functional or image benefits. A strong brand will have a strong emotional appeal that results in loyalty, repeat patronage, or other positive responses in the marketplace.

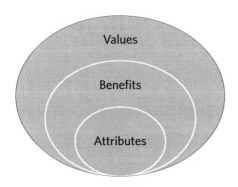

FIGURE 4-1. Brand Elements

For small business entrepreneurs who must compete with much larger enterprises with considerably more resources, their marketing arsenal often includes emotional branding. The entrepreneur's story is woven into the business so that it has meaning for marketing the

enterprise. It strives to persuade the customer to connect with the business or business owner. With minority entrepreneurs, this is relevant because many have overcome significant barriers to beat the odds to become successful. Their struggles become part of the fabric or essence of the business. Successful minority entrepreneurs are often pioneers for their communities, and many contribute to the welfare of others by creating jobs where none were available before. These individuals become role models for younger people to emulate. Their stories are inspiring.

Emotional branding can be helpful when competitors are offering products with a similar value proposition. Even if a business has competitive pricing and high quality, it needs something to set it apart. The bootstrapping owner of a fledgling business can use her personal story to get customers to take an interest in the business. This can be the differentiating factor in getting a foot in the door.

Logo. A logo is a graphical representation of the company that embodies its brand image from customers' perspectives. An ideal logo will say volumes about the company in a very economical way. Often, emerging businesses are so busy producing goods or delivering services that they do not take the time or spend the money to develop a logo that draws new customers and forms attachment with existing customers. For the first-generation immigrant entrepreneurs who come from different business cultures where branding logos are not valued, creating these may not be viewed as important.

In the US context, every company should have a logo that is appropriate to the business and communicates clearly and unequivocally what the business wants its customer and community to think of the business. It is preferable to get professional help in designing the logo, but talented student teams have developed excellent logos. Once the company has decided on the logo, it should be tested on customers and vendors. If it communicates what the business wants, the logo must be trademarked. Then all company communication, marketing programs, and collateral elements (stationery, business cards, postcards, brochures, etc.) should make use of the logo in a consistent manner.

SELLING STRATEGIES

An entrepreneur serves as the firm's main salesperson in its initial years; therefore having strong sales skills is

CASE STUDY 3
Salvadorean Bakery and El Comal

Cultural Expansion to New Customer Markets

"It's not just a bakery, it's an institution."

Visit the Salvadorean Bakery in Seattle's White Center neighborhood and you will find authentic Latin cuisine: pupusas, empanadas, plantains, and tamales. Aminta Elgin and Ana Castro, co-founders, are sisters and business partners. When the sisters emigrated from El Salvador to the United States, they moved with the dream that people could continue tasting the traditional foods and baked goods of their home country. In January 1996, they opened the Salvadorean Bakery and Restaurant and began offering traditional Latin dishes inspired by family recipes. White Center is a diverse community, with a nearly 22% Hispanic population compared to Seattle's overall Hispanic population of approximately 6%.[1]

It is a family business. In the early years, the entire family worked in the bakery. Today the bakery is run primarily by Aminta and Ana. Their mother still likes to stop by to enjoy a pupusa. They recall that their father was very proud of them. "He felt that [his] life was complete" and was happy that his daughters could live their lives the way he was not able to in El Salvador.

Aminta and Ana use their strong family roots as a foundation for their marketing program, which relies heavily on word of mouth, a colorful website, social media (i.e., Yelp and Google reviews), and community outreach. Ana is very active in the local White Center community and other local organizations. Their donated cakes often bring in the highest bids at local charity auctions.

In 2009, Aminta and Ana opened a second restau-

rant, El Comal, in Bellevue, an affluent suburb of Seattle. This expansion addressed the lack of Central American restaurants in the area. Compared to their main bakery, El Comal is an upscale restaurant and bar. The food is presented more formally and the menu is more expansive. While Bellevue is home to about 7% Hispanics, this area caters to a much different clientele than the bakery's White Center location. They estimate that they serve mostly Caucasians and Asians (60%) compared to Hispanics (40%).

In 2010, Ana and Aminta brought in a student consulting team to develop marketing strategies to promote their new restaurant. The students conducted a survey that provided good information about customer demographics and, more importantly, what they liked and did not like about the restaurant and menu. Recommendations included website design and a revised menu. Upon the completion of the project, Aminta said she felt more confident about her business strategy. Business is picking up at El Comal, in part due to the student team's recommendations.

The success of Salvadorean Bakery and El Comal restaurants is attributable not only to flavorful food and pastries but also to hard work, perseverance, and strong community relationships.

---

1   US Census Bureau. White Center: http://quickfacts.census.gov/
    qfd/states/53/5378225.html. Seattle: http://quickfacts.census.
    gov/qfd/states/53/5363000.html. Retrieved 4/10/12 from
    census.gov.

crucial to a new business's success. The founder of the company is the main salesperson in 82% of ventures. Sales skills are all the more essential because almost 90% of a fledgling enterprise's early sales are from direct sales.[1]

The key to any successful sales strategy is discerning the needs of the customer and finding the product or service to meet that need when information is not perfect. It is in this role that the business owner can iterate his or her way to meet the undefined requirements of a new and upcoming market niche. Being the frontline salesperson for the firm allows the entrepreneur to have direct access to customer wants and needs. It allows him or her the opportunity to customize offerings as needed to get the sale. Having this close contact with the customer provides a significant advantage over large firms, where sales departments do not connect so intimately with product development or manufacturing teams.

In executing a sales strategy, the business owner must have the tenacity to get a foot in the door. For this reason, having worked in the industry before provides a strong advantage if the business owner had a customer-facing role prior to starting the new business. Because of past relationships with the owner in another capacity, potential customers may be more willing to begin a new business relationship with the small business.

Networks. A major constraint with small businesses is the lack of financial, human, and other resources. Bootstrapping with a small staff and hiring whoever is available in the employment pool, the business owner does not have a reserve of sales support to fall back on. To overcome this, business owners need to develop networks. Such networks or clusters have been found to work very effectively in developing economies to such an extent that they can compete globally with much larger enterprises. For example, small businesses in Brazil have developed clusters to compete in the shoe industry.[2] During boom times, the business is able to outsource to other businesses in its cluster to meet demand. Businesses pass sales leads that they cannot fulfill to other companies in the cluster. They group together to purchase equipment. The same benefits

have been found in immigrant businesses in the United States. For example, clustering among Korean American entrepreneurs has assisted in creating a pool of capital to start businesses.

Sales pitch. It is very important that the business owner develop a sales pitch that effectively sells the company to any potential customers or referral sources. Some business owners who come from Asian and other cultures where it is inappropriate to "boast" about oneself may initially find this difficult. The owner also has to learn to ask for the order, overcome objections, provide information on how the product matches the needs of the customer, and close the sale. These may be behaviors that are contrary to his culture. The owner must be taught to be diligent in getting as much information as he can from the customer so that the sales pitch can be tailored to the needs of the specific customer. Basic to a good sales pitch is a strong belief in, and indeed a passion for, the product and company. Additionally, the owner must back this up with impeccable customer service. Every employee who has contact with customers must show the same diligence and impeccable service.

Customer Relationship Management

The concept of customer relationship management (CRM) came to the forefront when technology allowed businesses to track all customer activity. Because the software allows the enterprise to customize by individual customer using an automated set of rules, it made the servicing of micro-markets economically viable. In effect, at its best, CRM eliminates the advantages of economies of scale enjoyed by larger enterprises and levels the playing field for emerging businesses (see Table 4-3).

Customer Value Proposition

Providing customers something of value should be one of the cornerstones of a firm's marketing effort. The basic idea is straightforward. A business should

TABLE 4-2. Customer Value Proposition

Selection, quality, service, price	
Customer benefits	Customer costs
Product	Price
Service	Cost of acquisition
Image	Maintenance
	Disposal

---

1 Amar Bhide, *The Evolution of Businesses*. New York: Oxford University Press, 2000.

2 Michael Porter, *Competitive Strategy*. New York: Free Press, 1980.

TABLE 4-3. Customer Relationship Management

CRM Concept	Description	Emerging Business Issues
Create a customer value proposition	Knowing the customer well and creating a value proposition for the customer that is uniquely identified with the business.	Often there is a disconnect between what the business assumes and what the customer truly finds of value. It is important for businesses to determine customer needs and tailor products/services to be of value to a market segment that is seeking these benefits.
Target customer share versus market share	It is less costly to retain existing customers than to acquire a new one. Use customer lifetime value to evaluate which customers to target.	Emerging businesses often focus on gaining new customers rather than selling more products and services to existing customers.
Cultivate the customer	Use the customer life cycle to increase customer share and acquire new customers.	Without major resources for marketing programs, the best way for businesses to grow is by growing the share of its existing and adjacent customer bases. This can be done by testimonials and referrals, especially through the use of social media.
Manage information about your customer	Maintain a customer database and use every opportunity to add to the database.	With low-cost options for customer databases, smaller enterprises can compete effectively. Emerging businesses must develop the discipline to collect, maintain, and mine customer information.

want to be known for how it is better than its competitors. Typically, the customer value proposition centers on selection, quality, service, and price. If the business offers the best customer service in the local market, that could form the basis of the customer value proposition. Although most small businesses have a customer value proposition, they fail to articulate it. This omission can result in a lack of focus in its marketing efforts and indecision when it comes to what direction to take. In other cases, the business owner may wrongly define its customer value proposition. For example, one African American coffee shop owner thought his customer value proposition was high-quality coffee. When a focus group was conducted with his customers, they stated that the quality of the coffee was inconsistent; rather, they purchased coffee there because it was convenient.

Customer Share

A fledgling business typically targets an underserved niche market. Customer requirements for the product or service may be fuzzy, so the business makes its way by selecting paths that require relatively low amounts of invested capital but show the promise of high returns, even if the probabilities of success are low. New businesses often rely heavily on the sales skills of the entrepreneur to persuade customers to take a chance on a new business. Customers are acquired one by one; thus, each plays a large role in the success of the business.

Given this scenario, there is much evidence to suggest that the concepts of CRM can be beneficial to emerging businesses. The first tenet of CRM is to know the customer. In an initial direct sales contact, the business owner should collect as much information as possible on the customer and put this information into a database. In the experience of the student consulting program, even fledgling businesses with a small customer base sometimes do not know the customer. For example, a catering company owner may know that she sells 500 meals a week. But she might not be clear as to which customer is buying the most meals. The owner may also not be able to answer a range of other customer-related questions, including:

- How many customers are also buying from a competitor?
- Which competitor(s) are customers buying from?
- What other kinds of food do these customers like?

If the customer spends $4,000 on catering a month, the business owner might only be getting 10% of that customer's business. Focusing on growing customer share rather than market share will lead the business owner to focus on selling more products or services to high-

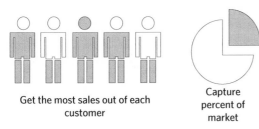

Get the most sales out of each customer

Capture percent of market

FIGURE 4-2. Customer Share versus Market Share

potential existing customers. If a business owner can get 50% to 80% of a customer's business when each customer spends $4,000 per month, it will take only 500 existing customers to generate $1 million in revenue rather than thousands of new customers.

A careful analysis of customer sales can also yield more profits. A business that has 80% of its customers generating 20% of the sales is in a different position than one where 50% of the customers are generating 30% of the sales. Because new customers cost more to acquire than it costs to sell more to existing customers, it is advantageous to focus on increasing sales with existing customers. A rule of thumb estimates that it costs five times more to acquire a new customer than it does to maintain an existing customer. To get new customers into a store, there might be the cost of placing an ad in the newspaper, the cost of discounting a product to draw them in, the cost of printing and mailing postcards, or the cost of using a web-based coupon service. For all these costs, the business may get two to three customers for every 100 people it reaches through the marketing. Getting more sales from existing customers will cost considerably less. If the business is able to capture the most ardent customers of the product and is able to get that customer to buy most of their product from the business, the highest profitability will result.

Ironically, the mission of CRM is to return the large enterprise to its small business roots. Yet small businesses tend to forget how important it is to manage the customer life cycle by cultivating the customer. To conceptualize CRM, take the example of the family Mexican restaurant in the neighborhood. When entering the restaurant, the customer is greeted by name and shown to her favorite table. Instead of being handed the standard menu, the owner recommends a dish that is based on the current availability of the freshest ingredients, careful to avoid the customer's dislikes, and with a good sense of what the customer might prefer on that day, given the time of year and the weather. The owner automatically brings a glass of the customer's favorite wine and ensures that the water has a fresh slice of lemon just as the customer likes.

The owner knows that the customer has a family celebration coming up and suggests that he can host the dinner party at the restaurant or cater the event at her home if she so desires. He spends time talking to the patron and knows all the other restaurants that she patronizes. He knows how often she dines out. He knows all the major events in her life that might require a dinner party. On her birthday, he will prepare a special cake as a present.

This kind of personalized service can do much to engage the customer, and it is quite conceivable that the business owner has a large share of this customer's restaurant spending. For higher-end customers, recent surveys show that the accumulation of experiences is more important that the convenience factor of dining out. The customer most likely recommends the restaurant to all her friends. The owner can easily charge a premium to the customer for this level of service, and the customer will gladly pay for it. From her, he finds out the "hot" preferences of people like her who are likely to frequent his restaurant. He is able to adjust his menus to meet their requirements and draw more customers. This small example demonstrates the customer life cycle, as shown in Figure 4-3.

FIGURE 4-3. Customer Life Cycle

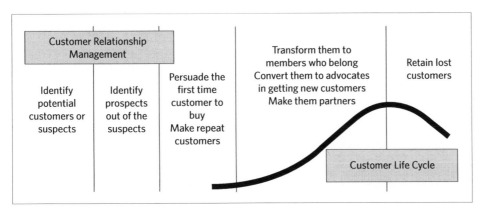

A similar story is told by other entrepreneurs. Great benefits can come when they focus on the customer. For example, one business owner described how he started his business subcontracting for a large Fortune 100 company. He got to know his customers well and found out that they were outsourcing other kinds of production and services. The business owner followed up by providing whatever the customer wanted, often pursuing products or services that were completely different from the core business. By providing for customer needs, the business was able to grow quickly and discover new markets.

Customer Lifetime Value

The concept of customer lifetime value is an important one to develop within a business. When a customer walks into a business and buys a product or service, most businesses value the customer for that single transaction. The next customer who buys a product or service is valued for that single transaction. In fact, when a customer walks into a business, he or she represents many more purchases than that single transaction. Take a customer who walks into a dry cleaning shop. He was drawn to the store by a 30% off coupon on shirts. The customer has $50 worth of cleaning done. Because 30% off was given, the profits on the sale were $10. Yet the value of the customer is not $10. In fact, this customer spends $150 a month on dry cleaning, or $1,800 a year. Over the course of living in the area for five years, this customer would be worth $9,000 in dry cleaning revenues. If the enterprise were selling insurance, a customer could be worth $500 a year in house premiums, $1,000 in car premiums, and $200 in other insurance premiums. Over the course of ten years, this is $17,000 in premiums. Additionally, that customer might recommend two or three other customers to the business.

To properly determine what a customer is worth, innovative and successful businesses will calculate a customer lifetime value. For large and sophisticated enterprises, this is often done with statistical modeling. The model will incorporate the customer's past performance plus other factors such as demographics, preferences, or psychographic factors that might determine how much the customer will buy and for how long. The model is updated using information about similar customers. This is possible in large enterprises because they have databases that capture all customer transactions, which they can combine with other databases they acquire. It is even

$$\text{Customer Lifetime Value} = \sum \frac{\text{Profit} + \text{Other Benefits}}{(1 + \text{discount rate})^n}$$

FIGURE 4-4. Customer Lifetime Value

simpler for a small business. The key is to capture the information through customer databases.

Once the amount of purchases and frequency of purchases is determined, these can be incorporated into the calculation of a customer lifetime value. Basically, the customer lifetime value is the net present value of the cash flows related to that customer (see Figure 4-4). It would include the estimated marketing costs of acquiring that customer, the profit margin less the cost of maintaining the customer. To properly calculate the customer lifetime value, it is important to have accurate costs.

As an example, take an online handbag store:

- This business acquires customers by direct mailings and print ads.
- For every 100 mailings it sends out at $1.50 per mailing, it gets two customers. Thus the cost to acquire each customer is about $75.
- The business expects to keep each customer for five years, and each customer is assumed to buy about $60 in handbags per year.
- The average gross margin on the handbag is 30%.
- The business spends about $5 a year to maintain the customer.
- Through a "friends" promotion, this customer recommends two customers to the business.

All the revenues, costs, and profits related to this customer are projected over a five-year period. Using an 8% discount rate, the net present value for each year is calculated. These are summed as the net present value. A tabulation of the lifetime value of the customer for this business appears in Table 4-4.

As with any model, it is important to continue to test it. If the customer does not stay for five years, does not purchase $60 per year, does not generate a 30% gross margin, or costs more than $5 to maintain a year, this will affect the calculation.

Also critical to the usefulness of this model is making sure that the costs are correct. When marketing programs are designed and implemented, it is important

TABLE 4-4. Customer Lifetime Value Analysis

Year	0	1	2	3	4	5
Customer acquisition cost	-75					
Revenues		60	60	60	60	60
Cost of goods		-42	-42	-42	-42	-42
Cost to maintain		-5	-5	-5	-5	-5
Referral 1 profit		13	13	13	13	13
Referral 2 profit			13	13	13	13
Net cash flow	-75	26	39	39	39	39
Present value (8%)	-$75	$24.07	$33.44	$30.96	$28.67	$26.54
Net present value	$68.68					

to track all costs associated with it. This requires careful analysis. For example, although most businesses track what it costs to mount a store website, they fail to determine what additional costs they incur when fulfilling the orders. Order sizes may decrease, and more handling and shipping costs might be incurred. However, if it is assumed that handling and shipping are the same, these costs will not be included in the accounting of customer profitability. Additionally, the business must be careful to track all customers acquired through the program.

Tracking costs and customers meticulously will allow the business to determine the difference between the cost to acquire customers and the cost to retain customers. It will be evident in fairly short order that it is much more cost effective to retain a customer than it is to acquire a new customer. Even the most targeted marketing programs reach a small portion of the market. Each marketing program will differ in the number of customers it will generate. There is less information on new customers than on existing customers. Will they buy again? Will they recommend to other customers? These are open questions when new customers are acquired and depend on good customer relationship management. For existing customers, a history of buying behavior will help the business determine what is possible.

Once accurate accountings of "cost to acquire" and "cost to retain" a customer are obtained, the business can perform calculations on where to allocate resources. Often the business finds that it is much more cost effective to design and deploy programs to retain customers versus those needed to acquire customers.

Defining profitability. Businesses that have an accurate accounting of profitability by customer or customer type have a tremendous advantage over those that do not. It is possible for these businesses to differentiate customers. The 80/20 rule, while not actually a rule like supply and demand, often holds when customer sales are analyzed. Some customers buy many times and recommend to their friends. As such, this 20% of customers may account for 80% of revenues. These are the customers that the business wants to cultivate with customized marketing programs or offers. Other customers buy infrequently, and when they do, they complain, they require much support, and they return the product more frequently than others. These customers cost the business time, expense, and morale. With emerging businesses, often these high-maintenance customers will occupy a large part of the business owner's time. They are unlikely to be profitable and in fact take up resources that could be used to generate profitability elsewhere. Some business thinkers feel these customers should be "fired."

It is important to divide all customers into groupings that define their profitability. The business should identify good customers and give them the attention they are due. Some businesses will assign staff to high-value customers. They take the opportunity to develop a deeper relationship with these customers. They will call them to get feedback on their experience. They will thank them for being good customers. They will collaborate with them to customize the product or service so that it better fits their needs. They can be targeted to be viral marketers of the business by recommending the business to their friends through social media.

Groupings can also be used to organize the business's customers so that the business is responsive to specific needs. Most minority businesses serve a combination of ethnic and mainstream markets. These markets cannot

FIGURE 4-5. Customer Touchpoints
Source: Yankee Group

be treated in the same way. It is important that the business define groupings and focus staff, customer service, and marketing programs appropriately. In the same way, the business must market to and service different age and gender groups.

Touchpoints. For the fledgling business, every interaction between the business owner and customers is important in building the relationship with the customer. There are many opportunities to interact with the customer, and each customer "touchpoint" should be exploited to get the maximum amount of information. The key touchpoints that are found useful in consulting projects are illustrated in Figure 4-5.

Direct sales are the main route for getting information on a customer. The business owner should make sure that each meeting allows enough time to get to know the customer. What are the goals of the customer? What problems is the customer trying to solve? Who does the customer partner with? Who does the customer buy from? All this information should be kept in a database for future reference. The fledgling business wants to be an integral part of the customer's value chain.

E-mail ranks next in terms of getting information, and the business owner should make sure that the employees responsible for responding to e-mail make note of any relevant data. Additionally, customer service (which may include e-mail, telephone, and face to face) is another

major touchpoint for customers. Customer service staff must be courteous and integrate any information they obtain from the customer in the database.

Website and social media site visits are also important, and many businesses give incentives to their customers to register when they come to the site. Often this incentive could be access to information about new products in advance of other customers, access to order status, or access to other information. Having customers identify themselves when they enter a web or social media site will help the business track information on what kinds of questions they have about products, or their browsing may give indications of other types of products in which they may be interested.

For much of business-to-business marketing, trade shows play a crucial role in getting information out about products and services. It also provides direct contact with buyers. There are approximately 11,000 trade shows every year. Businesses must be aware of when their industry's main trade shows are scheduled. In some industries, buying is predominantly done at trade shows at certain times of the year to coincide with the selling season. As buyers can encounter fatigue with this venue, it is important to develop ways of appearing fresh and new.

Finally, surveys and focus groups can be used to elicit customer information. For the emerging business with no resources, the student team survey can provide invaluable information to help the business move forward. More information on these specific tools is presented in the section on market research.

The business needs to make sure that each transaction is tied to a customer. Use-of-frequency programs ("for every ten you buy, you get one free") will allow the business to log every customer transaction. Often, promotions or sweepstakes will be tied to filling out a survey. Surveys may also be handed out at trade shows or events.

Customer Complaints

Since repeat customers typically provide higher profitability for a business, consultants working to improve business profitability should help the business owner focus on resolving customer complaints. When a customer is unhappy, he could tell on average 8–10 other people that he is dissatisfied. With the help of social media like Facebook and Yelp, this number can grow exponentially.

It is in the best interest of the business to have complaints surface early and be caught before they become too serious. Good businesses give customers lots of opportunity to give feedback. This is more easily done through social media such as Facebook. Often customers are excellent at pointing out systemic flaws. When the business responds to this feedback, they improve their products and services for all customers. Paradoxically, making complaining easier can be a positive way of building the business. The best feature of social media is that it allows the business to listen to its customers. It is important to note that if a customer complains, businesses must be responsive. Involving the customer in the statement of the problem and collaboratively coming up with a solution is the best way of resolving a complaint. Customers who undergo this process tend to be more loyal.

If a customer complains on the web, the business should respond immediately to the customer in the web forum with a message that includes an apology and a plan to correct the problem. Then the complaint should be taken into a private arena, either by personal message, e-mail, or voice mail. When any customer complains, the business should research every single transaction the customer has had with the business and talk to all employees who have had contact with the customer to determine the nature of the customer relationship. A review of customer profitability may be necessary, as well as a determination of whether it is a product or service quality problem. Finally, the business should talk to the customer one-on-one and take action to improve the customer's satisfaction.

Managing Information

Customer relationship management encourages responsiveness to customers' needs, but it does not mean the business gives concessions to the customer. If used properly as demonstrated in the previous examples, CRM should result in the business charging the customer a premium for better service and the customer being happy to pay more. It also follows that a business will not launch marketing programs such as free promotions, discounts, or giveaways unless it has done careful analysis of a program's cost effectiveness. Will the program bring in high-value customers? What will it add to the bottom line in net present value?

Periodically, a business should contact former customers to gain feedback about why the customer left. Small businesses, with their lack of resources, are often the last to commission a customer survey, but they also can gain valuable information from conducting one.

Creating Customer Knowledge

The process and system of CRM requires a coordinated and integrated framework for organizing and understanding customer knowledge. Small businesses typically have their accounting system databases but often fail to develop any other databases that will help them compete. Technology advances are leveling the playing field for many small businesses when it comes to information management. The small business should take advantage of technology to organize its customer information.

Each business should maintain a database of its customers. It should organize data that are already available in existing systems such as purchase, invoicing, and payment information. Additionally, it should gather information from sales calls, customer service contacts, e-mails, surveys, focus groups, and more.

There is no standard way of organizing the information. Databases should be designed to be compatible with other business processes and information systems. However, it is important to organize this information early. As the business grows, managing this information becomes cumbersome. It must be kept accurate, with any errors corrected quickly. If it is not well organized from the start, the business will incur all kinds of expenses to convert the information into a form that is usable, or worse, it may not be able to use the information at all.

USING THE MARKETING MIX

Segmentation, targeting, positioning, and branding goals should be accompanied by specific measurable objectives. For larger businesses, this might be articulated in terms of an increase in market share. For smaller businesses, this may translate into number of customers. An action plan that makes full use of the marketing mix must be put in place. *Marketing mix* is a term coined by Neil Borden in 1965 to cover the elements of marketing tactics.

Depending on the personality of the entrepreneur, the tendency may be to focus on too many or too few elements of the marketing mix. Developing too many tactics with not enough resources dooms the plan to failure. For overachieving entrepreneurs, it is important to focus efforts on those that are most easily accomplished and will give the best return. Achieving one or two initial successes will likely lead to more in the future.

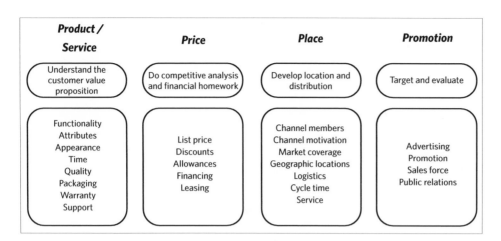

FIGURE 4-6. Elements of the Marketing Mix

Product / Service	Price	Place	Promotion
Understand the customer value proposition	Do competitive analysis and financial homework	Develop location and distribution	Target and evaluate
Functionality Attributes Appearance Time Quality Packaging Warranty Support	List price Discounts Allowances Financing Leasing	Channel members Channel motivation Market coverage Geographic locations Logistics Cycle time Service	Advertising Promotion Sales force Public relations

For others, previous experience may be in a very narrow band of tactics. These entrepreneurs continue to work with what is most familiar and neglect other areas that may yield greater opportunities. It is important to consider all elements of the marketing mix and to think outside the box when developing tactics. It will be productive to review the full checklist of elements presented in Figue 4-6.

Product

Once the customer value proposition is articulated, product or service features are created to address customers' needs. To be effective, the business must have an objective analysis as to what is important to the customer. Why does the customer buy the product or service? What functionality does it serve? In the case of an African American beauty salon, the African American woman can get her hair styled in a way that is consistent with her concept of beauty. This may not be possible at other salons. Along with this functionality, the woman may be looking for a chance to socialize, an important attribute of beauty salons in her culture. The appearance of the salon and the people who serve the clientele may be important. Time may be a critical factor. It might be assumed that shortening the time cycle is what the customer wants when, in fact, the customer might want to luxuriate in the salon similar to how people want to enjoy a coffee experience at Starbucks. The quality of the service must be suited to the customer's expectations. Service must be consistent. Clients will not return if the client perceives the hairstyle or cut to be excellent one time and a disaster the next. If a product is sold, the packaging, warranty, and support may be a factor. These factors must be considered along with a cost-benefit analysis to properly assess product value.

The articulation of the customer value proposition for services is particularly difficult for emerging businesses. Minority business enterprises that have operated solely in ethnic markets may lose the value that close identification brings as they expand to new customers in different racial/ethnic markets. Shifts in population or increasing sophistication of ethnic markets may take away location as a customer value proposition. As such, the MBE must develop and communicate a different value. This could be customized services or personal attention. Successfully delivering these values may require a major redesign of its service.

Pricing

The main influences on pricing generally include customer demand, competitor actions, quality and related services, costs and other factors such as laws and regulations, technological conditions, and capacity or other resource constraints. Company responses to such influences are shaped by its strategic and operational decisions. These include pricing objectives, strategies to accomplish those objectives, the structure of prices offered by the firm, and general pricing conditions in the markets in which the firm competes.

Important questions to ask about pricing include: What is the value of the firm's offering compared to competitors? How are the firm's products or services perceived by different segments? Are there sustainable competitive advantages that can be identified for the firm? Answers to such questions will provide clues regarding how much discretion, if any, management will have in its pricing policies and decisions.

TABLE 4-5. Pricing Tactics

Strategy	Description
Value Pricing	Adjusting prices to offer the right combination of quality and service at a fair price. This requires competitive analysis to determine what constitutes the right price for the value that the business gives. Small businesses (despite the fact that they often have cost advantages) should not attempt to compete on price alone.
Cost-based pricing	Cost-plus and mark-up pricing, return on investment, or other cost methods may be used to determine price. This requires the careful accumulation of product costs to include both variable and fixed components. Costing based on variable cost only can pave the way to bad pricing. Small businesses sometimes do not track product line profitability. However, this can be easily gleaned from looking at financial statements and speaking to the owner. This can be educational for the business owner.
Competitive pricing	Matching prices with the firm's main competitors is a common method of pricing. Most small businesses do not have the time to get a complete listing of competitor prices. This analysis can be invaluable in determining how the firm stands competitively. This includes finding the price ceiling or highest price and the pricing floor or the lowest price. In several Business and Economic Development Center analyses, this strategy has shown that the business charged prices that were too low.
Promotional pricing	A business may cut prices to gain customers in the short term. This is done by the industry as a whole at certain times of the year. For example, furniture is typically discounted in the summer when sales are low. For any promotions, it is important to assess the benefit achieved. If prices are lowered but no new customers or sales are gained, the promotion should not be repeated.
Discount pricing	Reducing prices to reward customer loyalty or purchase behavior and other incentives to reward for patronage is also common. As in other cases, when prices are reduced, it is important to evaluate the benefit.

Often with emerging businesses, the rationale behind the pricing is the entrepreneur's desire to make a certain profit margin regardless of what customers are willing to pay for the product or service. Prices may have been set in reaction to competitors or based on other factors. Some common pricing strategies are illustrated in Table 4-5. In most businesses, one strategy will be used in combination with another. All pricing strategies should be evaluated against competitors. Financial analysis is mandatory on any pricing changes, and the effect of the changes should be monitored and adjustments made as necessary.

An analysis of competitive pricing lets the business know how it is positioned against the competition. In the case of an African American coffee shop, the consultant team walked a ten-block radius of the shop and found 17 competitors. They mapped the locations of each of these. Next, they collected pricing information for the most frequently purchased types of coffee. They found that the business was in the 10th percentile of pricing. Pricing coffee lower than the competition may unnecessarily give away profits or convey inferior quality when convenience is the key factor in their customer base.

When dealing with large volumes of customers, small businesses may have to offer volume discounts. Going into these negotiations armed with the correct numbers will let the business owner know the price range in which he or she can negotiate. Allowances, financing, and leasing may be other ways that small businesses can assist their customers in meeting the price.

Distribution

From a cost standpoint, distribution processes are extremely important activities. For example, it is widely quoted that as much as 20% of what consumers pay goes toward the physical distribution of goods. Thus, a significant distribution management objective is to minimize the costs of performing these order-filling tasks while delivering goods to customers. Overall, the goal should be to perform these activities in order to insure the swift, safe, and low-cost delivery of goods and services to customers.

The first step in a good distribution program is a detailed market analysis to identify the locations of the target market, such as a mapping of customer locations. With emerging businesses, there is no room for any waste. Often a detailed neighborhood market analysis can identify significant savings for a small business. Careful business process analysis (covered in Module 6) can be very helpful in determining what improvements can be made in distribution. In the case of a parking lot cleaning service, the business was able to reduce travel time significantly by mapping upcoming jobs and taking the most efficient routes. This reduced costs of staff time and gas, while also allowing the company to book additional business due to the increased efficiency of staff time.

Suggested questions to ask about place or spatial attributes include:

- How accessible is my place of business for customers compared to my main competitors?
- Is my location compatible with the other elements of the marketing mix that I offer?
- Am I making the best use of available marketing channels for delivering goods and services to customers?
- Can I afford to gain more control over the marketing channels that are currently being used?

As an emerging business, it is tempting to focus on a narrow part of the distribution channel. For example, an Indian American promotional products firm provides products that companies give away to enhance the customer relationship or promote a product. This could include eye-catching T-shirts or pens with the company logo. The company could focus on providing products only when the customer asks for them. If, for example, the customer has a trade fair in two months and wants 2,000 mugs as giveaways, the company must scramble to find a source for the mugs, print the logo, and get the shipment to the customer on time. This makes the business very reactive and subject to short lead-time requests. If instead of reacting, the business, in close relationship with its customer, suggests an innovative high-tech giveaway that it has already sourced in anticipation, logistical problems are reduced significantly. At the same time, the business better serves the customer. This is a win-win situation for the business and its customer. It took a broad view of its customer's overall marketing strategy. Then it recommended effective products and promotional campaigns to help its customer achieve her goals. In the process this promotional product firm created circumstances where it fulfilled orders most profitably.

As with other parts of the marketing mix, it is important to explore all feasible options in developing a distribution program. Look within the company for how warehousing, inventory management, shipping, and order processing are achieved. Analyze vendor and customer processes to determine where the value is in the chain and what efficiencies could be achieved.

Promotion

Promotion tactics included in this section focus on programs that are more effective with emerging businesses, in multicultural markets, and in hyper-local markets. The use of broadcast media is less effective for small businesses because those methods are expensive and often not effective in reaching a targeted hyper-local market or a niche business-to-business market. For some first-generation immigrant consumer markets, promoting a product or service though their native language media is critical to success. At the same time, even though most immigrant Asian Americans and Hispanics read English, they sometimes prefer to read in their native language. Ethnic press can be a more effective means of attracting customers from ethnic markets than the mainstream press.

Promotion programs include a wide range of communications and relationship-building activities, including personal selling, advertising, sales promotion, direct mail, public relations, trade shows, and event or organization sponsorship. For most small businesses the first four are most relevant.

Suggested questions to ask about promotion programs and strategy include:

- Are our promotion messages clear, concise, consistent, and compatible with our position in the marketplace?
- Have we designed our promotion strategy in ways that are cost effective in achieving our order-getting objectives?
- Are we evaluating our promotion efforts to ensure that we get "the best bang for our buck"?
- What changes should we consider making in our overall marketing communications strategy?

TABLE 4-6. Promotion

Media	Method	Cost	Small Business Advantages
Direct mail includes flyers, postcards, and e-mail.	Use of word processing software allows personalized mailings, and use of desktop publishing allows the business to design its own materials.	Costs typically range from $1.50 to $5.00 per mailed piece, with additional cost for mailing list acquisition when seeking new customers. E-mailing can cost considerably less.	Advantages include an effective way to communicate with current customers, with research showing that e-mail marketing is most effective when targeting existing customers rather than new customers, and this provides an opportunity to communicate with different customers in their native language.
Print media	Create ads and place in local newspapers.	Ethnic newspapers and magazines can be of reasonable cost due to lower circulation than mass media publications.	For small businesses moving to adjacent markets, ethnic newspapers are an effective way to reach another multicultural market, and ads can be placed in different languages.
Yellow Pages	Place ad or listing in Yellow Pages. Often this arrangement includes a listing on the online yellow pages as well.	Can range from a few hundred to over $1,000 a year depending on the size of the ad.	In general, business-to-consumer companies that compete on price or service time availability find advantage with this strategy.
Outdoor	Billboard, awnings, or other signage in high-traffic areas.	Cost runs about $1,000 a year.	Can be very effective for reaching local markets, especially if signage is placed in high-traffic areas. Local zoning laws need to be checked to see what is allowable.
Sales promotions, including online coupons, contests, samples, point-of-purchase displays	Sales promotions can be in store or part of mailings or ads.	Determine costs and exposure or reach prior to use or rollout.	The small business often works with very little margin for error. Inexperienced business owners may want to pursue promotions because they think that will generate new business. A break-even analysis should be conducted before application to insure new business generation.
Social media	Business can promote via Facebook sites, customer review sites, blogs, and Twitter.	The most significant cost is staff time to update information and correct errors or respond to customer complaints.	This strategy encourages customer intimacy and requires little out-of-pocket expenditures beyond staff time.

- Have we adopted state-of-the-art integrated communications methods and media?

Table 4-6 summarizes various promotional strategies.

Public Relations

Marketing to ethnic markets may take the enterprise into religious and community institutions, where it is important to generate goodwill. For African Americans and Hispanics, the church may be a good place to reach key market segments. For other groups, family associations and community service organizations may be effective. Affinity groups are an excellent way to reach markets, and people are less apt to be skeptical when reached within their own community. However, sensitivity must be exercised in approaching these respected institutions. The communication must be authentic and appropriate, and it is most effective when delivered by someone from within the community.

Public relations, also referred to as earned media as

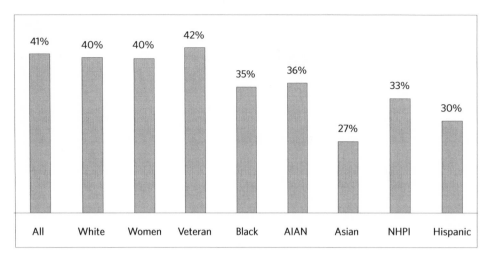

FIGURE 4-7. Portion of Businesses with Websites

Source: "Statistics for All US Firms That Had a Website," 2007 Survey of Business Owners Survey_Business_2007.xlsx

opposed to the paid media associated with paid advertising, can be an effective way of implementing an emotional branding strategy. The business owner who has overcome the odds can be an excellent story for the local press. In the case of an architectural firm, a photo spread of a design in a local magazine's home section is much more effective than running a generic ad in the same magazine. Having a comprehensive website with extensive information about the firm can be a good way of generating press interest. Reporters conduct Internet searches on community-related topics. If the website is professional and includes all the excellent credentials of the business owner, the reporter will often follow up for more information.

Simple and low-cost steps can be taken to create an effective public relations plan. The business can issue regular newsletters to its community or the local and ethnic press about its activities. It can participate in or sponsor community events. It can apply for any awards that may be given by the local chamber or other community associations. It can host open houses where it invites the community to visit its premises and meet its staff. Business anniversaries and other landmarks can be celebrated with the community. Developing partnerships with nonprofit organizations may provide name recognition in press releases issued by the nonprofit. Heartfelt participation in the community will create trust within the community for the business.

WEB MARKETING

In a 2011 survey, the Pew Internet and American Life Project found that 78% of the US population uses the Internet. This ranges from 95% of people aged 18 to 29 to 42% of those aged 65 and older. Those who are more affluent are more likely to use the Internet, as are those who are more educated. Of Internet users, 78% research a product online and 71% will buy a product online.[3] Despite this, the 2007 Survey of Business Owners found that only 41% of businesses had websites, and the proportion fell for MBEs, as shown in Figure 4-7.

As an indication of the shift to the web, online ad spending was 17.7% of all ad spending in 2011, surpassing newspapers at 13% and magazines at 17.3%, and is projected to grow at rates of 12% to 14% until 2014. US mobile ad spending is projected to grow at equally high rates. The use of paid online searches (or placement on search engines through words searched) will continue to be a large component of online advertising, as shown in Figure 4-8. E-mail, classified, and display ads are contracting. Another noticeable trend is the increase of rich media or video.

As advertising moves increasingly away from print to the Internet, small businesses are given the opportunity to compete effectively with large companies, as it is possible to target very small segments of the market. This requires that small businesses better segment their potential customer base and conduct analyses to determine strategies to best reach their target customers.

In addition to the use of websites, *Inc. Magazine* found that of the companies in the Inc. 500 (a list of fast-growing companies with at least $2 million in revenues), 78% use Facebook, 78% use LinkedIn, and 73% use Twitter.

---

3   Pew Research Center, "Internet and American Life Project Spring Tracking Survey," conducted April 26–May 22, 2011. http://pewinternet.org.

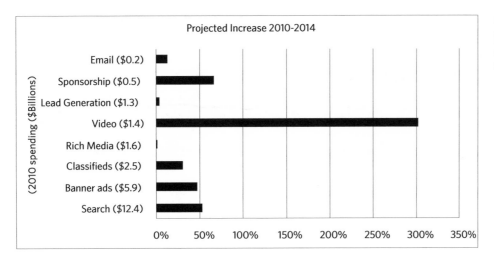

FIGURE 4-8. Trends in Online Ad Spending

Source: "US Ad Spending: Online Outshines Other Media," eMarketer, December 2010

TABLE 4-7. Search Engine Share

	Share
Google sites	66%
Yahoo! sites	16%
Microsoft sites	14%
Ask Network	3%
AOL, Inc.	1%

Source: comScore.com, June 2011

Although MBEs lag white firms in use of the web, there is no doubt that the increasing use of the Internet among minority populations and the increasing migration of MBEs from their own ethnic markets to adjacent and larger markets make it imperative to use the Internet as a major component of their marketing strategy.

Social media such as Facebook, LinkedIn, and Google+ are fast becoming a standard of websites. Implementing these features on a website is usually not costly. The premise behind social media is that recommendations from friends are the best way to sell a product or service. Nielsen found that 76% of US Internet consumers said they most trusted recommendations from personal acquaintances, while 49% trusted consumer opinions posted online. Those two forms of "earned" advertising were also cited as the most relevant to consumers when they are looking for information on products they need and want. Forty percent of respondents also ranked "e-mails I signed up for" as one of the top three most trustworthy forms of advertising.[4] However, despite

the buzz about social media, searching continues to be the main driver of revenue generation. According to a report in the Media Industry Newsletter (Smith 2011), 41% of website traffic comes from searching as compared to 11% from social media.

Large enterprises such as Starbucks and IBM use social media as a means of listening to their customers. Listening in social media can assist the enterprise in adding wanted product and service features, developing new products, projecting future trends, and anticipating possible negative trends or crises. Some low-cost means of listening include Google Alerts, Technorati blog searches, Twitter searches, Facebook searches, and YouTube searches on keywords that may be of interest to the business.

Additionally, social media may be used as a form of advertising. The "like" app on Facebook allows customers to signal to friends that they like the business or support the brand. Customers use social media to receive promotions, to get updates on future projects, to learn more about the company, and to be informed about upcoming sales; all forms serve to advertise and promote the business.

Creating a Business Website or Social Media Site

A business web or social media site can be an effective marketing tool. Businesses must have very clear goals that they want to achieve with their websites. Websites provide the opportunity to improve relationships with existing customers. A company can provide in-depth

---

4   Neilsen, "State of the Media: Trends in Advertising Spend and Effectiveness." June 2011. Retrieved 12/20/11 from http://www

.immagic.com/eLibrary/ARCHIVES/GENERAL/NLSN_NL/ N110610S.pdf.

detail about its products and services at very low cost. A web or social media site provides the small business with the ability to reach new markets both nationally and internationally. It can cut costs and increase efficiencies by allowing customers to access information at any time and from anywhere.

When properly designed and used, company web and social media sites are very effective in reaching current and new customers. As with every aspect of marketing, the design of a web or social media site starts by asking the customer what he or she wants and insuring the ease of finding this information in a manner that can lead to a sale.

For the most part, it is recommended that the business contract a web design company to create the website. Student teams that are working with a small business can assist in developing the content as well as the architecture of a site by asking the following questions:

1. What is the objective of the site? Is it to be an e-commerce or brochure site? To develop relationships, gather market research, manage events, build awareness, or gather sales leads?
2. What type of visitors will the site attract?
3. Is the website effective in meeting its established objectives?
4. What are the aesthetics and overall visual appeal? Is the website memorable, well-differentiated, or fairly standard? Are the branding, aesthetics, and information on the website consistent with all other touchpoints?
5. What are the key differences (positive or negative) between this website and competitors' sites? Differences could be in terms of aesthetics, ease of use, extent of information and options, or any other aspect of website evaluation.

Search Engine Optimization

Search engine optimization (SEO) is a means of bringing traffic to the business owner's website. Potential customers overwhelmingly use search engines as a means of finding the products and services they need. These search engines will provide and funnel the traffic based on a number of factors that the business owner should seek to maximize.

There are two different types of SEOs: off-page and on-page. The on-page SEO relates to the business web-

site's ability to increase search engine keyword performance in producing frequency of visits or hits and usage. These are "organic" results, not results from Ad Words or other paid sponsorship programs. Web designers suggest that phrases, not words, be used. Google Analytics is a tool that can be used to identify which words are most effective in drawing traffic to the site. Google Keyword can be used to do analysis of the type of keywords for which customers are searching. By using a service called Websitegrader (websitegrader.com), the team can input the business's URL and three to five competitors' URLs to generate a report that will provide some simple suggestions on how to improve the website. Using another site (tools.seobook.com/general/keyword-density), the business can see the density of keywords on the homepage. Ideally, keywords should have a 2% to 3% density. Alexa.com is another site that will rank the URL.

The off-page information is critical for SEO and is done outside of the website. It maximizes the website's performance on search engines by relating on-page keywords and content in off-page direct links. The top off-page elements to engage in are submission of the business website to search engines, social networking sites bookmarking submission, article submission, press release submission, blog creation and postings, and forum postings such as Facebook, LinkedIn, and Twitter. To evaluate off-site optimization, use siteexplorer.search.yahoo.com and search for the business's URL to determine the number and quality of links.

The key is to get the business website link on as many other sites as possible and have those inbound links direct traffic to the site. This includes creating free listings on sites such as Yelp, Google, and the Yellow Pages, as well as industry-specific websites. Search rankings are based on link popularity. The more clicks on the link, the higher the resultant ranking. Business owners should also limit the number of outbound links that take people off the business website. The business could track website traffic by using free services such as Google Analytics and improve search engine optimization tactics as necessary.

Social Media

Social media have become major forms of marketing. Examples include forums, blogs, comments, review sites, and Twitter. For example, most business owners start by using Google Alerts to track any keyword or brand mentions. This communication tool informs business owners

16 Copenhagen

Creating a Relevant Cultural Brand with Creativity

Rachel Valdez, founder and CEO of 16 Copenhagen, contends that her team is not just a website developer and branding agent, but Design Mixologists™ who inspire imagination through designs with purpose. 16 Copenhagen's portfolio of services includes website design and development, print marketing media, professional photography skills, interactive media products, search engine optimization, and training solutions. It provides services to a diverse client base, ranging from emerging businesses and public entities to large global clients.

16 Copenhagen is a unique brand name that captures the essence of the firm: creativity, imagination, good fortune, and modernism. $1 + 6 = 7$, and 7 is a lucky and significant number across many cultures and contexts. The number 7 is also related to the activation of imagination. The 16th is Valdez's birth date. Copenhagen represents the firm's global reach and image; the city represents modernism, great use of small spaces, and a progressive community.

Valdez launched 16 Copenhagen in December 2008. Like many small business owners, she wanted to follow her entrepreneurial ambitions and dreams and recognized an opportunity to offer competitive services with superior customer satisfaction. She was also motivated by a personal goal—to be a role model for other minority-owned businesses. Valdez is active in her local community and mentors other multicultural and women business owners. She described her seven values:

1. Relationships with external stakeholders
2. Trust: encouraging open dialogue and passionate debate
3. Fun: laughter stimulates creativity
4. Be a good neighbor in the community
5. Innovation: free flow of ideas

6. Diversity and inclusion: all voices welcomed and diverse talent cultivated
7. Fiscal responsibility: solid, responsible, and profitable business foundation with integrity

In 2009, a group of student consultants worked with Valdez and her team to identify high-growth market segments, to strengthen her financial management oversight, and to enhance her social media strategy. The student team conducted a market segmentation analysis and identified three growth industries to target: health care, education, and renewable energy. Although 16 Copenhagen was in a relatively healthy financial state, the student team recommended regular meetings between Valdez and her CPA and opening a line of credit (she opened one before the project was completed). The student consultant team also recommended adding a blog to the 16 Copenhagen website, which could strengthen her search engine optimization (increase number of search results), as well as provide valuable information to her customers. Upon completion of the student consulting project, Valdez hired one of the student consultants as a marketing intern to help implement the team's recommendations. Among other responsibilities, the student intern was responsible for executing the company blog. The blog continues to be an integral part of 16 Copenhagen's website.

16 Copenhagen blends a unique combination of creativity, innovation, and diversity in its branding strategies and website development: www.16copenhagen.com is a bilingual website.

of the specific keywords that customers search for when looking for their products or services. This information can be used to adjust the keywords attached to business websites.

Twitter is the real-time media that keeps users current on happenings and various types of chatter. This might be the first place a rant or rave will be mentioned. From Twitter, posts can quickly go viral and make it difficult to implement the right damage control (for example, a customer may post a complaint about the business). Business owners should monitor Twitter and other social media sites to determine both positive and negative feedback on the business.

Creating a blog for the business is another way to drive traffic to its website. The more content and density on the business website, the higher its search engine rankings will climb. Businesses should encourage their loyal customers to post reviews on sites such as Yelp.

Online coupon services such as Groupon and Living Social have been used to drive new customers to businesses. It is important to do a careful break-even analysis to determine at what level couponing is effective. Review services such as Yelp can also bring customers into the business. It is important that the business encourage loyal customers to post reviews. At the same time, the business should monitor reviews so that any negative reviews can be dealt with quickly. Location-based apps such as Facebook Places or Foursquare allow customers to share their current location with friends.

Businesses on Facebook have created stores. Businesses have used LinkedIn to create a community with

which to promote products and services. For example, Small Biz Nation, ostensibly an advice site for small businesses, is maintained by HPQ. Caution must be exercised with the use of social media; it requires that the business owner maintain the social media. If no posts are made and no activity is registered, this can be more damaging than not using social media at all.

Maintaining the Website

For most small businesses, it makes sense to use an Internet service provider (ISP) to host the website rather than rely on the business's own servers. It is difficult for a small company to ensure that servers are up 24 hours a day, seven days a week, and that it has adequate security to ward off malicious hackers or other online criminals. In fact, large companies spend a significant amount of money to insure security. For relatively low cost, a small business can get enough space at an ISP to satisfy all its web requirements. If a small business buys broadband service such as a DSL line, the provider may include a website as well.

Neglecting a website may lead customers to distrust the company. Out-of-date websites are the number one turnoff for customers. Customers may perceive the company to be disorganized and to not care about its products, or worse, not care about its customers. The business must maintain the website regularly. Monthly reviews to check information accuracy and links are very important. Make sure someone within the business has been trained to do this and that they are accountable for what they do.

REFERENCES

Kotler, Philip, and Gary Armstrong. *Principles of Marketing.* Upper Saddle River, NJ: Prentice Hall, 2009.

Peppers, Don, and Martha Rogers. *The One to One Future.* New York: Currency/Doubleday, 1996.

Williams, Jerome D., Wei-Na Lee, and Curtis P. Haugtvedt. *Diversity in Advertising.* Mahwah, NJ: Lawrence Erlbaum Associates, Inc., 2004

DISCUSSION

1. Using US Census data on the zip codes surrounding the client business, compile a profile of the most attractive target markets. Select one of the targeted groups and identify how it could be reached effectively through a local advertising medium.

2. Emerging businesses often need to have very low-cost marketing programs that reach a local market. Brainstorm some ways that a business could use low-cost methods to promote the business.

3. Review the section on web marketing. Create a checklist and evaluate the current effectiveness of the client business's URL. Suggest ways in which the client can use social media to increase customer engagement.

4. Analyze and discuss how the client incorporates the customer life cycle to increase revenues and profits.

Discuss specific programs at each phase of the customer life cycle.

5. Based on what you know about your client's community engagement activities and relationships, what public relations program could be effective at relatively low costs?

5. Marketing Research

ABOUT THIS MODULE

This module illustrates the methods and techniques used in conducting business and marketing research. Most consulting projects require some form of research to obtain information and data needed to effectively solve problems and make sound business decisions. Small businesses rarely have the luxury of using paid, professional consultants to conduct their research. Consulting by teams of business students, supervised by faculty and business professionals, offer client firms and organizations valuable access to research that otherwise would not be available to them (see Module 3). The completed research studies can often have a sizable impact on current operations and future strategic directions. The information is typically most useful to businesses when it is presented in terms of analytical results and relationships that they can understand and apply.

In the first part of this module, task and functional research questions are used as a way to illustrate how the process works. The questions illustrate how and why certain methods and techniques are used in carrying out the main tasks of research. The second section focuses on secondary research. Compiling information from published sources or using data collected by someone else can be a cost-effective means of getting valuable information. The third section covers primary research whereby the consulting team will collect the data. Qualitative research, which emphasizes the context and content of what is being reported rather than what is counted, measured, or quantified, is covered in the fourth section. Observational methods are included in this type of research.

Business and marketing research is a systematic process of collecting, analyzing, interpreting, and presenting information or data on a defined question, issue, or topic pertaining to market exchange transactions and relationships. The findings and results produced from the research process are used mainly to support decisions and solve problems.

After Studying This Module

When the student consulting team has reviewed this module, it will be able to frame key questions that business owners ask to move forward. Such questions need to be answered based on research rather than on guesses, hunches, and intuition.

After studying this module you will be able to:

- Define, select, and compile published (secondary) information.
- Design, use, and analyze the results from a survey questionnaire (called primary research).
- Describe, use, and interpret the results of focus group interviewing, ethnographic studies, and other qualitative research methods.
- Apply standard research methods to help solve multicultural business and marketing problems.
- Help a small business answer an important question.

RESEARCH PROCESS

Questions in Figure 5-1 provide a way to explore the research process. The sequence of questions begins with how the research can help to accomplish project objectives and moves through to the evaluation of the costs and benefits of the time, talent, and other resources

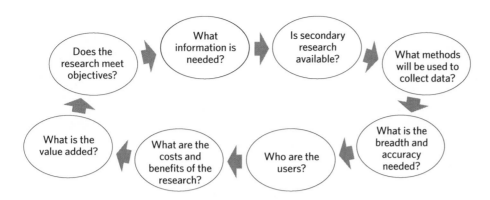

FIGURE 5-1. Key Questions About the Research Process

required to complete the research. For emerging businesses with few resources, even the time involved in completing such a survey can represent tremendous cost to the business. The results must justify the costs or the research should not be done.

Does the Research Meet the Objective?

In completing the consulting project on time and within budget, the consultant cannot afford to engage in any activities that are not directly relevant to the project mission. The initial question asked is: What are the basic objectives of the project that require information to be collected and analyzed? Answers should focus on the definition of the problems that the consultant is being asked to investigate. Very likely there will be issues related to finding new opportunities in the marketplace (e.g., different markets to serve or ways to increase sales and revenue among present customers). If the needs of the business have been described in terms of finding new customers or increasing the frequency of store visits of existing customers, the research will need to provide reliable information for taking appropriate action. From the beginning to the end of the project, the aim should be to provide information and knowledge that will help the client make better decisions.

What Information Is Needed?

In answering this question, it is important that the consultant team cover the full range of factors that affect the business. A sampling of these factors is shown in Table 5-1.

TABLE 5-1. Categories of Marketing Information

Customers	The Firm	The Market

Demographic
  Age, race, national origin, ethnicity, education, household size, gender, income
	Financial
	  Growth rates, financial characteristics, business model
		Economic Conditions
		  Local employment, economic growth, housing starts

Geographic
  Region, state, county, city, community, census tracts,
	Competitors
	  Branding, positioning, merchandising, locations, advertising, product offerings, pricing, size, and resources of competitors
		Industry Trends
		  Sector growth, industry dynamics

Socioeconomic/psychographic
  Lower, middle, or upper class, lifestyle, occupation
	Experience
	  Human capital, owner's capabilities, successes
		Regulations
		  Federal, state, and local regulations

Cultural
  Religious traditions, ethnic customs, music preferences, artistic sensibilities
	Managerial
	  Benchmarking or other performance measures, elements of strategy
		Sociocultural Issues
		  Official observance of community celebrations, ethnic holidays

Business
  Industry, length of supply chain, sales cycle
	Businesses
	  Place in the supply chain, cash flow needs
		Businesses
		  Industry trends, sustainability issues, resource costs, outsourcing trends

These relationships illustrate that marketing itself is very broad in scope. The more clearly information needs are identified, the more effectively the consultant will be able to define and follow steps in the business and marketing research process. With MBEs, it is important to supplement the information obtained through analysis using the above format with information on racism and the effect of discriminatory practices on buying from particular companies. This type of information can be crucial to understanding the barriers the business faces in the current marketplace.

Are Secondary Data Available?

Data are generally classified as primary or secondary. Primary data are collected directly from the group, sample, or population of interest. Primary data include all forms collected by a researcher such as surveys, focus groups, observational, or other qualitative data. Data collected or compiled by someone else are called secondary data. US Census data are a commonly used form of secondary data. Census data can provide secondary data on the trade areas covered by any business. Racial/ethnic composition of the market area, including household size or other demographics, is also available through census data sources. The Census Bureau, the Department of Commerce, and a range of private sector sources publish information on businesses and industries that can be used in secondary research.

What Methods Will Be Used to Collect Data?

Secondary data such as client financial statements can be useful in defining benchmark standards for the firm. Other examples include store invoices, sales records, and other company documents. There may be additional internal sources of information such as marketing materials or reports. Other data will be collected from external sources such as government websites, newspapers, periodicals, and library databases. Local government economic development agencies are an excellent source of secondary information. Keep in mind that the detailed niche information required for ethnic small businesses may not be available in mainstream sources. In these cases, it may be helpful to identify industry benchmarks. Secondary sources should include community/ethnic newspapers and the Yellow Pages.

Methods used to collect primary data include observation, focus groups, ethnographic studies, and surveys (by telephone, mail, and personal interviews). Primary data regarding customer preferences and shopping experiences could be collected by customer "store intercept" interviews. Survey questions can also be asked of preselected customers (or convenience samples) and others who shop near where the data are collected.

What Are the Breadth and Accuracy Required?

This question gets to the heart of asking what kind of research will be conducted. There are basically three categories of research: exploratory, descriptive, and causal. Exploratory research is broadest in scope because its purpose is to define and clarify problems, gain insight into situations and relationships, and form hypotheses that can be examined in more rigorous and narrowly defined research.

Descriptive research focuses definitively on answering specific questions about who, what, when, where, and how in relation to a topic or problem. It is generally considered to be more rigorous than exploratory research and should provide answers regarding product choices and decisions, provide estimates of what will occur in the future, and generate an empirical basis for understanding the problems and issues being studied.

Causal research is the most rigorous of the three types because the results are expected to yield explanations of the cause-and-effect relationships between and among variables. Under ideal conditions, causal research is conducted through laboratory and field studies using experimental designs.

1. If the research is exploratory, your scope will need to be broader and more tentative than when it intends to describe, evaluate, or confirm a previously established condition or relationship.
2. If the research is descriptive, it will be more rigorous and definitive than if it is exploratory, but it is generally less rigorous and more inclusive than explanatory research.
3. If the research is causal, it will focus on meeting the requirements of experimental design and manipulation of variables to ensure the valid determination of cause-and-effect relationships among the variables being studied.

Of the three types, descriptive research is the most inclusive as to methods and uses. It ranges from basic statistical analysis of means and frequencies to more elaborate multivariate methods of statistical analysis. Often statistical software packages such as SPSS will be used to execute the analysis. Explanatory research is less likely to be used in project studies and research because of time, resources, and its generally more theoretical and analytical orientation and purposes.

Two other types of research—qualitative and quantitative—should also be included in this discussion. They are related to the types of data and methods of analysis that are used in the research. Qualitative research focuses on answering research questions based on the content and context of understanding people, behavior, or other aspects of business and marketing. This is done through the use of observational studies, open-ended interviews, focus groups, and ethnographic studies. These methods provide important emotional and contextual understanding of behavior and relationships.

Some observations should be made about sampling methods. In quantitative research using surveys, it is expected that those selected for inclusion in the research will be representative of the population being studied (e.g., sample). The size of the sample is a strong determinant of validity. Validity is important because it means that the results actually and accurately describe what they purport or claim to describe.

The trade-off between cost and accuracy may be the main determining factor in selecting sampling methods. If general background information is needed that will be broadly representative of the larger population in the community, a convenience sample might be adequate. But if precise statistical estimates are to be developed with specified levels of confidence in the estimates that are to be presented, more rigorous statistical or probability sampling must be developed.

In such a case, the expected results would be accompanied by a precise statistical calculation about the expected error or confidence that is associated with the numerical results. The terms applied to such a relationship or concerns are the validity and reliability of the results of the study. Clearly, if decisions involve considerable risks, substantial investments, or commitments of resources, higher levels of reliability would be imposed. This means that the sampling could be duplicated and that comparable results would be expected.

Who Are the Users of the Research?

The primary users of the research are typically the business owners or clients. However, the business owner may make use of the research to achieve other objectives, such as justifying financial projections to bankers and investors. The results may also provide evidence for the size of a market niche.

The design and execution of the project must meet generally accepted analytical standards. This could include a certain number of years of financial data to establish a trend, designated size of a sample survey to provide a given level of confidence in the statistical results, or other measurable categories of relationships and outcomes of the research. Such standards are likely to be indicated and applied by the mentors and advisors as well as the professors who are supervising a given project. In conducting the research and analyzing the results, all these audiences should be considered.

What Are the Costs and Benefits of the Research?

Many forms of research can be quite expensive and particularly prohibitive to small businesses. Care should be taken to make sure that the methods used are appropriate and cost effective. Businesses want to make the best use of all their resources. The costs should not be any higher than what is needed to provide the necessary information. It should also be recognized that benefits from research can be quite subjective and even intangible. The value to the client should be determined, not assumed. The expectation should be that the benefits will be greater than the costs.

Costs to the client would be the owners' time and any financial support that is provided to cover the out-of-pocket costs, such as travel for personal interviews or incentives for participation. Consultants, whether they are paid or not, should quantify their time spent in completing a research project.

Benefits from marketing research are commonly associated with gains that the business can realize from using the results of the research. In a retail gift shop project, for example, the owner needs to be able to make better selection decisions in buying merchandise. This can lead to improved inventory control, reduced inventory carrying costs, increased efficiency of allocation of financial resources, and ultimately increased sales.

Broadly speaking, the benefits associated with such research are increasing sales and market/customer share, uncovering needs and preferences, finding alternative ways of attracting and serving customers, and reducing business risk.

What Is the Value Added?

The final work product of the business and marketing research is a written report to the client. This will be evaluated with respect to its technical, managerial, and other dimensions that lead to increased profitability. By technical evaluation, it must be ensured that the coverage includes the most up-to-date information that is deemed adequate to solve the problems being studied and support sound marketing decisions. In managerial terms, the business improvement ideas generated from the project should be sound and help guide buying decisions and sales projections or meet other managerial needs. The owner must be able to implement the recommendations that were supported in the research. The reported results should be actionable and effective.

SECONDARY RESEARCH

Whatever the questions, problems, or issues that need research, the process should begin with secondary research. Most likely the first search will be on the Internet to identify relevant information sources. This can sometimes prove overwhelming. More productive searches begin with library resources that limit the search to more fruitful areas.

The research objective needs to be as clear as possible. If the topic has not been fully clarified, ask advisors, team members, and faculty how to gain greater clarity. This is especially pertinent with small businesses that are inexperienced with the consulting process. It is important to spend time figuring out exactly what needs to be researched. Time taken at the outset to ensure clear problem definition and project focus will save time for completing other tasks later in the process.

It may be beneficial to re-ask the question about how the research results will be used. If the research is completed, what difference will it make? What actions can be taken on the basis of it? Inexperienced consultants are often enamored with "nice to know" data. If the results of the research are not actionable or do not directly answer project questions, then it should not be done. What value will be added to the business when the information is obtained? Take the time to come up with the mission or objective in writing and share it with the business owner and advisors. Time is a scarce commodity on any consulting project, and the team needs to be right on target. Being slightly off target at the beginning can pull the team far away from the goal at the end.

Budgeting Time

The deadline for the finished project may be a few months away, but research takes time. There can be wide variation between teams in the amount of time used to complete projects. The amount of time can vary by a factor of five or six. Needless to say, the more time spent on the project, the higher the probability that it will be done correctly. In fact, it is possible to miss the mark completely if not enough time is spent. Beginning researchers are likely to make missteps or run into dead-end paths before finding the right direction. They should allocate even more time for task and project completion. The more experienced the researcher becomes, the less time needs to be allowed for misdirected effort.

Start early and budget blocks of time (2–3 hours) adequate to do serious searching. It can take 40 to 60 hours to thoroughly research a relatively small topic. Finding the information itself is not difficult once the important sources are known. Filtering, sorting, organizing, and coming up with relevant conclusions can take considerably more time. If the consultant is new to a research area, she or he needs learning-curve time to process and better understand the information being generated. It is necessary to build a framework for processing the information in a meaningful way. Often the framework does not become clear until the consultant has "lived" with the data for a while. Starting early also allows time for more feedback from the business owner and advisors on the analysis.

Use the Library Effectively

The library is an invaluable information resource for several reasons: (1) it is readily accessible to most individuals, (2) the costs of using the library are minimal from the user's perspective, and (3) the services available are personal, technical, and substantial. For these reasons it would be an important missed opportunity to take on a research project without making effective use of the library. Recognize that a university library or any other professionally staffed one may have a reference librarian available. Any approach to secondary research that avoids the proper use of the library is likely to be more costly but less effective than the library.

After reviewing major business publications, refer to trade journals for the industry being researched. A trade publication is a periodical that covers topics in a particular industry. Three examples in retailing include

Stores, *Chain Store Age/Executive*, and *Progressive Grocer*. For multicultural entrepreneurship the list of trade publications would include *Black Enterprise* and *Hispanic Business*. Many mainstream publications also carry articles about multicultural entrepreneurship and marketing. Just about every industry has a trade publication, and many are available at the local library. Often there is an annual issue that gives statistics for the year. Student teams have the added advantage of industry mentors who often have access to expensive market research done by private firms. These are available only through subscription or membership. They include directories of firms in an industry, restaurant association summaries of cost structures, and projections of industry growth.

Reading articles on a subject helps the beginning researcher become more familiar with the literature and what others are writing about the topic. Reading may suggest ideas and connections that can lead to better answers to research questions. Such processes are also likely to provide a framework for the hard analysis that comes after all the information has been gathered.

Before striking out on an Internet search, refine the topic and make a list of keywords. Make use of connective words (i.e., AND, OR) to extend or distinguish between keywords in your search; these are logical connectors and could also include NOT or NEAR. Search engines such as Google, Yahoo, and Bing canvass the web to collect an index of websites. When the keywords are typed, the engine searches its index for possible web pages and produces a list. Most search engines offer advanced functions to make searching more specific; it is well worth reading the help files of each. Search engines have gone through much consolidation in the past two years. For a recent and complete list of search engines see www.searchenginewatch.com. Google (www.google .com) is the one most frequently used.

Evaluating Research

The key to business research is to find recent information. For most business topics, information older than twelve months may not be very useful. It is also important to evaluate sources for credibility. If it is one of the major business publications, it will be fairly reliable (although they have been known to be wrong) but may be biased. If it is a company publication or industry association publication, assess the potential accuracy of the information. The mission of an industry group is to promote the indus-

try; thus its information might paint a much brighter picture than is actually the case.

CARS (credibility, accuracy, reasonableness, and support) is a simple acronym that helps evaluate research. A summary checklist is provided in Table 5-2.

Consumer Data

Having basic demographic data on potential customers and using it to inform marketing strategies are essential to any business's success. Yet small businesses are often in the dark as to their exact customers. This is especially ironic because much of this information is readily available to the public.

Many examples of national data sources and references are described in the following list. While all of them may not be as readily available as census sources, they are still quite accessible and generally considered to be economical sources of information.

- Statistical Abstract of the United States. Published by the US government, this book is the best place to get a compendium of key data if researchers are not familiar with what is available. It offers a wealth of demographic information for the United States and other countries. Sources for each table are often valuable sources of additional information. The Statistical Abstract is available at http://www.census.gov/ compendia/statab/.
- US Bureau of the Census. This US Department of Commerce site (census.gov) provides a huge amount of demographic information and is likely to be the most valuable source of data. Using the Census Bureau site, it is possible to create custom reports for specific communities and their population, housing, economic, and other data. Information can be retrieved for state, county, and city levels as well as by census tract and zip code. Detailed information such as the number of African Americans living in a specific census tract (equivalent to a neighborhood) is available, but the search may take time to figure out. The minority-specific links are particularly helpful for ethnic data.
- Current Population Survey (CPS) (census.gov/cps/). A monthly survey of about 50,000 households conducted by the Bureau of the Census for the Bureau of Labor Statistics. The CPS is the primary source of employment status of people 16 years and older. Data include employment, unemployment, earnings, hours

TABLE 5-2. Checklist for Evaluating Research

High	Low
Credibility	
Author's education or experience relevant to the issue	Anonymous author
Contact information given	No contact information
Organization the author or the website belongs to is reputable and unbiased on the issue	Periodical not well known; known or suspected bias in content or authorship
Author has reputable position	Reviews are mostly negative
Author has good reputation	Author is not convincing
Periodical is of good quality in content and presentation	Writing contains bad grammar and numerous misspelled words
Accuracy	
Up-to-date information; dates are current	No date or old date
Any historical data includes the latest year	Use of vague or sweeping generalizations
Comprehensive; many sources of data; cites all relevant sources of information	Limited information or sources; limited coverage of topic
Considers the audience for the information	Hidden messages of persuasion; inappropriate for audience
Reasonableness	
Fair; presents all sides	Angry or spiteful tones; not balanced
Objectivity; controls biases, discloses any conflict of interest	Conflict of interest
Moderateness; most truths are ordinary. (Some truths are not, but check to see if they are real.)	Sweeping statements
Consistency; writer avoids contradictions	Writer exaggerates or over claims
World view; writer identifies his or her religious, political, etc. points of view	Writer obscures his or her biases and viewpoints
Support	
Source of information is cited	No identified source for numbers
Corroboration; may want to triangulate; find three sources of information that agree	Absence of documentation when it is needed
Agrees with outside sources of information	Cannot find other sources that agree with information

of work, and other indicators. They are tracked against demographic characteristics including age, sex, race, marital status, and educational attainment. They are also available by occupation, industry, and class of worker. Additional characteristics to produce estimates on a variety of topics include school enrollment, income, previous work experience, health, employee benefits, and work schedules.

- Demographic Statistics (fedstats.gov/). This FedStats site offers links to current demographic statistics on a wide variety of American population factors from a dozen US government agencies.
- Consumer Expenditure Surveys. This Bureau of Labor Statistics site (bls.gov/cex) provides data about consumer spending in the United States. Demographic information, such as average number in consumer unit, percent male and female, education level, age,

and income, is detailed along with average annual expenditures consisting of 14 main categories: food, alcoholic beverages, housing, apparel and services, transportation, health care, entertainment, personal care products and services, reading, education, tobacco products and smoking supplies, miscellaneous, cash contributions, and personal insurance and pensions.

- Survey of Consumer Finances (SCF) (federalreserve .gov/econresdata/scf/scfindex.htm). This triennial survey of the balance sheet, pension, income, and other demographic characteristics of US families also gathers information on the use of financial institutions.
- American Housing Survey (AHS) (census.gov/housing/ahs/). This survey collects data on the nation's housing, including apartments, single-family homes, mobile homes, vacant housing units, household char-

acteristics, income, housing and neighborhood quality, housing costs, equipment and fuels, size of housing unit, and recent movers, National data are collected in odd-numbered years, and data for each of 47 selected metropolitan areas are collected about every four years, with an average of 12 metropolitan areas included each year.

- US National and State Data. This Population Reference Bureau site (prb.org) provides annotated links to sources of national and state data on the web, including Bureau of the Census population data, the Urban Institute, and many other organizations.
- Tax Stats. This US Internal Revenue Service site (irs.gov/taxstats/) offers information about the financial composition of personal, business, nonprofit, and other taxpayers.
- Simply Map (simplymap.com). A web-based mapping application that enables users to develop interactive thematic maps and reports using thousands of demographic, business, and marketing data variables. It may be available through local or institution libraries.
- Pew Research Center (pewresearch.org). The Pew Foundation has funded extensive research aimed at informing the public, improving public policy, and stimulating public life. Areas of research include arts and culture, children and youth, computers and the Internet, corrections and public safety, economic policy, education, environment, family financial security, health, Hispanics in America, media and journalism, religion, science, and civic initiatives.

Competitive Information

Company descriptions or profiles, financial performance, and other information can be useful as "competitive intelligence." Knowing what competitors are doing can be important in making decisions about how to seek and sustain a competitive advantage. Examples in this category include the following sources (unless the website is given, these databases are available at libraries that subscribe to them):

- Hoovers Online. Hoovers has brief information on several dozen industry sectors and four dozen industry snapshots, available by clicking on the "Companies & Industries" button at the top of the screen. Hoovers Online also includes extensive information on 14,000 companies worldwide, both public and private.

- ReferenceUSA. This provides directory information for 12 million companies in the United States. Companies can be searched by name, business activity, size, and location. With this database, it is possible to identify businesses by geographic area and type of business, as well as by number of employees and gross annual sales.
- Dun and Bradstreet. D&B is another directory of information on companies. It covers 1 million US companies with sales greater than $1 million or total number of employees greater than 20.
- Telephone Directories. The yellow pages are an excellent source of competitive information. Online and hardcopy versions can be searched to determine who local competitors are and where they are located.
- Bizstats (bizstats.com). This site provides information compiled from IRS data about business profit and loss and balance sheets. It provides enough detail for businesses to benchmark their financial performance against businesses of similar size.
- Google Maps (maps.google.com). If a business category is entered into Google Maps, the site can map all competitors within a determined radius.
- Inc Magazine (inc.com). This small business magazine focuses on small business issues. The Inc 500/5000 can be used to find companies that may qualify as high-impact companies and provide competitive information.

Small Business

The focus up to this point has been on sources that are national in scope. Yet most projects are likely to be highly localized. Thus familiarity with local resources is quite important. Key sources and references are as follows:

- Kauffman Foundation (kauffman.org). Funds extensive research on innovation and entrepreneurship. The Foundation maintains an entrepreneurial index and continuing studies on a number of business issues.
- Small Business Administration (sba.gov). This site provides tools such as business plans and other resources for small businesses. The Office of Advocacy has studies on a number of business issues.
- Survey of Business Owners. The US Census Bureau (census.gov/econ/sbo/) provides extensive data from the 2007 economic census on ownership of business enterprises by minorities and women. The economic census is conducted every five years.

- Minority Business Development Agency (mbda.gov). Part of the US Department of Commerce and provides information on various trends pertaining to demographics, industry characteristics, exports, and other important dimensions of minority enterprise small business.
- The National Black Chamber of Commerce (nationalbcc.org). A nonprofit, nonpartisan, nonsectarian organization dedicated to the economic empowerment of African American communities. The NBCC reaches 100,000 black-owned businesses.
- The United States Hispanic Chamber of Commerce (ushcc.com). Works to advocate, promote, and facilitate the success of Hispanic business. The Hispanic Chamber of Commerce has a network of nearly 200 Hispanic chambers of commerce and Hispanic business organizations.
- The US Pan Asian American Chamber of Commerce (uspaacc.com/web). This national nonprofit association represents Asian and non-Asian American businesses and professionals in business, sciences, the arts, sports, education, entertainment, community, and public service.

Industry or Trade Associations

Just as there is a trade journal for just about every industry, there is also a trade or industry association for just about every industry. Some of these associations may publish yearbooks that give industry statistics. Some will answer inquiries by e-mail. Many have websites. Just remember that industry associations try to paint the industry in the best light, so it is important to evaluate the information given. To contact trade associations, use the *Encyclopedia of Associations* or try the Internet Public Library list of associations (ipl.org).

Trade associations could also include country trade associations. Their purpose is to develop trade for their country. In order to do this, they might maintain extensive statistics. To get a listing of international trade associations, access the Federation of International Trade Associations at fita.org/index.html.

Social Media

Social media can also be mined for consumer research. Monitoring Twitter posts can reveal shifting trends or moods. It is possible to search the thousands of groups of LinkedIn to find out how communities are formed around products or services. Facebook sites for other companies can be accessed to monitor consumer feedback. Reading customer reviews on Yelp can give an idea of a business's strength and weaknesses and those of its competitors. Monitoring books and topics on amazon.com can give an indication of trends. In certain high-tech industries, influential blogs are the best source of information. Research should also be conducted on discussion forums.

PRIMARY RESEARCH

Once secondary research has been completed or is well under way, consideration can be given to primary research. One of the most basic and widely used methods of primary research is a survey of an identified group of respondents (i.e., a sample). Surveys can be very labor intensive and costly. They should be defined, designed, and completed with these factors in mind. Recognize that professional marketing research firms typically price telephone surveys at $50 per completed call, while a mall intercept survey may cost anywhere from $20,000 to $50,000, depending on the sample size, length and complexity of the questionnaire, and standards applied regarding validity and reliability of the results. The team should ensure that the right direction is taken before starting the survey process.

Preliminary Research

Most small businesses serve a local market, so it will be necessary to understand local factors as well. Make sure to carefully explore available market data. This refers again to secondary research. Before refining a primary survey instrument, talk informally with a few customers. Ask open-ended questions or questions that provide more insight or details. For beginning researchers, it is important to gain enough knowledge to ask the right questions in the finished survey. Ask customers why they buy the product or use the service. Talk to potential customers as well. Ask them why they do not buy and what they buy instead. Talk to suppliers; they are great sources of information about the industry and competitors. Allow enough time to pretest the survey with a small group of likely respondents before deciding on the final set of questions to be used.

Refine the Purpose

There is a balance that must be struck in creating surveys. If too few questions are asked, the purpose will not be achieved. If too many questions are asked, the respondents experience fatigue. The optimal path is to ask just the right number of questions. This should be based on getting the most essential information needed and the amount of time it takes to complete the survey. Creating an effective survey is similar to hitting a small bull's eye. It is important to focus on the "need to know" versus the "nice to know" questions.

There are additional complications in conducting research when dealing with relatively unsophisticated businesses. The client business is likely venturing into new and unfamiliar territory. The business owner may not be quite sure what she wants to know or do. The consultant has to make sure that the business owner also goes through the educational process. As the business owner learns more, she will want to be more involved. The scope of the project can change. However, projects can be refined to perfection and not accomplish anything. It is important to stay focused on what must be accomplished. At the same time, allow the increasingly educated client to inform the process. This should help to build his or her confidence in the project. In some ways this could be considered as part of the effort to get his or her buy-in to the final results and recommendations of the project.

Who Is to Be Surveyed?

First, avoid the common mistake of surveying people (respondents) because it is convenient to do so. This may seem to be a low-cost approach, but it is likely to be an incorrect one that produces misleading or even useless results. This could mean asking the right questions of the wrong people and getting obviously irrelevant answers. Such a survey would likely miss the people who should be targeted and questioned.

Consider the consequences of surveying the wrong group. The first is that it results in a misuse of time and effort. It also means omitting or overlooking the correct segments of the market that should be questioned. As stated, the information obtained is likely to be incorrect or irrelevant.

Two examples highlight the issues involved. One relates to a mall intercept survey and the other to a telephone survey. A consumer is intercepted in the mall and is asked a few questions. Marketers may use the results from this survey and extrapolate to all consumers. However, there are major drawbacks to this. If respondents are limited to mall intercepts, people who do not shop

at malls are excluded, as are those who work during the times malls are open.

Similar exclusions can occur with telephone surveys. People who are not at home during the times calls are made are excluded, as are people who screen calls. Omissions may be even more basic. It could be that by using these convenience sampling methods, the wrong people are sampled. These survey design errors can result in getting the wrong information. It is important to think carefully about who is to be surveyed and how best to reach the targeted population.

For example, a consulting team was trying to learn about gardeners and their interest in high-quality, premium-priced cutting tools. The client is the manufacturer of such tools. She would like to sell to a kind of specialty consumer market. The challenge would be to identify how this target group could be reached. Getting to know the buying behavior of garden club members would be one possibility. Participants attracted to garden shows might be another. Patrons of certain nurseries could be another. Clearly the emphasis is on reaching the serious gardener who would want quality tools. Casual gardeners who find gardening a chore will not be interested in paying a premium for tools. For most small businesses, the challenge will be similar. The researcher must devise a method of surveying a small segment of the market.

After doing secondary research, the team determined that serious gardeners join associations so that they can enjoy their pastime together. The team identified the Master Gardener program as the best population from which to choose their sample. Master Gardeners are volunteers who instruct people on gardening. There are 50 Master Gardener associations, approximately one in every state. The team located the Master Gardener coordinator and was able to get a list of serious gardeners to survey.

What Do You Need to Know?

Trying to define exactly what the client needs to know is not as trivial as one might think. With the example of the team working with the cutting tool business, the business needs information about the consumer gardener. Demographics may not be one of the need-to-know questions. Secondary research is the best way to get demographics and is considerably more efficient than administering a survey. How about the growth rate of the market? This is likely to be obtained from secondary research. So get as much data as you can from secondary sources. Then compile a list of what is missing.

The team did this, but many questions still remained. What kind of cutting tools are important to gardeners? How do they judge quality? Would the gardeners pay a premium for the tool? Do serious gardeners use the Internet to purchase items? There still may be too many questions for the survey to be effective. Questions have to be filtered, and the researcher must get agreement from the business on what is actionable.

With regard to the "guerrilla" marketing research that is often necessary given the short period of time of the consulting engagement, Brooks Gekler, former executive of a major consumer-products company and a professor at the University of Washington–Bothell, determined seven key principles to keep in mind when designing market research:

- Behavior-based. Make the survey behavior-based instead of attitude-based. It is more important to know what the customer is going to do as opposed to what the customer prefers. Attitudes often do not match behavior. Answer behavior questions: What have they bought? What will they buy?
- Actionable. If the business cannot do anything about the issue, do not ask. Make sure that all questions will lead to actions that will improve circumstances for the business.
- Extendable. The instrument should allow the researcher to redirect the focus on the business. Ask questions that test this. Which tools are most highly valued? Is brand loyalty an important factor in buying?
- Focus. The survey should focus on what information is needed to achieve the goals of the project. There should not be any extraneous questions. Most respondents will only give a small window of time, and the researcher must use this to the best benefit of the business.
- Validation. Beyond the specific questions, use the survey instrument to validate one issue in the marketing strategy. Determine what this is and then incorporate questions that will address it. Do not miss the opportunity to validate the strategy.
- Directional. This survey is directional rather than empirical. It is a convenience sample, fast and furious. As such, be careful how the results are used.
- Repeatable. Make an instrument that can be reused by the business. The business environment changes often, and surveys have to be redone. Create an instrument that the business owner can use again, and give instructions on how often it should be used.

Type of Survey

Professional researchers will choose between regular mail and e-mail and online, telephone, or face-to-face surveys. When making these decisions, they weigh the cost of the survey against the likely or expected response rate. They also must take into account the complexity of the questions and kind of information being requested and how the results will be used. For good examples of survey questions, check out surveys used by the Pew Research Center.

It should be recognized that response rates vary widely, even for a specific type of survey. The prospective respondent's level of involvement determines the extent of participation. With a high-involvement respondent (someone who cares about the issue), response rates will rise. Some researchers and writers suggest that mail survey response rates can range from 2% to 20%. Mail surveys tend to have the lowest response rates and take the most time to administer and complete; but in terms of out-of-pocket costs, they are the least costly, in the range of $5–$10 per completed response.

Web surveys are generally expected to yield a response rate of about 10%. The format should include an initial explanation, an invitation to prospective respondents, and possibly an accompanying incentive offer to respondents. Much higher rates are sometimes reported for topics that generate unusual interest. However, even when invitations or requests for participation are made by telephone, often just over half of those who agree to participate will actually return the e-mail questionnaire. Internet surveys must be shorter than mail surveys and must be personalized rather than sent as part of a newsletter, flyer, or other form of communication. Costs are also relatively low per completed response. Under special circumstances, costs can be much higher. For example, in a Hispanic tax-preparation service, the business owner entered all survey respondents into a drawing for a DVD player.

When considering methods that involve direct contact by telephone, there are distinct advantages over impersonal, pencil and paper, or even Internet interactive contact. Telephone surveys have the advantages of flexibility and ability to deal with topics that could not be addressed in regular mail or Internet surveys. Response rates also tend to be much higher, in the range of 20%–40% or more depending upon the topic. But they must usually be brief (15–20 minutes or less). They are relatively expensive, at $30 to $50 per completed interview.

Face-to-face interviews can cover the most complex and sensitive topics. Response rates can be very high. An expected range is from 20% to 80%, with an average of about 40%–60% for consumer surveys and higher for business-to-business surveys. They are obviously labor intensive, as allowance must be made for travel time and other incidental expenses of the interviewers, along with the actual cost of interview time.

In large national surveys (such as national opinion polls completed by telephone) it is customary to interview about 1,000 randomly selected American adults. These results are generalized for the entire population of the United States using mathematical relationships involved in calculating standard errors of means and proportions in randomly selected samples. As a practical matter, random sampling is not feasible in most small business consulting projects. It is far more likely that convenience or judgment samples will be used. The team will target a local segment that pertains to the trade or market area served by the client.

But even with convenience and judgment samples, careful consideration should be given to the selection of survey respondents. Who should be surveyed? Often one of the most difficult tasks is finding a viable list of customers to survey. Customer lists should be tested to ensure that they are not "dead" lists or do not have a high rate of wrong contact information. Sometimes student teams will contact community groups to survey their members. Nonprofit associations are often sympathetic to student projects. Industry advisors and mentors may call upon their networks to come up with a list of possible respondents.

The short timeline involved in academic consulting assignments makes it likely that either an e-mail, online, or telephone survey will be selected. There are all kinds of tactics that can be used to improve the response rate. Mailing a postcard before and after, using first-class mail, addressing a letter personally to the respondent, having a person of authority sign the letter that accompanies the survey, making a charitable donation if the respondent answers, making follow-up phone calls, or running a sweepstakes can increase the response rate. Affiliation with a community organization or university can also increase the rate.

Direct mail surveys were specifically omitted because of the long turnaround time involved. The required pretesting, mailing, follow-up requests, and other tasks of completing a direct mail survey would be far too time-consuming to undertake.

For exploratory surveys, adhering to strict random-sample design is not expected. It is likely that teams will survey far fewer than 500 respondents in a convenience sample. Although the findings cannot be inferred to the entire population, such sampling is often more than adequate for the bootstrapping MBE. In many student consulting projects, a sample size of 30 is adequate to provide acceptable results. Surveying fewer respondents would definitely be considered a small sample. But even this might be sufficient for some forms of qualitative research.

Keep in mind that the more concise the survey, the higher the response rate. If the survey is online, it should be completed in five to seven minutes. For a telephone survey, two to three minutes may be all the time that respondents will give. Face-to-face interviews can be longer. It is important to set expectations beforehand; if the survey instructions state that there are ten questions and it will take three to five minutes to complete, respondents are more likely to comply.

Formulating the Questions

Once the content of the survey is decided, the researcher can proceed with creating the questions. Survey questions must be worded very carefully. It is easy to introduce bias or to direct respondents to an answer if care is not taken. Poorly worded questions can give bad information, which is costly, since it is likely to be misleading.

Take, for example, the simplest kind of question: one that respondents answer either yes or no. Do you approve (disapprove) of the way the president is handling the economy? The way the question is worded, the respondent is more likely to say yes. In order to overcome this bias, marketing research firms like the Gallup Poll rotate the order of approve and disapprove when they ask questions. Be aware that respondents may have other ways of reacting to questions that give the wrong information. For example, if a list of TV brands is presented, some respondents will say they own the most prestigious brands even when they do not. It might be more accurate to ask them to list or rate the brand(s) that they own. But recognize that this option might increase the costs of coding and completing the data analysis. Yet such trade-offs are commonplace in research and in life.

Include at least one question on demographics or

Unbalanced scale with named categories for each point on the scale:			
Would you buy this product or service?			
Definitely will not buy	Probably will not buy	Probably will buy	Definitely will buy
1	2	3	4

Balanced scale, without naming the intervals or points on the scale				
How important to you is the availability of a sales associate in shopping for hardware?				
Not at all important				Very important
1	2	3	4	5

Balanced scales, with naming of intervals or points on the scale				
To what extent are you satisfied with this store?				
Very dissatisfied	Somewhat dissatisfied	Neither satisfied nor dissatisfied	Somewhat satisfied	Very satisfied
1	2	3	4	5
What is your position on this issue or statement?				
Strongly disagree	Somewhat disagree	Neither agree nor disagree	Somewhat agree	Strongly agree
1	2	3	4	5

Figure 5-2 Sample Rating Scales

characteristics of the customer. Have more important questions in the middle or at the end for when people are already invested in the interview process and are unlikely to stop or walk away. Although not everyone will comply, ask for a contact e-mail in case the research team has a lingering burning question.

Open-ended questions provide valuable insight into directions that the research might not have pursued otherwise. But the questions should not be completely open ended or the customer will not be able to answer them. Provide guidance as to the direction or choices.

If a fair number of surveys are being administered, it is more efficient to have answers fall into categories like a rating scale (sometimes called a Likert scale). This makes the tabulation of results easier.

Some of the common types of questions that involve the use of rating scales are illustrated in Figure 5.2.

Five-point Likert scales are the most common types used in marketing and business research. There are technical and analytical reasons for using seven- and even nine-point scales. Basically, choices focus on how much sensitivity or scope is allowed for measurement and what effect the extended scales have on reliability.

When using a rating scale, be aware that the midpoint or the "neither satisfied nor dissatisfied" rating can be misinterpreted. Some respondents use that rating to mean the middle. Some believe it represents a neutral position. Some respondents who do not care or do not want to answer will use that rating as well. Researchers sometimes eliminate the midpoint rating so that they can do a majority count of either positive or negative. Others include a "Don't Know" rating so that respondents who cannot answer the questions can be properly categorized. A "Not Applicable" designation can also be provided to accurately capture situations in which respondents are not in a position to answer a question appropriately.

Rank-order questions can determine what is more important to respondents. They can be used to determine product, feature, and attribute preferences. But they are limited in terms of statistical analysis and may not give information on how much the respondent likes one option over the other. For example, a college student was asked to rank order his favorite beers; the options included Coors, Bud, and Miller. It could be that the respondent likes Coors much more than the other two or that he likes Coors just slightly more. It would be impossible to determine this from his answer. One way to get around this is to ask respondents to allocate a specific number of points (for example, 100) to their choices. In that case, the respondent may give 75 points to Coors, 15 points to Bud, and 10 points to Miller. This gives a better idea of how much more important one beer is than the other.

Another popular tool is semantic differential, which uses opposites to gauge psychological impressions. This can be used to determine the subtleties of brand imaging or consumer attitudes. For example, a company may test the impression given by its website using the following semantic differential:

	1	2	3	4	5	
Modern						Traditional
Unreliable						Trustworthy
Friendly						Unfriendly
High quality						Low quality
Bargain						Expensive

FIGURE 5-3. Semantic Differential Tool

Be aware that bias can be created in a semantic differential question by putting all the positive words on one side. The respondent becomes accustomed to checking certain ratings and continues without really reading the words.

Once questions are formulated, assess whether the wording and meaning are clear ("How many bottles of beer do you drink in a week?" might not generate the information wanted if the bottles of beer are different volumes), that the language is accessible to the respondent ("How many containers of alcoholic liquids do you imbibe in a week?"), and that questions are not biased ("Are you pleased with the great taste of Coors?").

To determine if respondents are being truthful, researchers often incorporate several questions asking for the same information. If the respondents answer the questions differently, this may be an indication that they are less than forthcoming. This respondent may be eliminated from the sample.

Most of the surveys will be of an exploratory nature and will have a relatively small number of respondents (i.e., fewer than 500). For quantitative information, ask respondents to give number answers rather than predetermining categories. For example, instead of creating categories like "fewer than one," "two to five," "six to ten," and "over ten," ask the respondent to give the exact number. This gives more raw data that can be categorized by the researcher. Include some open-ended questions to capture information that otherwise would not be considered.

The exception to this is demographic data. Be aware that respondents may be especially sensitive to demographic questions. For example, who likes to answer the question: How old are you? To overcome this, use age categories and keep them as broad as possible. The same can be done with income level. Some researchers just use two categories, over and under $50,000 in household

income, to differentiate households with discretionary income. By asking for zip code, it may be possible to use census data to deduce income levels.

Psychographic information requires the clustering of information to create profiles of customers. Interpreting or giving meaning to the answers from a psychographic perspective could be based on some categorical description, such as whether the respondent is considered to be an achiever, a person who is successful, work oriented, and favors established products that showcase their success, versus a striver, a person who has the same aspirations but is unable to achieve them, among the market segments responding to a survey. Such categories are used in comparison with demographics and socioeconomic categories to understand groups of people from a lifestyle or psychographic perspective. These are two groups in what are called VALS-2 types of psychographic segmentation. Be aware that most established psychographic profiles do not routinely consider multicultural populations. Often such groups do not show up in psychographic profiling because they do not meet income levels considered attractive by marketers. As such, student teams have the opportunity to create new profiles of use to marketers who see the opportunity in these markets.

Typical questions in student projects focus on:

- How does the customer get information about the client?
- What attracts the customer to the client?
- What are the customer's reasons for using the product or service?
- What product or service features are desired?
- What does the customer like about the client?
- What competitive products are used and how much?
- How does the business compare to competitors?
- Why does the customer prefer the competitor over the client?
- What factors are important in making the buy decision?
- What price is the customer willing to pay for various attributes?
- What mode of communication or marketing does the customer prefer?
- What is the optimal timing and frequency of marketing promotions?
- What is the level of customer satisfaction with key attributes of the product or service?

ISLAND SOUL RESTAURANT SURVEY

In order to help grow our business and understand our valued customers, please take a moment to complete this short survey (1 per table). Your responses will be anonymous. Upon completion of the survey, we would be happy to give you one of our famous corn muffins.

Today's Date _____

1) What is the reason for your visit today?

☐ lunch ☐ dinner ☐ appetizers/cocktails

2) How many times have you been to Island Soul?

☐ First time ☐ 2–4 times ☐ 5+ times

3) How far did you travel to dine at Island Soul today?

☐ Less than 2 miles ☐ 2–5 miles ☐ 5–10 miles ☐ more than 10 miles

4) How did you hear about Island Soul?

☐ Newspaper/magazine ☐ Island Soul website ☐ Social media (e.g., Facebook)
☐ Word of mouth ☐ Third-party website (e.g., Yelp) ☐ Drove by ☐ Other: _____

5) What day of the week are you visiting Island Soul?

☐ Monday ☐ Tuesday ☐ Wednesday ☐ Thursday ☐ Friday ☐ Saturday ☐ Sunday

6) What time of day are you visiting the restaurant?

☐ Before 3:00pm ☐ Between 3–5pm ☐ Between 5–7pm ☐ After 7pm

7) Rank (1–4) your favorite element of Island Soul (4 = Most Favorite to 1 = Least Favorite)

_____ Service

_____ Food

_____ Atmosphere/ambiance

_____ Live music (if applicable)

8) How was your overall experience at Island Soul **today**? (circle one number)

Very poor   1   2   3   4   5   6   7   Very good

9) How much did you spend on average (per person) today?

☐ Less than $10 ☐ Between $10–15 ☐ Between $15–20 ☐ More than $20

10) Please share any additional comments or feedback:

Thank you for your time and valuable feedback!

FIGURE 5-4 Sample Survey Questionnaire

- What improvements would the customer like to see?
- What are customer characteristics, such as age, gender, income, or frequency of purchase?
- What incentives will motivate sales staff?
- How can relationships, processes, or pricing with suppliers be improved?

Ordering the Questions

Most projects do not allow the luxury of a list from which good respondents can be selected. Usually the first questions on a survey are used to screen respondents. For most consumer research, interviewers will look for women between the ages of 18 and 54. They are most likely to be the decision makers in a household

TABLE 5-3. Question Order

Screening	Used to qualify respondents for survey
Warm-up	Easy questions to get respondent in the mind space of answering questions
General	Related to survey but not difficult to answer
Difficult	These questions take more thinking and effort to answer
Classification and demographics	Some respondents find demographic questions to be sensitive

when it comes to buying goods and services. There may be other types of screening questions, depending on the objective of the research. For example, in a gardening survey administered by students, the screening question asked was: How many hours do you garden in a month? Those who responded with more hours were more likely to be serious gardeners.

Once the researcher has screened the right respondents, it is important to begin with a question that the respondent wants to answer. With the gardening survey, the team started out with the gardener's area of specialty. Gardeners want to talk about what they are interested in, and asking this question opens up the respondents and makes them more willing to respond. Then the survey moves on to more general questions that warm the respondent up. These questions might get the respondent to start thinking about the product or service. The middle of the survey is the place for the questions that require more thought or consideration. Timing is very important. Consider whether the respondent will be tired or bored and incorporate strategies to keep interest up. Tough and sensitive questions (like demographics) are placed last. Respondents are less likely to walk away when they have invested all that time and effort in answering the questions. And even if they do, some valuable information will already have been gathered.

If the survey is to be administered over the telephone, have a script for the survey administrator to use. It is important that each survey be administered in a consistent manner.

Pretest the Survey

The best way to ensure that the survey works is to pretest it on a few typical respondents. Incorporate this pretest in the timeline for the project. All kinds of problems can be uncovered when the survey is tested. Respondents might interpret questions to be completely different from the intended meaning. They might misread words. They might be confused. These all need to be corrected. Test respondents under the same conditions that actual respondents will experience. Gather information on what happened. Meet with the team and spend sufficient time revising the questionnaire. In revising, ask hard questions about the objective of each question and whether the objective was achieved.

Evaluate the Research Process

Review the results with a strong critical eye. Does it make sense to act on the findings? Does more research need to be done? Be aware that the biggest flaw about surveys is that people do not always do what they say they will do.

Checklist for Completing a Survey

1. Conduct secondary research first. Typical research instruments may be available, or trade associations may have done research already.
2. Conduct preliminary research. If the survey involves customers, find a few customers and ask them exploratory questions. If the primary research involves businesses, ask the client to recommend some representative businesses. The goal is to understand as completely as possible the issues that are to be studied. Recognize that it is more helpful to ask open-ended questions with the preliminary research.
3. Insure that respondents are available. Pretest any customer lists to see if they are viable.
4. Create a research instrument and review it with mentors and faculty. Specify the objective of each question. Revise the instrument based on feedback.
5. Pretest the instrument on a few typical respondents.

CASE STUDY 5
Explorer West Middle School

Creating an Identity in the Education Marketplace

Education is about creating an experience that will change a student's life. Explorer West Middle School redefines the experience of middle school by offering a distinct award-winning program that focuses on sustainability and outdoor education. Explorer West attracts a diverse student body of about 90 students per year and nearly 25% students of color.

Every seven years, Explorer West participates in the Pacific Northwest Association of Independent Schools accreditation process. The process begins with a self-study, which is an opportunity for the school to self-reflect and examine its mission and philosophy. The result of the self-study process is a comprehensive document that highlights the school's self-identified strengths and weaknesses, in addition to a self-assessment on how the school is fulfilling its mission. This self-study is shared with a peer review team of educators who then provide a report of their findings to the association's accreditation committee and board of governors.

In order for a school to begin the self-study, it must provide an assessment of how the school is meeting its major standards, such as its mission and core values. Typically schools outsource this task to professional consultants. However, in 2009 Explorer West called upon a team of student consultants to conduct this crucial assessment in preparation for the school's self-study. Evan Hundley, the head of the school, notes that the student team conducted an assessment on the most important major standard, the school's mission statement and core values.

The student consultants conducted an extensive series of surveys with Explorer West students, faculty, administration, and stakeholders such as parents, alumni students, and board members to inform the forthcoming self-study. The results from a SWOT (strengths, weak-

nesses, opportunities, and threats) analysis and surveys provided insight into Explorer West's strengths and areas that needed improvement. For example, a survey of seventh and eighth graders, alumni students, and parents revealed that the outdoor education program contributed to higher levels of self-esteem. The majority of eighth graders, alumni students, and parents also reported that Explorer West helped prepare the students for high school.

The student team conducted a thorough evaluation of the school's mission statement. Specifically, they tested the validity of core phrases in the mission statement among the various stakeholders. The team observed that although the school was highly committed to cultural diversity, the mission statement did not reflect this important focus. It recommended that Explorer West look for more opportunities to inform the community about its commitment to diversity. As a result of the student team's recommendations, Explorer West revamped its mission statement. The improved and more representative statement also affected the school's curriculum. For example, the school faculty evaluated the course curriculum in light of the new mission statement and made necessary adjustments.

The student team presented its findings to Hundley and to the school's board of directors. Hundley notes that the research conducted by the team of student consultants was comparable to that of professional consultants and proved to be invaluable to their reaccreditation process.

TABLE 5-4. Types of Qualitative Research

Method	Benefits	Limitations
Focus groups: Usually a group of 6–12 people who are led by a moderator in a discussion of a specific topic.	Provides information (opinions, experiences, etc.) to understand what people want, like, and how they respond to new ideas and products.	Subjective and judgmental; difficult to quantify results; relatively expensive to administer, record, and complete.
In-depth interviews: Long, probing individual interviews without the use of a formal questionnaire.	Designed to uncover motivations or reasons behind behavior, attitudes, and perceptions.	Data based on thoughts of a single individual; heavily reliant on the meaning given by the interviewer.
Ethnographic studies: Participant-observer exchanges that reveal insights into the psychosocial and cultural aspects of behavior.	Uncovers the lived expressions and meanings that explain behavior in defined cultural contexts, groups, and institutional arrangements. Can be important in understanding the cultural context of a multicultural market.	May require considerable academic and technological resources (understanding of ethnography, videography) to use effectively.
Observational studies: Obtaining information by observing and recording behavior.	Captures behavior as it occurs in the moment.	Insights limited to what can be observed; description that requires attribution and explanation.
Mystery shopping: Interviewer simulates buying or other transactions in a store.	Provides detailed evaluations of actual performance and shopping satisfaction.	Heavily reliant on interviewer recall from the interview experience.

Revise the instrument based on observations and feedback.

6. Submit the instrument to mentors or faculty for final approval. Include a description of what the sample will consist of and how the respondents will be selected.

7. Administer the instrument.

QUALITATIVE RESEARCH

The term *qualitative* refers to methods that focus more on the context and meaning or subjective aspects of information than on the numerical or *quantitative* aspects of what is being studied. Data collection and research design procedures are shaped by the purposes and uses of qualitative methods. With regard to MBEs and promising businesses in new markets, these methods can provide valuable insights into the direction of the market. They are also more cost effective and can be accomplished in a relatively short period of time; therefore they are more relevant to the guerrilla marketing environment of most of these enterprises. These methods are summarized in Table 5-4.

Focus Groups

A focus group is 6 to 12 people who are led by a moderator in an in-depth discussion on a topic. The discussions are exploratory in nature. They may be used to learn and understand how people feel about an issue, product, or service. Interaction among the people in the group is important. One person's response can be the stimulus for another person to speak. This major strength of focus groups can also be its major drawback. Individuals can dominate the discussion or lead others to think like them. Nonetheless, the researcher can experience the reaction of the respondents in ways that are not possible with surveys. He or she can catch nuances and emotions that are impossible to capture in a survey. An example may include determining how assertive a person is relative to being an innovator and adopter or a follower and laggard in responding to ideas, products, and brands.

Typically, a researcher will form a group of about eight and run the focus group for one and a half hours. Most people are paid to participate. For a small business, free meals or low-cost giveaways can serve as incentives for customers to participate. Focus groups can be done quickly and are sometimes less expensive than surveys. The moderator is crucial to a successful focus group. She or he needs to demonstrate unconditional acceptance and positive regard. Any negativity will stifle discussion and elicitation of responses. The moderator needs good observational skills to manage the discussion and accomplish objectives. In some instances, focus groups are videotaped so that the moderator can focus solely on leading the discussion. Moderators cannot exhibit a bias toward any point of view and must be neutral in discussion. They cannot impose or suggest direction to any questions asked, and they need the ability to make quick decisions as to how to direct the discussion to get the most out of it. Often moderators show the ability to become trusted quickly.

In preparation for a focus group, the researchers will create a discussion guide. The first step is to explain the purpose of the group and what the researcher wants the participants to do. It is important to disclose all recording devices or whether people are watching from behind two-way mirrors. Initial stages of the focus group may concentrate on introductions and getting people to participate. The middle part of the focus group is the most intense. Participants will discuss the major issues. The final stage might be to summarize the discussion and get clarification. A focus group can be a combination of writing and discussion. Sometimes moderators will ask participants to put their feelings in writing first, followed by a more thoughtful discussion. This insures that important comments are not lost.

The transcript of the focus group is analyzed by coding the respondent comments and summarizing patterns that emerged in the discussion.

One-on-One In-Depth Interviews

The thought of 30 minutes or more for an interview with one respondent may seem like an unacceptably costly or time-consuming method of obtaining information from a small group of individuals. Yet for some studies this could be an acceptable trade-off between the relatively brief period of per-respondent time in focus group research. The argument for the in-depth interview is that it offers more quality and quantity of information per respondent. By definition, it allows a topic to be explored in greater depth than other techniques. By providing more detailed information, the results can also be representative of the feelings and perceptions of the respondents. Thus, it can be argued that there is more value in the information that is obtained. Those who use this method argue that it offers more information for less money without some of the limitations imposed by focus groups.

The method is especially strong when key informants and gatekeepers are the targets of the investigation. For a project in which a considerable amount of risk is involved or in which relationships should be examined with especially detailed critiques, this method should be considered. As with focus groups, it is important that interviewers have adequate knowledge of the subject being investigated as well as familiarity with interviewing techniques.

Ethnographic Studies

Both surveys and focus groups have their drawbacks as research methods. Typically, low response rates for mail and telephone surveys make them less effective. Focus groups may be dominated by a few individuals, or participants may feel pressure to say the "right" thing. Market researchers are increasingly turning to ethnographic studies to gather information. Ethnographic study is a well-established form of research used by anthropologists.

An ethnographer begins with extensive reading on the topic. Once knowledgeable about the topic, she or he proceeds to do the research in the natural environment. He or she may administer questionnaires in the field (swap meet) or take photographs of the participants and their surroundings. The process involves videotaping the subjects while they use products or go about their normal tasks. The researcher interviews and records observations while participating and observing the subject's environment.

Ethnography is the subjective alternative to the quantitative approach of behavioral research. The ethnographic method acknowledges that the researcher is immersed in the process. Researchers like to use it because it may bring about more original ideas. Long open-ended interviews allow people to tell their stories. In this case, the researcher does not follow a script. Respondents are allowed to say anything they want. Ethnographers believe that these very open-ended interviews capture spur-of-the-moment thoughts as well as deep truths that the respondent feels. The respondents speak in their own words and are free to roam to any subject.

The researcher may watch the respondents act naturally in their environments. In one case, the researcher was interested in consumers' relationships with their motorcycles and with other riders. He actually joined a Harley Davidson owner's group (HOG) and became immersed in the environment alongside the consumers. BMW dashboard designers rode in cars with customers to see what was important to drivers. Researchers observed drivers talking nonstop on cell phones, writing notes, eating lunch, and shaving while driving—all activities that they would not have known about otherwise.

This type of participation helps researchers get very close to the subject and allows them to notice potentially important areas for new ideas on positioning. When they

FIGURE 5-5. Mystery Shop

Mystery Shopping Experience and Evaluation Questions

An individual unknown to store staff is contracted to conduct a mystery shop.
The person will enter the store as a customer and log the following information:

Date and time.

Shopper is greeted by sales staff after how many minutes in the store?

Salesperson's dress and appearance. (Appropriate? Clean? Name tag?)

Store appearance. (Display attractive? Tidy?)

Did the salesperson assess the shopper's needs?

Did the salesperson know the product and how it would satisfy the shopper's needs?

Did the salesperson persuade the shopper to try the product?

Did the salesperson suggest a cross-sell?

If the product was not available, did the salesperson suggest an alternative?

Was every effort made to service the shopper?

Did the salesperson close the sale?

How long did the shopper have to wait in line to purchase the product or service?

Did the salesperson address the shopper by name?

participate in what the subject does, they see firsthand the objects, movements, gestures, and processes that help them understand what the customer thinks and feels. The researchers may even recreate the environment in which the subject uses the product. They might collect articles that are used in conjunction with the product.

Some researchers will focus on the product and follow it throughout its life. This tells the story of what happens to the product from the time it is designed to when it is discarded by the consumer. A more complete understanding of what the product means to the customer is created. Most businesses focus on the relationship only at the time of purchase or when it is used. Understanding the whole process might produce breakthroughs in marketing.

Ethnographic studies are based on the understanding of behavior within the context of cultures and cultural influences. Broadly, this could be the norms and customs associated with music, art, and language. In a marketing context, more concern is placed on material culture. The functions, symbols, and status associated with products and brands are artifacts of material and consumer culture. Thus ethnographic studies are particularly pertinent to ethnic markets. It is important to be familiar and com-

fortable with, if not immersed in, a group-specific cultural environment to understand how to best communicate and market to these communities. For students, hip-hop and punk-rock cultures might be familiar terms to focus on where ethnography would be an effective way of understanding how being a part of these cultures influences aspects of lifestyle and consumption behavior.

Observational Studies

In situations where customers or users can be watched in the buying or consumption process, observational studies could be especially valuable. Mystery shopping is a form of observational study. It is commonly used by most large retail chains to assess the quality of customer service. People are contracted by the store to behave as regular shoppers. As they proceed with trying to buy an item, the mystery shoppers will make notes of how service is delivered.

The exact measures for assessment differ depending on the type of store. Some businesses have specific requirements of their sales staff, and they will measure against these requirements. One set of evaluation questions is illustrated in Figure 5-5.

While mystery shopping is the most popular form

of observational study, there are other uses of this type of qualitative research. One student team observed, recorded, and later questioned customers at a local fast-food restaurant about their wait time, ease of ordering, and shopping experience. Based on their results they were able to design a more customer-friendly and effective layout of the reader board. Customers and the client firm benefited from the faster order processing, better service, and reduced transaction time. They were able to combine their marketing research results with business process analysis (discussed in Module 6) to help the business improve operations and increase sales. The relevance of this brief summary is to suggest that if customer responses in an actual store setting can serve as a guide to improving the business, consider how an observational study might be used.

REFERENCE

Hague, P. *A Practical Guide to Market Research*. 2006. B2B International. Free e-book available at b2binternational.com/b2b-blog/ebook/practical-guide-to-market-research.pdf.

DISCUSSION

1. Go to the Pew Research Center website. Choose a study and describe its survey methodology. Evaluate the purpose of the survey. Indicate the extent to which each question in the survey relates to the purpose. Look at the questions and summarize the following aspects of the research: use of open-ended questions; clarity of the answers obtained; whether the survey missed any important questions.

2. Create a survey to satisfy a purpose. Administer the survey to five people. Analyze whether the survey was effective. Suggest improvements.

3. How would qualitative research be used to find out crucial information about the client that could not be obtained by quantitative research?

4. With three other students, conduct a mystery shop of four different retail stores in a shopping mall. Compare and contrast your results. Which store had the best customer service?

5. Create benchmark metrics to evaluate the client business against its competitors.

6. Emerging Business Consulting

ABOUT THIS MODULE

The key role played by consultants in any enterprise is that of change agents. Consultants are employed when the business does not have the knowledge resources to capitalize on an opportunity or solve a business problem. The consultant provides that knowledge, but knowledge in itself is not enough. More often than not, the business needs to transform itself to take full advantage of the opportunity. The process of change involves education, commitment, and execution. It is the consultant who must spark this within the enterprise. With small business consulting, the relationship between the consultant and the business owner is pivotal to the consultant being an effective change agent.

The first part of this module deals with fostering a productive client-consultant relationship. Once the relationship has been established, the consultant moves to executing the assignment. This phase requires the use of various tools and techniques that we summarize in this module. A SWOT analysis provides a useful strategic framework from which to begin. This module also includes elements of business process analysis along with related techniques of accounting and financial analysis. The experience of student consulting teams is that business process analysis has been effective in helping emerging businesses make the leap from marginal to promising businesses. Having inefficient or inconvenient operations and customer transaction procedures often constrains an emerging business from growing quickly and may prevent it from growing at all. Completing a good business process analysis does much to document what the business does. Efficiency improvements can be highlighted. A template for replication is created that will allow the business to reach escape velocity.

Sloppy bookkeeping and poor financial management have contributed to the demise of many small businesses. Starting early to implement good bookkeeping and accounting procedures can prevent problems and facilitate growth. In addition, other tools such as benchmarking, best practices, and force analysis are used across marketing, operations, and finance. They provide an analysis of the business processes that points immediately to solutions.

After Studying This Module

Students will learn how to:

- Use knowledge and skills from the fields mentioned above to define and solve business problems. Be able to create a concise and comprehensive statement that defines a business problem or opportunity and suggests alternative responses and feasible solutions, gather information, and develop a strategic evaluation framework using SWOT analysis.
- Apply selected concepts and techniques of business process analysis, accounting, finance, and managerial decision making.
- Develop financial projections for a new opportunity.
- Evaluate and integrate research findings; write recommendations and an action plan that measures success and includes a timeline for implementation.
- Communicate research and consulting results effectively in a client-focused presentation and final report.

NATURE OF EMERGING BUSINESS CONSULTING

Major differences exist between approaches for consulting with small enterprises and approaches with large enterprises. Most small businesses do not have the financial resources to pay for highly specialized departments with highly skilled teams. For example, a family-owned restaurant will often have a management team of one to three generalists who are responsible for setting the company's vision and direction. They will also oversee all aspects of marketing, accounting, financial management, operations, and human resources. In smaller businesses, it is the entrepreneur who performs these business management functions.

Essentially, many entrepreneurs bootstrap to make effective decisions with limited information, capital, and human resources. When working with small enterprises, the consultant has to address all business and operational processes rather than delving deeply into one area of the business. For example, in a large enterprise a consultant may complete research to identify new market niches for a company to enter. The consultant can assume that, once identified, the large company has the skilled managers to examine and plan for the impact this expansion will have on company operations, financing needs, and staffing. The small business consultant, however, cannot assume that the business has managers with these skills and so must address them herself. It follows that the small business consultant must be more of a generalist than a specialist and must be able to address all areas of the business.

Entry

The entry phase of the consulting project is when the goal and scope of the consulting project are defined. Prior to defining this, consultants must learn as much as possible about the small business to determine its primary area of need. Be aware that often what the business owner initially articulates may not be the actual goal. Often business owners are acutely aware of symptoms but may not have worked through causes. As an example, a four-person architectural company sought help from a team of student consultants to conduct market research and develop a marketing plan to reach private commercial development clients. Through discussions with the CEO over a four-week period it became clear that the lead architects knew whom to target and how to target them, but they lacked sales and networking skills. As a result of digging deep into the company's operations and history, the student consultants were able to focus directly on the underlying issue rather than address the initial surface concern.

Throughout the initial interview, the consultant is creating ground rules for the consulting engagement. These may include establishing expectations of their working relationship. Issues that may surface include the amount of information the business owner is willing to share with the consultant. Obviously the more information made available to the consultant, the more effective she will be. However, business owners are often hesitant to be forthcoming with certain information, such as financial statements. Unlike public companies, where financial disclosure is required, outsiders are not privy to the financial information of small businesses. Often small business finances are tied very closely to the personal finances of the business owner. Disclosure about earnings becomes a very sensitive matter. The consultant needs to be aware of this privacy concern. This is often dealt with in the consulting contract. A confidentiality clause will state that information will not be shared with any outside parties.

In order to be an effective change agent, the small enterprise consultant needs to develop a strong bond of trust with the business owner. The first step is to ensure that confidentiality will be maintained. The team cannot betray this trust by discussing business matters with any outside parties.

At the entry phase, the consultant has the exciting task of finding out as much as he or she can about the business and crafting an agreement that will become the signpost for the entire engagement. Often the leader of the team will be tasked with finding out about the business and developing the consulting contract. This involves an in-depth interview covering history, legal structure, and a broad range of business functions. A framework for an initial in-depth interview follows:

1. *What is the mission of the business?*

2. *Who are the stakeholders?*

3. *What is the business?*

- Industry? Size of industry? Number of competitors? Mature or growth industry? How many new entrants? Nature of competition (large or small)?
- How does the business fit in? What products or services will it offer? What is its history? Is the legal structure appropriate? What trademarks or patents does it hold? Who are the key managers, and what do they contribute?
- What products and services does the business

offer? What are its brands? What segment of the market does the business target? What are its prices, and how do they compare to those of competitors? How does the company manage the customer life cycle? What kind of customer service is given?

4. *What is the market?*

- What market is being targeted? Who are the customers—demographics, geographic location, and psychographic profile? What do customers value? How is the value proposition presented to the customer? What is the relationship with the customer? What is the quality of the buy experience? How do customers feel about the firm? How does the business acquire customers? How does it measure customer satisfaction? What is customer profitability? What is customer retention? Describe the customer life cycle using relevant measures.
- What is market share? How is the business positioned in the marketplace? What is the image and reputation of the business? Does it have brand equity? Describe how the business is positioned on functionality, quality, and price measures.

5. *What are company processes?*

- How does the company develop new products and services? How long does it take? How much does it cost? When is breakeven reached?
- Who are the key vendors? What resources (materials, etc.) have to be used?
- What is the distribution system?

6. *How does the company learn and grow?*

- Who are the employees? Do they understand the mission of the business? How productive are they? Are they empowered? Do they have the skill sets to succeed? What is employee turnover? What kind of technology does the company use? What steps are taken to use technology to achieve goals?

When working with any small business client, it takes time to build trust in order to get to the place where real information about the struggles and opportunities that a company faces can emerge. Consultants need to learn about facets of the business that a business owner may not wish to reveal during initial conversations. This hesitancy comes from the fact that the business is often the "owner's baby." All of the business's strengths and weaknesses are the result of the actions of the owner and the management team. Many business owners are reluctant to reveal the true weaknesses to outside "experts" for fear of being viewed negatively or considered inadequate as an owner or manager. Student teams will often spend considerable time hearing about the business owner's personal history. In certain cultures, this is an important part of trust building.

Experience also shows that the racial and ethnic background of the client, as well as the consultants, plays a big role in how easily and quickly information is shared. For example, due to generations of mistrust on financial issues, Native American–owned companies may be reluctant to show financial statements to white consultants working with government agencies. Similarly, new immigrants from Latin America, Asia, Africa, or Eastern Europe find that the systems of financial management and recordkeeping in their home country are very different from the systems in the United States. Thus consultants operating from a US-based system of accounting find it a challenge to get the necessary financial information from these prospective clients.

Another challenge is that early-stage enterprises often lack experience in working with consultants. Typical of their bootstrapping nature, owners of small enterprises will seek to get as much from a consultant as possible. This can lead to conflict for any project, but especially one where the time frame is fixed. During the entry phase, a careful discussion of the scope of the project and timelines will greatly aid work throughout the rest of the engagement. Of course, it is important to be somewhat flexible in the process. Conditions, problems, and needs of the client may change, or unforeseen circumstances may occur. Adaptive responses must be made in order to be effective in the consulting process. First and foremost, consultants must be professional even when they are firmly drawing the line on what will be done.

Contracting

Once the business challenge has been identified and the scope of a project has been discussed, the consultant drafts a contract that will clearly define work areas, timelines, and resources needed from the client. For some student teams, this contract has been discussed and partly developed through prior work with faculty or staff from a sponsoring institution. This may occur because of the short time-frame involved with a quarter- or semester-long project. These work areas will focus on several specific results that will benefit the client.

Student consulting projects most often focus on marketing opportunities (feasibility of a new market, moving into adjacent markets, providing consistent branding through websites and other marketing materials, etc.). Reviewing and recommending improvements to business processes is another prime area. This includes streamlining operations, standardizing procedures, and acquiring systems so that the business can expand. Although the menu of possibilities is quite large, the selection of student projects is based on fit with the skill level and expertise of the student consultants and compatibility with the resources available to the client. Additional consideration is given to the constraint that actionable solutions must be delivered within the time frame required by the business and consultants.

Many small business owners have little or no experience working with a consultant and thus often hope that all of their organizational needs can be addressed by one consultant. In a real-world consultant engagement this is possible, as the client will be paying on an hourly basis for the work to be completed. When working with student consultants whose time is limited by the academic quarter or semester and who have numerous other competing priorities, it is important for the client and the student consultants to strike a balance between all the needs and the depth of investigation and analysis. With the fluid nature of fledgling enterprises, it is strategically more beneficial to address all areas of the business at a moderate level of depth than to address only one area very deeply.

Another primary challenge for student consulting teams is that they may lack the full set of skills necessary to fully meet the desires of the business owner. Client satisfaction is maximized when the full scope of work can be accomplished. Thus, it would be better to deliver benefits to the client from a small project that is well done than to deliver partial results from a broad-based project. Having one success leads to others. Failure very likely would keep the business at a standstill. It could also set the business back.

A statement of the work areas of the student consulting engagement defines the project goals. Typically, two to four work areas are specified with subtasks listed.

In selecting the work areas, attention should be placed on projects that can be completed by student consultants and that the business commits to executing. The business owner and student consultants must keep these goals clearly in mind throughout the life of the engagement.

Bearing all this in mind, the contract may include the following:

- Agreement of the business owner to provide information and to attend meetings (typically scheduled weekly).
- Commitment of the students and mentors to keep all business information confidential except for discussion in class.
- An understanding that the work is provided pro bono and that execution of any solutions is the sole responsibility of the business owner. No claims on gains can be made by students, faculty, or mentors, and no claims for liabilities can be made by the business owner.
- Obligation of the student consulting team to complete the work within the academic period.

When finalizing a contract, consultants should remember that written agreements are understood differently in low-context cultures and high-context cultures (see Module 2). In low-context cultures (such as white non-Hispanic or European cultures) where the emphasis is on the written word, e-mailing the contract for the client to read is often an effective review method. Groups such as Asians, Hispanics, and African Americans are high context. In high-context cultures, the interpretation of the message is heavily dependent on the nature of the relationship between the sender and the receiver, as well as on all previous communication. A face-to-face meeting to review and agree on the contract is recommended. Even revisions need to be discussed and agreed upon in face-to-face interaction. One consulting team that was composed primarily of non-Hispanic white students and their client, the owner of a multimillion-dollar African American insurance brokerage company, sought to clarify the meaning of contract language regarding research the students were to undertake to help design a new line of services. The students were focused on the exact words of the contract, whereas the client was focused on the underlying meaning and the possibility that the scope might be extended. Not until a face-to-face meeting was held could the different interpretations be understood and clarified.

It is important to note that in a very few instances, business owners are unable to overcome trust issues or to commit fully or agree to the scope and objective of the project. Given the limited time of the project and the need to complete the requirements of the course, student consulting teams may have to proceed without the full input of the business owner. Although this is less than optimal, student teams can still engage in a good learning experience.

DATA GATHERING AND ANALYSIS

In Figure 6-1, phases of research, analysis, decision making, and action steps are outlined. Each phase is essential to a good consulting product.

Data Gathering

The majority of the work for a consulting team is spent on collecting data and assembling information about the client, the business environment, and the strengths, weaknesses, opportunities, and threats faced by the company. A good motto for this phase is "leave no stone unturned." Prior to meeting with the client for the first time, the consulting team should have already conducted thorough secondary research to better understand the industry and marketplace in which the client is operating. Be aware that this research can take significant hours when individuals are inexperienced in researching these areas. Unlike academic research, which is more accessible, research into businesses is often proprietary and requires ingenuity to accomplish.

It should be recognized that novice consulting teams commonly make two major mistakes when it comes to gathering data. The first is that once the project plan is created, individual team members perform their tasks without maintaining adequate communications with other team members, mentors, and advisors. As a result, teams may produce deliverables that are disjointed and that do not contribute to a viable solution for the business.

The second major mistake is that, in the haste and pressure to complete the project, the team fails to budget enough time for information and data synthesis. The equally unfortunate result is that much of the data generated will lack coherence or relevance for use by the business. Unless extensive work is done to sift, sort, and

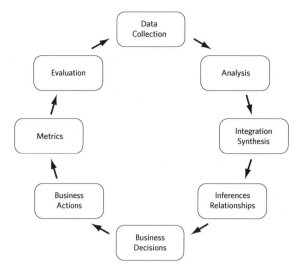

FIGURE 6-1. Overview of Data Gathering and Analysis Process

integrate data late in the process, the business receives a data dump as a finished product rather than an action plan that will capitalize on an opportunity or solve a problem.

Integration/Synthesis

Novice teams are often proficient at developing project plans and conducting secondary research via database and Internet searches, and they may even do well at creating and conducting primary research. Once all this hard work has been accomplished, these same teams may hit a roadblock when it comes to completing meaningful analysis of the information they worked so diligently to collect. Even more teams struggle to come up with viable and effective solutions or action steps for the business. Finally, with the rush to close, teams may fail to come up with suitable metrics to measure the results. All these phases are crucial to an effective solution. If analysis is flawed, the action steps will be wrong. If action steps are not viable, the business could waste time, effort, and money. If metrics are not defined, follow-up, which is critical to emerging businesses, cannot be performed. The business does not learn and will not be able to move to the next level. Fortunately, with knowledge and experience, these obstacles can be overcome.

Once students have collected all the data they need, the team should meet to review what they have learned. Often, novice consulting teams will find that they have to collect additional data because the information they have points to other areas of inquiry or opportunities for the company. It is important for the team to collect as much information as early as possible in the project and do continuous assessment as a team so that they will have sufficient time to gather additional data if needed.

It is possible to spend too much time collecting data, because data collection has to be balanced against other tasks that need to be accomplished in the short time frame of the project. Deciding when enough data have been collected is a judgment call. In terms of resources, consider the constraints of time and money and the importance of the decisions that are to be made. With respect to content, the information must be accurate and timely, and there must be adequate information to explore several possible options or solutions. A further consideration is to avoid collecting misinformation and to keep missing and redundant information to a minimum.

One student team was researching the feasibility of purchasing a $1 million printing machine for a package manufacturing company. The team had collected significant demand data and trend analysis from competitors and industry trade journals. When team members met to determine their recommendation to the client, they realized that they had failed to collect product pricing and equipment operating cost data. Although the project time was half over, they still had sufficient time to collect this information. If they had covered their data analysis process later in the project, it is unlikely that they would have had the necessary time to do the additional research.

Next, the team must go through a process of analyzing the business. The consultant has a responsibility to give a cold, hard, objective look at the business and what it does. It is important to focus on asking and getting complete answers to the right questions.

Inferences/Relationships

Working for a small business is such a rich experience for student consultants because most small business needs are mission-critical. Numerous student consulting projects have had a major impact on a business, with benefits ranging from increasing sales by 50% to the very survival of the company. Small enterprises do not have the financial resources to redo the work of consulting teams; for the most part, they will implement the recommendations that the teams develop. However, if consultants do not get it right, the business can suffer. The key is to deliver a product of beneficial gain to the client. In order to be of beneficial gain, the product must be actionable and pro-

vided with the necessary resources for implementation. Expected outcomes and benefits must be measurable.

As the team conducts its analysis, it should be briefing the business owner. These briefings serve to verify information, educate the business owner, and test the limits of what is achievable. Caution must be taken with how analysis is communicated. Most business owners are not accustomed to the objective and often harsh way in which analysis is conducted in academic settings. Presenting the business owner with a written report that heavily criticizes management practices can be destructive. In one case, presenting this report to a Somalian business caused the business owner to abandon the project completely. In general, it is best to present feedback face to face, being sensitive to the business owner's response to each issue. Any results and meetings of this sort should be reviewed with faculty and advisors prior to meeting with the business owners.

Business Decisions and Actions

Most small enterprise projects will require that the consultants carry them through to implementation. The team will develop implementation steps and get business owners started on implementation. For small enterprises, these steps may have to be specified in more detail than for larger enterprises. The team must devise a means of measuring gains and work with the business owners to be sure they know what the gains are and how they will be measured. Again, with minority businesses, because of language or cultural differences, it may be necessary (but in any case helpful) to take time to communicate carefully and clearly. At times it may be useful to repeat a point or issue and ask a question of the client to make sure that effective communication has occurred. Remember what is at stake in consulting outcomes—implementing results that solve problems to provide new opportunities and other value-added benefits.

Because small enterprises often do not have the human resources needed to follow up on solutions and recommendations, consultants may be directly involved in the implementation of a project plan. This type of involvement can lead to potential problems. Team members may be unclear as to what implementation means. There may be a lack of communication between the team and the business owners as to how far the team will go in the implementation. Other problems arise when the consulting team is not specific and detailed in the implementation steps. Finally, if individual team members have not totally committed to the officially proposed solution, this will make implementation more complicated and challenging. In the worst case it could get in the way of or prevent effective implementation.

To reiterate, the presentation and final report are important to developing the skill sets of the student consultants, and they provide a road map for implementation and an audit trail for measuring success. However, in themselves they will not communicate effectively to the business owner and, in fact, if given in isolation, they may thwart the effort.

More often than not, student teams that find that a particular product line (or an entire company) can never become profitable find it difficult to recommend that the business should divest itself of the product line or close the business entirely. The difficulty comes from the fact that the business owner likely spent many hours and much expense to launch and maintain the business or product line. The student team should consult extensively with mentors and faculty as to how this should be handled. Additionally, the business owner must be part of the entire process in making this decision so that it is as much his or her decision as it is the student team's. Sensitivity needs to be considered in how to communicate such findings. Under no circumstances should the student team begin to propose this without in-depth analysis and review by faculty.

Metrics

For small, underserved enterprises and with social values in mind, the goal is to help the business adapt and become independent. Peter Block, founder of Designed Learning and author of numerous books on consulting, talks about being an authentic consultant, one who is objective and will not make any recommendations that are detrimental to the client. In a sense, the consultant-client relationship is akin to the medical analogy of the physician-patient relationship. The doctor takes the oath that he or she will do no harm. For most small businesses, participating in the consulting project can in itself be a drain and detract from day-to-day essential operations. Vague analysis, nonactionable recommendations, or incorrect conclusions can do substantial harm to the business. This is especially true for small enterprises that do not have the reserves or resources to absorb and survive mistakes the way large enterprises can.

Metrics should be selected that match the work

areas of the project. Teams can select from the large library of metrics or key performance indicators (KPIs) that has grown with the increasing use of continuous improvement and analytics in large enterprises. These are available at repositories such as kpilibray.com. For example, in the category of sales, there is sell-through percentage, market share, repeat business turnover/revenue, conversion rate of marketing/sales campaigns, customer attrition or churn, average spent per customer, and average order size. In the area of production, key performance indicators include inventory turns, average production costs, manufacturing schedule adherence, defect or spoilage rate, on-time delivery rate, freight cost per unit, transit time, and customer order cycle time.

Follow-Up Evaluation

Although the student team may complete its work with the delivery of the final report, advisors and mentors may continue to track the business after the project has been completed. They encourage the business owner to overcome resistance to change and implement the recommended changes. They enhance the recommendations with additional information or by linking the business to networks that will increase its chances of successes. Often referrals are made to other sources of technical assistance or education. The bar is set significantly higher when the double bottom line—profitability and social value—is to be achieved.

THE BUSINESS MODEL AND THE BUSINESS CASE
Business Model

The business model is an articulation of how the company makes a profit and competes against others in the marketplace. The consulting team should have a clear description of the business model, because it provides a guideline as to what the consulting project should or should not focus on. Often the business model will illuminate how the business will create barriers to entry or how it will compete effectively against larger competitors. The business model should provide a good indication of how the firm will make money, including the level and timing of profit coming out of the projected life of the business.

The business model is defined by some as a summation of the core business decisions and trade-offs used by a company to make a profit.[1] The model should articulate different revenue sources. Among the key questions to be answered are:

- Are revenue models subscription, volume, advertising, licensing, or transaction based?
- In addition to payroll, inventory, rent, and advertising, what are other important cost drivers? Are they fixed, semi-variable, variable, or nonrecurring? What is their relative size and importance? How do they change over time?
- What type of investment does the business need to grow?
- What are the critical success factors for the business? Is it the ability to acquire new customers? Or is it the ability to reduce costs to improve profit?

When a business does not have an effective business model, as often happens when small business owners jump at an opportunity without detailed planning, problems will ensue. For example, one café was started because the business owner was able to obtain cheap rent on a location. He decided that he would invest substantial funds in making the space very attractive. There was no analysis done on the market to determine demand, the type of food that would be served, the competitive environment, and foot traffic in the area. The business owner tried several formats and was unable to recoup his investment in renovating the space. Taking the time to create a business model would have saved the business owner much aggravation and considerable expense.

Business Case

Just as the business model provides the beneficial rationale for the business, the business case provides the beneficial rationale for the consulting project. The business case must convincingly argue the value that the consulting project will bring to the business. This value must be measurable. Conventional wisdom says that the consultant will conduct research, gather data, analyze the data, draw conclusions, and then come up with a solution at the end of the engagement. In fact, good consultants determine very early in the consulting assignment what the business needs and the shape of the solution. They

accomplish this by conducting a very quick market, financial, and operational analysis. Even though information may be incomplete, the team needs to take it and apply judgment in coming up with the business case. The business case must be compiled with objectivity. The key is to come up with the business case early and to reevaluate it several times throughout the course of the project to ensure that it is still valid.

One restaurant owner thought his key issue was attracting new customers to his existing customer base of low- to moderate-income families. Through discussion and analysis of the previous two years' performance, it became clear that food and labor costs had escalated. In response, the restaurant needed to raise its prices. But the price increases were more than what the customer base could afford, since many customers had jobs that paid less than $30,000 per year on average. Additionally, because of gentrification, many of the restaurant's clients had moved out of the surrounding neighborhood. The neighborhood had been transformed from what was formerly a low- and moderate-income neighborhood into a neighborhood with above-average levels of rent and housing prices.

In order for the restaurant to continue to serve its traditional customers, it had to reduce prices below a profitable level. An alternate strategy of pursuing the newer upscale residents in the neighborhood seemed self-defeating as well. The restaurant would have to change its product mix and restaurant atmosphere, which would result in a loss of many of the company's traditional clients. The consulting team considered all these factors and identified the goal of developing a strategy for a catering division. By creating a new division, the business would not alienate its current customers, yet it could pursue the opportunity to sell to business clients for whom quality food and service, rather than price, were the drivers.

In summary, the business case will state the problem or opportunity in a very succinct manner, outline the benefits or how money will be made, and point toward solutions. Once the business case has been outlined, the team can move productively into gathering information and evidence and formulating the detailed action plan. If a business case is clear and logical, the consulting team can proceed very efficiently.

SWOT ANALYSIS AND CORE COMPETENCIES

A commonly used tool to determine the mission-critical issues facing a company is a determination of the com-

---

1   J. M. Roberts, H. H. Stevenson, W. A. Sahlman, P. W. Marshall, and R. G. Hamermesh, *New Business Ventures and the Entrepreneur.* Boston: McGraw Hill/Irwin, 2007.

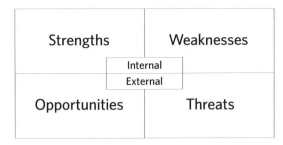

Strengths	Weaknesses
	Internal
	External
Opportunities	Threats

FIGURE 6-2. SWOT Analysis

pany's strengths, weaknesses, opportunities, and threats (SWOT). A SWOT analysis is a technique to structure group discussion to identify the internal and external forces that drive a company's position in the market. Used effectively, a SWOT analysis can organize data and information and determine the areas that a company needs to focus on in order to move forward. Student consulting teams find it helpful to conduct the SWOT analysis early in the consulting process, and most include this analysis in their final report.

The first step in developing a SWOT analysis is to gather the entire consulting team together and discuss the information that has been collected to date. Then, using a flip chart or white board, the group identifies:

- *Strengths.* Existing resources and capabilities within the company that provide a competitive advantage within the market in which the company operates.
- *Weaknesses.* Existing internal forces that lower or limit current or future asset value that would build competitive advantage within the market in which the company operates.
- *Opportunities.* Existing or emerging forces external to the company that, if captured, could provide the company with a competitive advantage.
- *Threats.* Existing or emerging forces external to the company that could inhibit the company's ability to gain a competitive advantage or maintain its current advantage.

Once a comprehensive list is developed, ideas should be clarified to insure that all team members understand all the concepts that have been listed. Then the challenge for the team is to determine which are the most important strengths, weaknesses, opportunities, and threats. Teams can use a five-point Likert scale to rank each item, with 5 being "most important" and 1 being "not at all important." The items receiving the highest overall rank-

ing become the ones that the team develops strategies to enhance, alter, ward against, or capitalize on.

A more extensive SWOT analysis can be created by combining it with another form of strategic analysis known as political, economic, social and technology (PEST) analysis. The analysis has been expanded to include environmental factors to complete the macro environment analysis. Also included are trends in the greater economy or society that may have an impact on the business (see Table 6-1).

Combining SWOT with Harvard Business School professor Michael Porter's Five Forces analysis provides a means of analyzing forces in a business's micro environment that would help it compete.[2] For the small business, this would include its local competition, customers, and vendors.

Assessing special internal factors can assist the team in identifying core competencies[3] within the business. The business can best grow by capitalizing on core competencies. It must also develop and enhance its core competencies so that it can continue to compete effectively.

Although SWOT analysis allows the student consulting team to get a comprehensive picture of the business, caution must be exercised in how this is communicated to the business owner. Often SWOT analyses come across as negative in presentations or reports. Since the primary role of the student team is to communicate and effect change, it is imperative that SWOT analysis be communicated in a way that does not create resistance in the business owner. For example, a weakness (i.e., lack of accounting skills) may be an opportunity for the business (i.e., outsource to a bookkeeper).

BUSINESS PROCESS ANALYSIS

Small businesses often fail to reach critical mass because they are unaware of the shortcomings or inefficiencies in their operations. Also, they may not understand their core competencies and core business processes. Typically, they have not documented their processes so that they can be replicated for regional or national expansion. They may not have considered the use of the Internet and the ability to link anyone, anywhere, anytime, in terms of

2 M. E. Porter, "How Competitive Forces Shape Strategy," *Harvard Business Review*, vol. 57, no. 2 (1979): 137–45.
3 C. K. Prahalad and G. Hamel, "The Core Competence of the Corporation," *Harvard Business Review*, vol. 68, no. 3 (1990): 79–91.

TABLE 6-1. Macro Environment SWOT

Macro Environment	Opportunities	Threats
Political/legal	Tax incentives for hiring veterans	Reduction in government spending; strict labor laws; higher corporate taxes
Economy	Low inflation; low interest rates	Low consumer confidence; difficulty for consumers to acquire loans
Social	Aging population; growth in multicultural market	Population shift to sunbelt; unfamiliarity of multicultural consumers' needs
Technology	Growth in consumers' mobile use; online customer reviews	Outsourcing to international firms; higher cost for smaller firms to implement new technology
Environmental	Climate changes; increase in recycling and reusable programs	Unpredictable natural disasters disrupting production

TABLE 6-2. Micro Environment SWOT

Micro Environment	Opportunities	Threats
Competitors	Distinctive products and services that are not easily replicated	Product technology may not be patentable; competitors have access to greater capital
Buyers	Low switching costs; loyal customer base	Customers are price sensitive; customers are concentrated in a declining market
Suppliers	Healthy competition among suppliers; efficient distribution channel	Suppliers are concentrated in a narrow market
New entrants	Low barriers to entry; low switching costs	Potential for new entrants to steal market share
Substitutes	Little product differentiation to encourage use of substitutes.	Potential for pricing wars

TABLE 6-3. Internal Environment SWOT

Internal Environment	Opportunities	Threats
Management	Good management team with ability to learn and grow	Small management team with limited expertise
Marketing	Excellent reputation in the community; good sales skills	Limited budget to promote brand message; outdated website
Operations	Efficient production process; high-quality products	Rudimentary operations that cannot accommodate growth
Finance/accounting	Good accounting and financial systems; generation of good cash flow	Business owner is not well versed on accounting and financial systems; lack of cash flow to fund growth
Human resource	Well-trained and motivated employees; employee handbook is used effectively	Lack of human capital in certain functions

increasing their part of the value chain with their suppliers and customers. Generally they have made little use of business process analysis.

The basic concept of a process is very simple: input, conversion, and output. According to the diagram in Figure 6-3, complexity is added based on the specific characteristics of individual businesses. In *The Balanced Scorecard*, Kaplan and Norton created an internal business process diagram to describe the processes within an enterprise.[4] The key to their model is that the processes important to the business are mapped out, at which point, it is possible to work on ensuring that each process meets stated goals and that the cycle time for each can be improved.

---

4 Robert S. Kaplan and David P. Norton, *The Balanced Scorecard.* Boston: Harvard Business School Press, 1996.

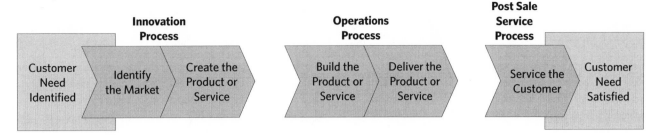

FIGURE 6-3. Internal Business Process
Source: Kaplan and Morton, *The Balanced Scorecard*, 1996.

In the area of systems analysis and implementation in large enterprises, business process analysis has been taken to increased levels of sophistication with certified training by organizations such as the Institute of Configuration Management. The following brief summary of *Configuration Management II*[5] is similar to the process described later in this section.

1. Determine the basic requirements for the system, including regulatory, business, mission, and objectives.
2. Establish all inputs and outputs for the system or process. Define stakeholders and what must be included and excluded. Determine what information and resources go into the system. Determine what information and resources are the product of the system.
3. Map out the process by establishing the link between inputs and outputs. Define how all information and resources are processed to satisfy the output requirements. Evaluate process for weaknesses and revise the process to mitigate weaknesses. Document the process and assign a process/document owner.
4. Plan the implementation of the process. Determine the impact of the implementation. Establish roles and responsibilities for managing the implementation.
5. Deploy the new process. Manage the deployment using good project management practices. Track and monitor progress of the implementation. Revise, document, and implement the changes necessary.
6. Evaluate the process. Establish metrics for system performance. Monitor the system performance to these metrics. Evaluate where improvements or changes need to be made based on how well the system performs.
6. Revise the system as needed. Define the scope

5   Vincent Guess, *CMII for Business Process Infrastructure*. Scottsdale, AZ: Holly Publishing, 2002.

of the change. Determine how to accomplish the change. Document the change and establish an effective date. Implement the change. Track and monitor the implementation of the change.

Who Are the Customers and What Do They Value?

In business process analysis, start with the top-level issues. Find out what the business is all about. This is not as simple as it seems. What the business is today may not be what the owner wants it to be in the future. Perhaps the owner has not thought about what it should be in the future at all. What is the mission or overall goal of the business? Business missions are about customers, so start by asking questions about the customer. Who is the customer? How has that customer changed in the past? How will the customer evolve in the future? What are the customer segments? What does the customer value? What does the product or service do for them? Look at the product life cycle in relation to the customer. Why do customers leave? Who are your potential customers? What do they want? What would make the customer's life easier? Determine where the product or service is in its life cycle. Look at the customer life cycle.

Once the answers to these questions are determined, a clear picture of business goals will emerge. The business goals then have to be broken down into specific business outcomes. Market share and profitability are common outcomes. These become key performance indicators or metrics for the business. It is important to note that metrics must be detailed at the start.

Target the Critical Processes

Once the business goals are determined and it is decided how these will be measured as outcomes, consider the business and determine its core processes. These processes are usually documented in block diagrams or flow charts. Typically, an analysis will start with a clear focus on the main steps in the process. These are mapped by asking questions, watching how people operate, and following the paperwork trail. Next, the steps are broken down into subprocesses. In complex organizations, the subprocesses are broken down into several other levels. A student consulting project with a photography studio has been selected as an example of business process analysis. This service business is similar in nature to other small businesses such as legal, financial, or health services.

Map the Top View. The core process of a photography studio is booking the client to come in for a photo shoot. Afterward, the client selects the proofs that she likes and the frames she likes, if a frame is desired. The photographs are processed and then delivered to the client.

Map Subprocesses. The clear focus on the overall process may appear straightforward, but even such a simple process is more complex than this overview suggests. These steps must be broken down into subprocesses. The consulting team spent time with the business owner and mapped out a process flow chart (Figure 6-4). They documented each step, how each step linked to or drove other steps in the process, and the amount of time taken. Like many bootstrapping small business owners, this business owner had higher turnover with her staff than a larger enterprise would have. She could not afford to provide the extensive benefits that larger enterprises could, nor could she afford high salaries. Often she would use interns to assist in her business. As a result, the business owner was often performing many of the tasks listed to keep the business going, without analysis as to what was important for her to do. Although the business was extremely promising and new clients called daily, this resulted in a major constraint in her ability to grow. Time tied up in these tasks was time taken from doing the core value-added task of photography shoots.

Mapping the subprocesses was the first step in analyzing where efficiencies could be obtained. The mapping showed that this business owner, although never trained in business, was very astute about payment. Clients were asked for payment upon booking the first appointment rather than upon delivery of service. This ensures that the client will turn up for the appointment, and it brings cash into the business immediately. The client pays the balance for the shoot immediately after the shoot, again

reducing the chances of bad debt and ensuring that the client will show up for the next stage of the process. By mapping such mundane tasks as invoicing and collecting payment, the team could also work to reduce the cash disbursement cycle (discussed in detail in the next section on analyzing accounting processes), increase the throughput of service processing, and shorten the service processing cycle.

An African American moving and storage company sought help from the student team to increase sales. Discussions with the owner pointed to possibly losing business due to poor customer service and poor follow-up to bid inquiries. The process chart in Figure 6-5 showed the process both prior to and after re-engineering. As can be seen from the figure, in the original process there was no follow-up, either on customers who did not respond to their bid or on customers who did contract their services. The consulting team proposed some simple changes to the process. They suggested that all inquiries for bids be logged into a database, that a quality assurance check be added for completed jobs, and that customers be contacted for follow-up business.

By adding a database, the company was better able to track clients, insure high customer satisfaction, and seek repeat business. Additionally, the database allowed the company to become a learning organization and to improve its pricing, service offerings, and customer service over time.

Map across Functions. A cross-functional analysis breaks down the steps by the function or person who performs them. In larger enterprises, the handoff between functions often results in inefficiencies that can be captured in process analysis. In this case and typical with small businesses wanting to grow, the tasks were not broken down by function. Most of the work was performed by the principals in the firm. This lack of differentiation made it difficult to delegate the work to others.

A careful analysis of the processes was mapped in Figure 6-5. It showed that processes could be broken down into crucial, value-added tasks that only the business owner could do and those that could be delegated. It was obvious that she was the only one who could do the photographic shoot. In addition, as is typical with promising businesses, the business owner was the firm's best salesperson. Therefore, it was important that she was the key touchpoint with the customer when buy decisions were made.

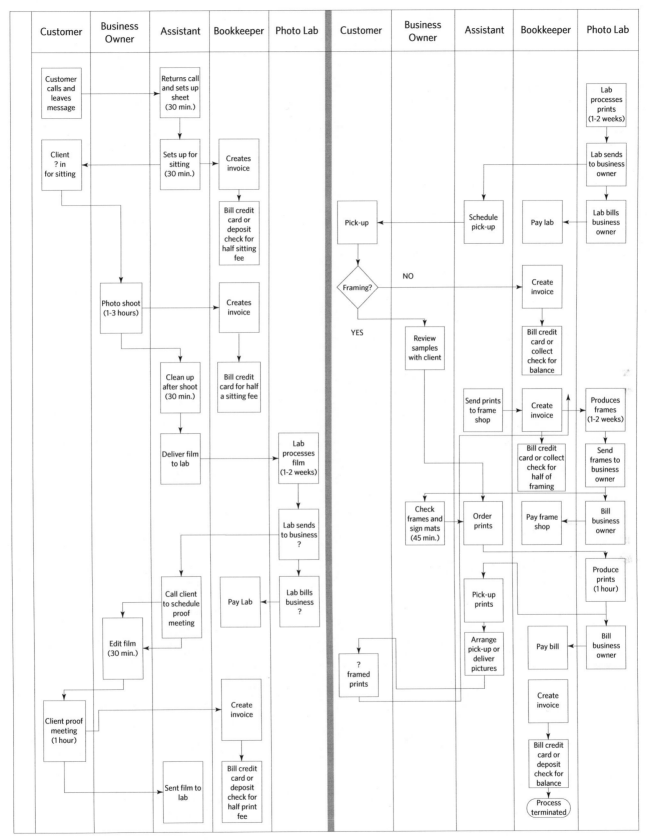

FIGURE 6-4. Photography Studio Mapped across Functions

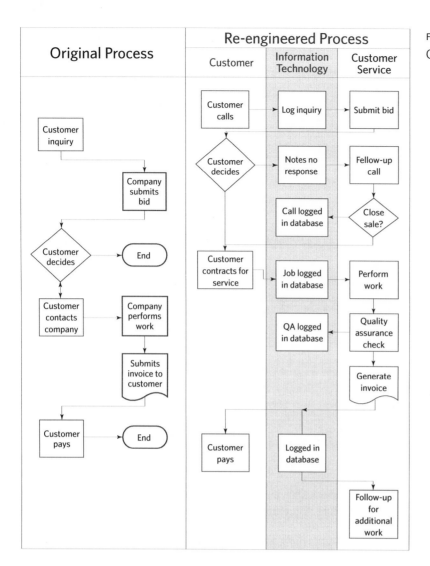

Original Process

- Customer inquiry
- Company submits bid
- Customer decides → End
- Customer contacts company
- Company performs work
- Submits invoice to customer
- Customer pays → End

Re-engineered Process

Customer	Information Technology	Customer Service
Customer calls	Log inquiry	Submit bid
Customer decides	Notes no response	Follow-up call
	Call logged in database	Close sale?
Customer contracts for service	Job logged in database	Perform work
	QA logged in database	Quality assurance check
		Generate invoice
Customer pays	Logged in database	
		Follow-up for additional work

FIGURE 6-5. Reengineering a Moving Company

Further, the analysis showed that an assistant could take care of the mundane scheduling and logistical tasks, while a bookkeeper could take care of the billing and payment tasks. The functional analysis also revealed the need for a photo lab and framing shop. With this business process, these outside firms played an important role in fulfilling the service. Although most small business owners would not think of these vendors as part of their business process, any improvement in the vendor's production time can decrease the business's cycle time, which allows the business to take on more customers and convert to cash more quickly.

Break Out the Value-Added. A detailed analysis of each step in this process will yield additional ideas for improving the process. Including the photo lab and framing shop would allow the business to explore improvement in their part of the value chain. Questions can be asked about reducing production time at both the photo lab and framing shop. Could the photo lab pick up and deliver, thereby reducing travel time for the assistant? Consultants could explore whether credit card processing could be faster or cheaper. Perhaps the customer could be asked to decide on the frame when the proofs are approved versus scheduling another appointment. This would enhance the customer experience by reducing one trip to the studio while decreasing the order fulfillment time.

Most important, the documentation of the process allows the business owner to easily delegate the tasks to others. If staff turns over, this documentation will reduce training time. Additionally, having the entire flow allows staff to see how each task is interdependent with the others. Staff will be better able to suggest other ways of improving operations.

Create Metrics. Most enterprises rely on traditional financial measures to evaluate their processes. They look at return on capital, return on investment, or net present value. These measures favor investing that returns fast and takes little risk. They are biased toward legacy systems. In order to survive for the long run, the business may need to do something risky and innovative. It is important that the student consulting team develop metrics that are understandable and manageable for the business owner.

Metrics need to be accurate, objective, and measure on more than one dimension. They need to make effective trade-offs. They need to be crystal clear to everyone up and down the chain of command. They must take into consideration the future, not the past. Robert Kaplan developed the balanced scorecard as an alternative to depending exclusively on financial measures. The balanced scorecard uses a combination of financial outcomes, customer metrics, internal processes, and enterprise innovation and learning. These measures have to tie into the specific strategic objectives of the business.

Gather Metrics. The business sees improvements from process reengineering with the development of metrics and measures that show progress. With process mapping, it is important that information be gathered to provide a baseline to measure changes. Often the information is there but it has not been used. Less easily available information can be obtained by sampling a segment of the population or data.

Once measurements are gathered, they need to be assessed as to how they contribute to the goals of the enterprise. It is helpful to divide the measurements into lead indicators (measurements that assist in predicting) and lag indicators (which measure whether goals have been reached). Lead indicators are similar to economic indicators like production capacity or housing starts that give economists an indication of what might be in store for the economy. A key lead indicator for a photography company, for example, would be client inquiries. Keeping track of all potential clients who called and how they learned about the firm is important but rarely done in small businesses. It lets the business owner know the effectiveness of individual advertising programs. For the emerging business, the effectiveness of a few thousand dollars in expenses can have a tremendous impact on the profitability and even the survival of a firm.

The percent of inquiries converted to appointments is the next important metric in the photography company example. If few inquiries are converted, the business owner will revisit the selling pitch. At the same time, he or she will track those that do not convert. Was it pricing or other factors that prevented the conversion? What could be changed about the business? Lead indicators give the business owner an idea of whether goals will be met. For emerging businesses, focusing on a breakeven number of clients is important to the survival of the business. For example, in the photography business, 50% of calls are converted to sales. If not enough inquiries are made in a given month, sales will not be achieved in the next month. Consequently there is a good chance that breakeven will not be reached in three months' time. This leading indicator signals the business owner to put more effort into generating initial inquiries rather than into converting inquiries into sales.

Once the shoot is completed, the business owner will track the effectiveness of cross merchandising. Did the client buy additional prints beyond what was in the original contract? Did the client purchase framing services? If not, the business owner will explore the factors that prevented these add-on sales.

Lagging indicators measure success or failure in reaching goals. They include revenue, profits, customer lifetime value, market share, and return on investment.

Map the Customer's Point of View. The picture is not complete until the process is mapped from the customer's point of view. This could be done by in-depth interviews with one or two customers and talking to them about their experience. Anyone who has gone through a service process can give a detailed description of its foibles. The best businesses will always look at the process from the customer's point of view. What can be done to make life easier for the customer? When the process is looked at in this way, it becomes obvious that there are many opportunities for improvement.

Who Owns the Process?

At the same time that core processes are being mapped, an assessment has to be made of the business's readiness to change. In larger enterprises, a survey is taken of the employees' attitude to new ideas or elements of the change, such as technology. Some test instruments will rank the enterprise on a scale of one to five as to readiness for change. With the small business, it is most important to assess the owner's attitude to change. The owner is the primary decision maker and key to the change process. Some owners are ready and even eager to change; others are reluctant. Keep in mind that just because the owner is not ready, this does not mean the change will not happen. Small business owners are smart and agile. Education can go a long way in making the business owner and the business ready for change.

The appropriate level of change is the next assessment made. With the abundance of technological solutions available, it is tempting to recommend the latest and greatest. Often the business is not ready to adopt this type of technology. Simpler solutions that employees can understand and maintain prove superior in many cases. For example, an Excel spreadsheet may be more appropriate than sophisticated accounting software.

In order to effectively implement change, the process owner needs to be intimately involved. The process owner is not always the business owner. There may be other key people in the business who are responsible for critical processes. Just because the business owner has bought in does not mean that everyone else is on board. The process owner is accountable for the process. She has the authority to make decisions. The process owner coaches and mentors others in learning the process. He or she is the advocate for procuring resources for the process.

Excellent processes have excellent process owners who are accountable for the outcomes of the process. They are responsible for a program of continuous improvement. They have a team orientation and value disagreement and opposing views. They make the best use of the business's knowledge assets.

So the consultant should make an assessment of process owners in the business. Evaluate their ability to lead excellent processes. Determine what kind of development is needed. If this will enhance support for process improvement, communicate what you have learned to the client or owner.

ACCOUNTING ANALYSIS

Proper accounting is vital to the success of any business. For small businesses, the importance of accounting is magnified by the impact it can have on the survival of the business. Resources are scarce. Business owners often operate with little margin for error. If the business owner has the wrong information regarding any number of accounting issues, it can be fatal for the business.

Accounting is also used to measure the performance of a business. It reports how large a business is, how much it is growing, and whether its parts are contributing their share. Accurate numbers can point the business in the right direction, while inaccurate numbers can put a business totally off course. It is common knowledge that bookkeeping is a frequent source of problems faced by small businesses.

Even the smallest businesses use an accounting system. For fledgling businesses, the system is often Quick-Books or Peachtree. A basic system can be purchased for about $100, with premium systems available for up to $500 per user. These systems are tailored for small businesses, and their features are relatively simple. Some industry associations have also developed accounting and other software systems for small businesses within their industry. The advantage of these off-the-shelf systems is that they are easily deployed with step-by-step menus to take the business owner through the process. It is not necessary to have a deep understanding of accounting or computers to install or use them. Their disadvantages are that the number of features is limited, and they cannot be used as the business grows larger because they do not allow for much complexity. More sophisticated systems run from $5,000 upward. Cloud computing applications are also available to business owners as another relatively low-cost option.

Accounting processes are fairly standard across businesses, as are the requirements for tax or government reporting. Resource-strapped business owners are often more focused on generating sales or providing services than they are about the more mundane tasks of keeping their accounting or tax situation under control. Often when the business is small, the entrepreneur takes a more seat-of-the-pants approach rather than systematically determining what makes sense in the long term. Since accounting issues are tied to cash management and cash management is the number one cause of small business demise, taking this tack is dangerous and myopic. Poor accounting can trigger time-consuming audits by government agencies that can tie up the entrepreneur for several weeks. It can also cause the entrepreneur to make the wrong decision about a growth strategy. By careful deployment of an accounting system, a business can improve its own processes so that minimum accounting requirements are met and growth can happen.

Flowers on 15th

Business Process Improvement

"We are not in the flower business. We are in the emotion business."

Flowers on 15th is a neighborhood flower shop in Seattle, Washington, owned by Alex Soto. As a young boy, he enjoyed playing with flowers; his dream was to pursue a career in which he would have enough flowers with which he could play and enjoy. He began his journey as an international flower broker. He recalls a life-changing experience that occurred while traveling in Hawaii to buy tropical flowers. Soto received a phone call from his father asking him to reroute his trip to San Juan, Mexico, as part of a religious pilgrimage. Soto carried out his father's wishes and traveled to Mexico. When he arrived in San Juan, he observed an array of carnations that were part of an offering to the Virgin of San Juan de los Lagos; he realized that he needed to follow his dream of "playing among the flowers." He returned to Seattle and opened Flowers on 15th.

None of the floral arrangements in the shop are premade. Although he sources flowers both internationally and domestically, the majority (about 80%) of his flowers are locally grown.

In 2008, a student consulting team provided Soto with recommendations to improve his business operations. The students identified several areas for improvement, including the website, the physical organization of the store, cross-merchandising, and the accounting processes.

First, the students created content for Soto's website and ensured that the site was fully operational. A good website is important because it is often a customer's first impression of the business. Next, the students conducted observational research in the flower shop. They determined that the physical layout of the store was too crowded and that it did not showcase the unique floral arrangement process. More importantly, the team recommended that he bring the flower design station to the front of the shop so customers could observe the staff creating the floral arrangements. The custom floral arrangements are an important differentiating factor for Flowers on 15th, especially given that there is a large grocery store across the street that sells predominantly bundled flowers.

Following the update to the shop layout, the students suggested that Soto cross-merchandise other gift items in the store. Soto heeded their advice and now displays a variety of items in his store on consignment. He is able to support other local businesses by promoting their products. The students also recommended that Soto reduce storage units (reducing his costs) and use both doors to enhance customer flow in the store (increase sales). Finally, the students helped Soto understand his accounting systems and encouraged him to look at his business objectively. He has been able to sustain his flower shop partly because he followed several of the students' recommendations.

Soto is dedicated to serving the community with his flowers. He attributes his success to his strong faith and happy customers. Each day, Soto is able to live his dream of creating something uniquely beautiful for his customers.

Setting Up Accounting Systems

Small business accounting systems have templates for typical sole proprietorships such as construction contracting, retailers, or health-care practitioners. It is important at the outset for accounting systems to be set up properly. Often this involves the creation of a set of files that provide the basis for transactions. These need to be logical for the business, consistent, and kept up to date.

Chart of accounts. A chart of accounts is the listing of accounts to which transactions are posted. They include the typical items that are part of financial statements, such as revenues, expenses, cash, and accounts receivable. Charts of accounts are specific to the business and, although the accounting system will suggest typical accounts, it is up to the business to ensure that there is enough detail to generate information to make relevant decisions. Typically, this is done by breaking accounts into subaccounts. For example, a business will separate sales, cost of goods, and other expenses by product line.

If the business owner sets up the chart of accounts without the assistance of an accountant, there may be problems with its logic and consistency. Even when book-keepers or accountants are used, the chart of accounts may be set up for tax reporting but might not allow for management reporting. It is helpful to review the chart of accounts to determine if changes are required to better fit the firm's needs. Business owners need profit and loss broken out by location, products, and customer to really understand how to grow.

Payroll. Processing payroll requires business owners to calculate compensation based on hourly or other rates. Social Security (FICA) and Medicare costs are included according to annual tables provided by the government for employees and the employer. A third category includes federal withholding taxes, state unemployment costs, and deductions for company benefits such as 401(k) savings or medical plans. Payroll checks have to be generated. Reports and payments to government are done on a regular schedule, and penalties and interest are assessed for inaccurate reporting and late filings. Another important reason for timely processing and deposits is employee morale. Not filing the proper forms will give the impression of disorganization or instability and can create problems that result in disgruntled employees.

Providing incorrect W-2 information will also lead to problems with the Internal Revenue Service. So it is in the best interests of both the business and the employees to make sure that payroll records are up to date and accurate.

Sales taxes. Sales taxes can be extremely burdensome to account for because they often involve hundreds of transactions. Some items are taxable, while others are not. Often sales taxes must be collected for more than one tax agency. Accounting systems will keep track of

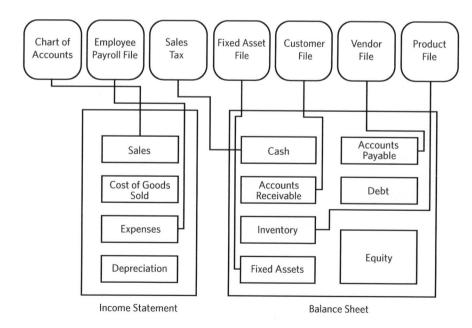

FIGURE 6-6. Setting Up Accounting Systems for Small Businesses

the sales tax collected and create the necessary forms to report and pay various tax agencies. Again, the key is for the business owner to ensure that these are done correctly and on time. The best way to do this is to employ an accounting system and diligently enter all sales into the system on a regular basis. Sales tax audits are extremely time consuming and can tie up a business owner for weeks.

Some cash-strapped business owners may divert for other uses the cash set aside for payroll requirements or sales tax payments in the period before they are due. These funds do not belong to the business (they are being collected for the government by the business), and this use of "diversion financing" should be limited and avoided, if possible. According to a study commissioned by the SBA, sole proprietors might not survive the first five years mainly because of cash-flow problems. Relying on these sources of financing may cause the business to improperly manage its other sources of cash generation.

Customer data. A simple customer database will include billing address, ship-to address, contact information, billing terms, current orders, and delivered orders for the past few years. These data should be accurate and up to date. Each customer will be tracked by a unique customer number. Customer files will also include customer payment information. Prior to taking on any business customers, it is important that the business conduct a credit check on the customer to determine whether terms should be extended.

One of the key tasks of a fledgling business is to develop its relationships with customers. A vigilant business owner will add other pieces of information about the customer that will help with follow-up sales. If this information is carefully analyzed and systematically collected at the early stages of the business, it can both foster and accommodate growth.

Vendor data. The vendor database should include contact information, payment terms, the business's credit limit with the vendor, and various levels of discounts for quantity ordered. If the vendor is a subcontractor, this will be noted on the file along with the requirement to generate a Form 1099 for IRS reporting purposes. Vendors may be categorized as cost of goods sold or expenses.

As small businesses increase their vendor lists, they may neglect to ensure their accuracy. Yet outdated or inaccurate vendor information will cause the business to pay

too much. If quantity discounts or extended payment terms are not used, the business has incurred unnecessary expenses. Other information should be added as the vendor relationship grows. The business should track delivery times, defects, and other measures of vendor performance. Vendors should be evaluated to see if better service and cheaper prices can be obtained. Many business owners do not feel they have the time to seek competitive bids, thereby losing an opportunity to save money.

Product data. Product files serve both the order processing system and the inventory system. Each product should have a unique product number. Linking the product to a vendor allows the business to differentiate between the same product provided by two different vendors.

Inventory systems will track products and will provide information on when the product has to be reordered. Keeping product supplies to just-in-time low levels can be a real benefit to the business.

Fixed asset data. A business needs to keep track of property, equipment, and other assets that it uses to generate revenues. As the business acquires these assets, they should be posted to a fixed-asset listing that is accurate and up to date. Often small business owners start businesses with their own funds or equipment and have not created a distinction between their personal and business assets. They may neglect to record every purchase of equipment. This can cause too much tax to be paid and other problems.

Order Processing and Fulfillment

Fulfilling an order is a process common to most businesses. As shown in Figure 6-7, a new customer is acquired through the hard work of the business owner or employees. A credit check is conducted, and terms are negotiated with the new customer. There may be additional negotiation on the specifications of the product to be delivered. A customer order is created. Since most businesses use an accounting system, the system will automatically assign a unique number to each order. This is important for tracking order progress. The business procures the materials it needs, employs workers, and produces what the customer wants. It ships the product. The customer is billed (again with a uniquely numbered invoice), and payment is collected.

In this instance, the business has targeted creditworthy customers who will repeat-buy. The product meets cus-

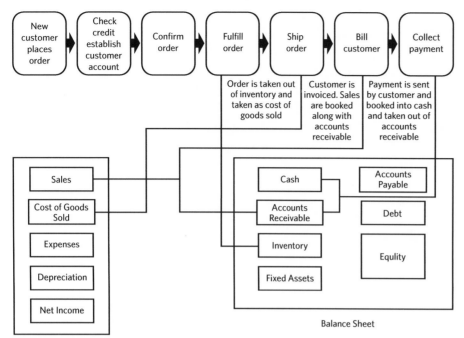

FIGURE 6-7. Order Processing and Fulfillment. Receipt Cycle

tomer requirements and is manufactured efficiently and with high quality. If business processes run smoothly, accounting is straightforward and automatic. Problems occur when the processes do not work as they should. For example, if the product specifications are not clear or if the business fails to deliver as promised, the customer will reject all or partial delivery of the product. If price and terms are not clearly communicated within the business, the customer will reject the invoice. If the order fails to arrive on time, this may cause the customer to demand a discount. If the customer is not creditworthy, payment may not be collected. It is obvious that these problems will have business consequences, including unwarranted shipping, redo, and administrative costs. Each of these must be dealt with on a case-by-case basis. Dealing with exceptions is time consuming and prone to error.

When businesses do not have an accounting system or if they use some combination of manual and automated systems, it is important that both orders and invoices be uniquely numbered and dated. (Often this is accomplished by using pre-numbered forms.) This allows for information to be collected on how long it took to fill the order and for the order to be tracked.

Purchasing: Disbursement Cycle

Most fledgling businesses begin with very little cash, so they need to be very resourceful in how they spend their money. Success of the business is highly dependent on how well the entrepreneur can bootstrap or do a lot with very little. In the purchasing disbursement cycle outlined in Figure 6-8, the business needs to find the vendor with the most value for the best prices. For most start-up businesses, being lean and mean is the only way of surviving. Some entrepreneurs were able to start their businesses for very little by buying high-end computer equipment from bankrupt dot.coms. Others scour the used furniture market for fixtures at a fraction of the cost of new. Businesses that do not spend the time soliciting competitive bids or comparison shopping often end up paying too much. Some business thinkers believe that bootstrapping for survival may be essential to business growth. Businesses that spend too much in startup are not resourceful enough to flourish and grow.

When the purchasing involves products or services the business sells to the customer, the vendor must be dependable. The business's reputation may be staked on the quality and timeliness of work produced by the vendor.

Often a small business with no credit rating will have to prepay for its orders. It is important to establish a good credit record quickly so that terms will be extended. Often the business owner will have to work directly with vendors to convince them that the firm has long-term viability and that favorable terms are warranted.

As with the receipt cycle, the better the business processes, the easier it is to manage the accounting. If terms

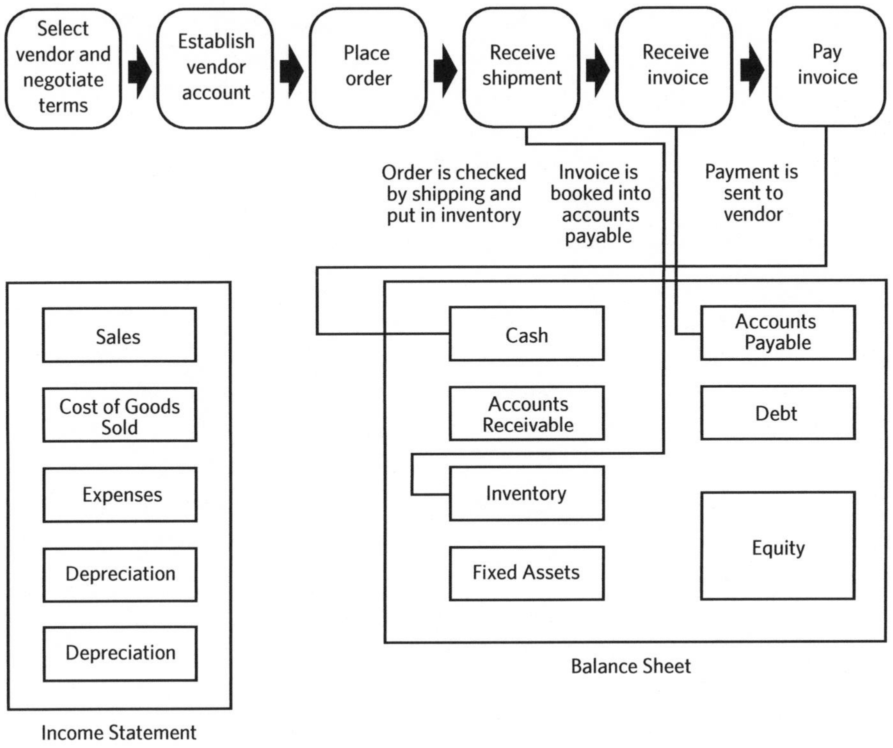
Select vendor and negotiate terms
Establish vendor account
Place order
Receive shipment
Receive invoice
Pay invoice
Order is checked by shipping and put in inventory
Invoice is booked into accounts payable
Payment is sent to vendor
Sales
Cost of Goods Sold
Expenses
Depreciation
Depreciation
Income Statement
Cash
Accounts Receivable
Inventory
Fixed Assets
Accounts Payable
Debt
Equity
Balance Sheet

FIGURE 6-8 Purchasing. Disbursement Cycle

are negotiated, the vendor data file is accurate, and the goods are received in quality condition, the accounting system will pay the invoice on the due date and book the transactions. If terms are uncertain or not entered correctly into the system, intervention is necessary. If the goods do not arrive according to specifications, both business and accounting problems ensue.

FINANCIAL ANALYSIS

The financial sophistication of the business owner sometimes determines the amount of financial reporting that the company does. Some business owners do their own bookkeeping. They ensure that transactions are recorded, prepare the financial statements, and generally have an intimate knowledge of the business's financial condition. These business owners create budgets to control the business. They perform cash flow projections to anticipate funding needs. A business cannot be properly managed unless its owner uses its budgets and financial statements. The more financially sophisticated the business owner is, the more credible he or she is to potential investors and lenders.

Other business owners hire an accountant or bookkeeper to do the accounting for the business. Hiring a certified public accountant (CPA) gives some comfort that financial statements are compiled correctly, but it is not a guarantee that transactions will be properly accounted for. Because of the cost, most business owners will hire bookkeepers to do day-to-day transactions and have accountants prepare the quarterly and annual financial statements and the tax returns. Having an accountant does not exempt the business owner from the understanding of and responsibility for the financial statements.

Corporations report financial statements following generally accepted accounting principles. These rules are set by the Financial Accounting Standards Board on how financial statements should be compiled. For the most part, small businesses do not have to adhere to all the same requirements as public companies. They are not subject to Securities and Exchange Commission regulations because they do not sell their stock to the public.

Most small companies will hire accountants to review their financials, but few will pay for a full audit by an accounting firm unless their bank requires it. Three financial statements are typically prepared by accountants: the income statement, the balance sheet, and the cash flow statement.

- Income statement. The income statement (also called profit and loss statement) gives an account of what

the company sold and spent in an accounting period. Sales (also called revenues), or what the company sold in products and services, less any expenses (expenses are divided into a number of categories) and less taxes equals the company's
net income.

- Balance sheet. The balance sheet is a financial snapshot of what the company owns (assets), what it owes (liabilities), and what it is worth free and clear of debt (equity). A balance sheet gives an indication of the company's financial health.
- Cash flow statement. For most small businesses, it is often more productive to start with the cash flow statement. Unlike the income statement, which may involve noncash entries, the cash flow statement deals only with what came in and what went out in cash. Looking at the actual cash flow gives an indication of how well the company can meet its cash obligations and whether it requires additional capital.

Not all the financial reporting has been covered here; for example, tax returns must be prepared. For its own internal purposes, the business will compile management reports that focus on locations, product lines, customers, other activities or projects. This allows the company to get a good picture of how profitable these activities are and how fast they are growing. If reports are not generated, business owners may not know if the activity is profitable at all.

All financial statements rely on the company exercising a certain amount of discipline in how it accounts for everything that occurs. A company needs to have careful procedures for bookkeeping, resolving exceptions and reconciling everything to cash accounts. Bad numbers foster bad decisions. Not instituting good accounting procedures when a business is in its early stages also creates a barrier to growth.

An in-depth analysis of a company's financial situation requires looking at the business's financial statements and their backup. For smaller businesses, it is possible to look at account registers and review the actual transactions, because they are relatively small in number, to find transaction details. For businesses with more sophisticated accounting systems, the general ledger (for details on administrative costs and cash balances), fixed asset listing (for details on property and equipment), accounts payable ledger (for details on vendors, timing of payments, and payment amounts),

accounts receivable ledger (for details on customers, timing of receipts, and receipt amounts), and inventory listing (for inventory by item, cost, and time in inventory) would have to be reviewed.

Before analyzing the financial statements, most consultants will make an assessment of how much they can rely on the numbers given. One quick check is to compare bank statements against cash accounts. Most auditors will take a random sample of transactions and assess whether they can trace them to the bank statements. If they cannot, it is likely that the financials are not accurate. In general, business owners should make it a practice to reconcile the bank statement to the financials on a monthly basis. Small and large errors can be caught and corrected quickly. Incorrect transactions that are allowed to remain on the books often develop into much larger problems.

With small businesses, accounting procedures should also be reviewed to insure completeness or to confirm that all transactions are tracked. A review of the account registers will show individual sales, expenses, and other detail. A random selection of transactions can be compared to documents. The account registers should also be reviewed for exceptions and how they are resolved.

A business owner's personal and business lives may be hard to separate; however, it is important that personal and business accounts be kept apart. Having personal transactions in business accounts is an administrative nightmare to untangle and can lead to inaccurate financial statements. It may also prevent objective decision making. The business owner needs distinct bank and credit card accounts for all business transactions.

Income Statement Analysis

Historical income statements should be analyzed for trends. Comparing monthly and annual statements for trends provides data for planning purposes. Trend analysis is essential for materials forecasting, inventory control, capital budgeting, human resource scheduling, marketing, advertising, promotional campaigns, and profit maximization.

Revenues. For small businesses, reaching a critical mass in revenues is essential to business survival. For food service establishments, only 64% of sole proprietorships were profitable in 2008. Of all these businesses, those with higher revenues are more likely to be profitable. Similar trends are seen in other industries.

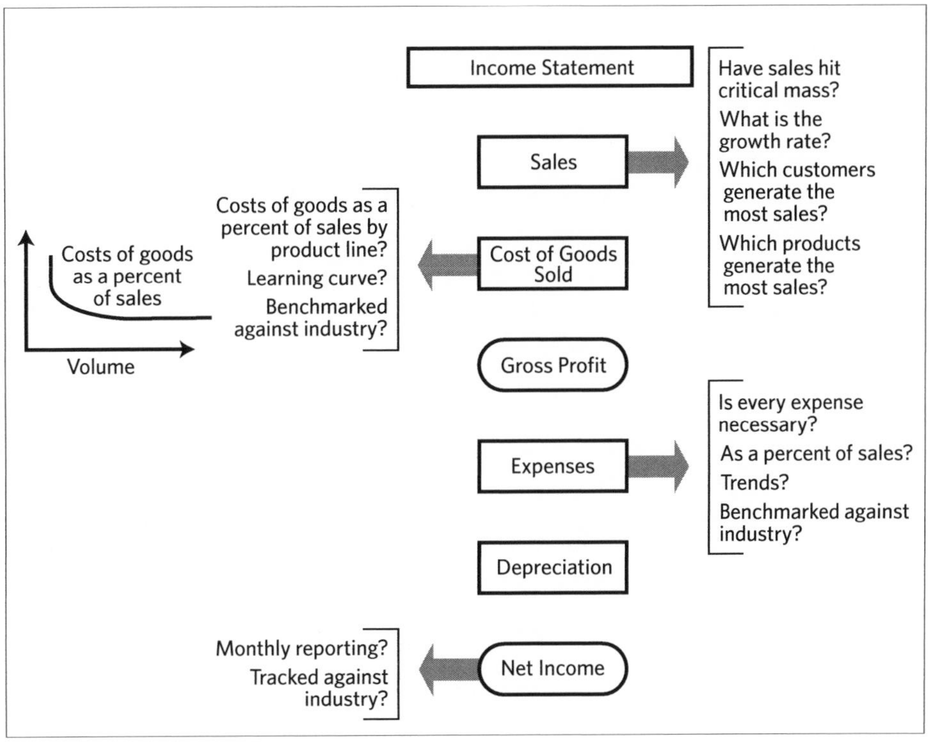

FIGURE 6-9. Income Statement Analysis

Whether or not a business will reach financial sustainability and hit critical mass depends on its sales and marketing programs. It will also depend on its competitive environment. A restaurant that is situated in an area full of competitors may have problems growing its sales.

The business needs to identify its profitable customers. Analyzing sales by customer will let the business know which customers buy the most. It will also identify the potential for additional sales. Matching this list with cost of sales and expenses associated with that customer will let the business know customer profitability.

By the same token, the business needs to categorize sales by product line. Businesses will often adopt products on an opportunistic basis without conducting an analysis of whether the product will be profitable. Unless sales and cost of sales are broken out by product line, the business owner will be unable to conduct an analysis. Profitability by product line lets the business owner know where to focus his or her efforts, identifies areas of best potential growth, and determines which products to drop.

Analyzing a small business's historical income statements helps in determining its future prospects. If a company's revenue grew at 15% last year, it might be expected that it would grow about 15% in the next year. But analyzing growth rates is not as simple as straight-line extrapolation. If growth was 10% two years ago and 15% last year, it might be projected that the business will grow at 20% next year. On the other hand, if growth was 20% two years ago and 15% last year, maybe growth will be 10% next year.

If sales growth slows or stagnates, serious analysis has to be done about the direction of the company. Companies with stagnant revenues may need to pare expenses and figure out more efficient ways to make the product and get it to customers. Even if sales are not growing, a business can still grow profits.

Cost of goods sold. The cost of making or buying the product a business sells is aptly named the cost of goods sold. In order to respond quickly to customers, businesses will have an inventory of products to draw from when they receive an order. Although these products may have been manufactured weeks before, they are not counted on the income statement or expensed until the product is shipped to the customer. This adheres to the accounting principle that expenses must be matched to revenues.

The calculation of cost of goods sold (COGS) as a percent of revenues (also called gross margin) is a key indicator of business performance. Over short periods of time COGS is typically a consistent percentage of sales. Over longer periods of time, if companies are growing,

COGS may decrease if the company is able to negotiate better terms for raw material inputs. Likewise, as commodity prices fluctuate on the world market, COGS as a percent of sales may fluctuate. Careful attention to COGS and its relationship to sales can lead to overall improved profitability.

Operating expenses. Operating expenses (sometimes referred to as selling, general, and administrative) is a catchall for every other kind of expense. It includes payroll, marketing costs, utilities, office supplies, insurance, legal costs, and the like. Many small businesses necessarily spend very little on these types of expenses. But there might be a tendency to spend unwisely because the business lacks the time or expertise to do proper research.

A process known as benchmarking is used to compare the business to its peers. The business will evaluate its spending as a percent of sales against others in the same industry with the same level of revenues. Benchmarks for common small businesses can be found at www.bizstats.com.

If a business has expenses as a percent of sales that are above or below the benchmark, it does not necessarily mean that the business is performing well. It could be that the business is underspending in the category or that it sells a different mix of products or services that drive the excess expenses. Essentially, benchmarking gives a business owner and consultant a chance to explore areas of potential concern more closely to determine ways to potentially increase profitability.

Profitability. Most small business owners are clear as to their overall profit, but they may not track profitability by customer or product line. The key is to redesign the chart of accounts so that sales and expenses are tracked by product line. Most accounting systems allow for customer profitability as long as the customer information is entered along with the expenses.

Timeliness. Income statements are required on a quarterly or annual basis for tax purposes, but owners of a business should have monthly budget and actual numbers at the tip of their fingers. These numbers need to be timely and accurate. Often variances in actual to budget can point to small problems that will throw the business out of kilter if they are allowed to continue.

Not knowing how the business is doing financially is a major reason for small business failures. Managing the

business by activating the accounting system, completing some basic financial analysis, and staying constantly in touch with the business's financial status is critical for adequate profit.

Balance Sheet Analysis

A company needs a variety of assets in order to operate, including inventory to sell, cash to pay staff and suppliers, and buildings to house its operations. The balance sheet summarizes what a company uses to operate (assets) and what it did to finance those assets (equity and liabilities). The balance sheet by its very nature measures financial health at a point in time.

There are a number of key ratios that are calculated and compared to industry averages. Knowing how a business compares financially helps the business owner who is seeking loans or expansion opportunities. Knowing that a business's financial ratios compare favorably to the industry gives the owner a psychological and planning advantage. It adds to the owner's general awareness of the industry and provides an early warning system for industry fluctuations and trends. A full balance sheet is complicated, but most small business analyses focus on a few elements.

Cash. Most businesses generate cash when customers pay for their goods. Having a healthy cash balance is a good sign because it means that the business is generating profit, but having too much cash can mean that the company is not deploying its assets to maximize profitability. Assessing a business's cash position and its ability to meet current liabilities guides a business owner in making decisions about how best to use the available cash.

Accounts receivable. In many types of business, customers have 30 days to pay a bill or invoice. While the company is waiting for the customer to pay, the outstanding balance appears on the balance sheet as an account receivable. As a measure of financial health, analysts often look at accounts receivable as a percentage of revenues. For some businesses a small accounts receivable as percent of sales shows that the enterprise is quickly collecting on its sales. Yet this can also mean that the company is forgoing sales due to its tight credit terms compared to competitors.

When dealing with accounts receivable, a business also needs to develop an aging schedule to monitor the timeliness of payments by customer. Because of the cost

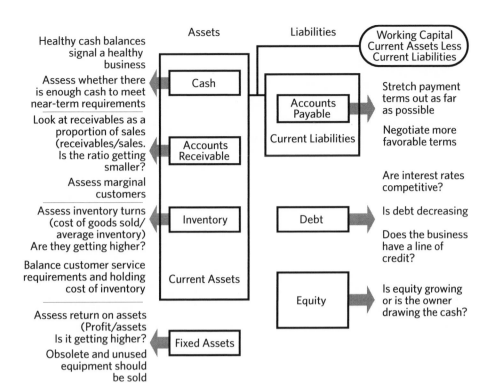

Assets

Liabilities

Working Capital
Current Assets Less
Current Liabilities

FIGURE 6-10. Balance
Sheet Analysis

Healthy cash balances
signal a healthy
business
Assess whether there
is enough cash to meet
near-term requirements

Cash

Look at receivables as a
proportion of sales
(receivables/sales.
Is the ratio getting
smaller?
Assess marginal
customers

Accounts
Receivable

Accounts
Payable

Current Liabilities

Stretch payment
terms out as far
as possible

Negotiate more
favorable terms

Assess inventory turns
(cost of goods sold/
average inventory)
Are they getting higher?

Inventory

Debt

Are interest rates
competitive?

Is debt decreasing

Does the business
have a line of
credit?

Balance customer service
requirements and holding
cost of inventory

Current Assets

Equity

Is equity growing
or is the owner
drawing the cash?

Assess return on assets
(Profit/assets
Is it getting higher?
Obsolete and unused
equipment should
be sold

Fixed Assets

to the business in financing accounts receivables, slow-paying customers may actually be unprofitable. If this is the case, the business should explore the potential of raising prices, altering credit terms, or discontinuing business with a particular customer.

Inventory. Most businesses want to fill orders quickly. To satisfy this customer service requirement, the business needs to have product on hand to ship to its customers as quickly as possible when orders comes in. Products or parts waiting to be assembled are kept in inventory in anticipation of these orders. On the other hand, companies may try to keep very little inventory because there are financing, maintenance, insurance, and administrative costs to keeping inventory. Striking an effective balance between maintaining high service levels and holding down costs is important in any business.

Inventory is sometimes measured by days of sales it will support. The fewer the number of days, the more efficient the company is, yet too few runs the risk of not being able to deliver products to a customer. Inventory turns is another measure used to determine inventory efficiency. Cost of goods sold divided by average inventory (inventory levels may be seasonal) gives inventory turns. A higher rate of inventory turns means that the company is operating at higher levels of efficiency.

Working capital. Working capital refers to current assets such as receivables and inventory less current liabilities. While this is not a balance sheet ratio, it is often computed to determine the business's cash requirements.

Fixed assets. These are buildings and equipment that the company owns and uses to make money. Fixed assets need to be productive. Assets that do not generate money tie up capital that could be used elsewhere and usually have financing and holding costs. While all companies need some level of fixed assets, a consultant can help a business owner determine the fixed assets that are necessary and those that aren't by analyzing the impact on the company's profitability if the asset were sold.

Accounts payable. Just as some customers get 30 days to pay their bills, so too do some businesses when they buy from vendors. Vendor payable accounts act as short-term financing for a business. Companies want to stretch this out as much as possible because it is an inexpensive way to borrow money, and others may want to pay early to receive discounts. A consultant can help a business owner determine the most profitable accounts payable strategy.

Debt. For each industry and each company there is an optimal level of debt as a percentage of equity. A consultant can help a business determine its debt-equity ratio, compare it to industry standards, and determine if the company is properly leveraged. A debt-equity ratio that is too high for a particular business can result in an inability to pay creditors, while a ratio that is too low means the business is using expensive equity financing rather than relatively low-cost debt financing. The debt-to-asset ratio (debt as a percent of total assets) can be used in the same way.

Equity. Equity, net worth, or book value is what the company is worth according to its books or balance sheet. Equity is what the business owner or other investors put into the company and any earnings the company keeps or retains to grow the business. Sole proprietors may draw from retained earnings rather than take a salary.

Bankers and investors look for book value to grow, signaling that the business owners are interested in reinvesting earnings to grow the business rather than drawing the cash for themselves. If the business is going to be sold, book value will be one of the determining factors in what price it gets.

Cash Flow Analysis

In larger enterprises, the cash flow statement is used to differentiate where cash is generated and for what it is being used. Cash flow is also used to determine whether the enterprise can meet its debt obligations. It is sometimes used to verify the income statement, because accounting is complicated with many noncash items.

Small businesses are less complex in scope, investing activities, and capital structure, and often their income statements are very close to their cash flow. However, it is still important to complete a cash flow analysis to determine if the business will be able to meet its obligations in the future.

Operating cash flow. The cash flow statement starts with the company's net income and then adds back any expenses, such as depreciation, that are not cash. If the business needs more cash for working capital, that is added in. Making these adjustments gives the operating cash flow. Operating cash flow tells how much cash the business generates.

Bankers look at operating cash flow to determine if the business can support interest payments on the loan it has taken or will take. An interest coverage ratio (earnings before interest and taxes divided by interest payments) can be calculated to give an idea of how well the company can support its debt.

Providing credit to customers can often increase sales volume and is standard practice in some industries. The business needs to take the time to do credit checks before extending credit to a customer. Not extending credit does not mean a sale is lost. Most businesses require new customers with no credit rating to prepay for orders until credit is established. If credit is extended, the business should have a written credit policy and it should enforce it. Otherwise the business stands to lose more money on bad debts than it can bring in in sales. Written credit policies can speed debt collection when discounts are given for early payments. Small business studies have shown

FIGURE 6-11. Cash Flow Analysis

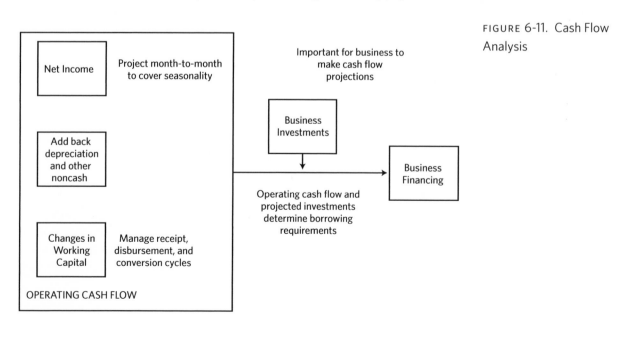

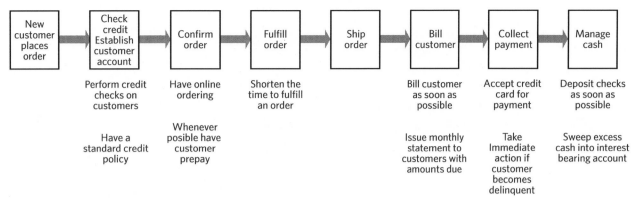

FIGURE 6-12. Managing Cash Flow: Receipt Cycle

a marked improvement in cash flow after credit policies were implemented.

Having an online ordering system can speed up the receipt cycle. In an enterprise, processing a purchase order can exceed $100 and extend over weeks. The longer it takes to process a purchase order, the slower the cash receipt from that order. Online ordering can be done 24 hours a day, seven days a week, and saves considerable administrative costs. Careful design of the online ordering system can eliminate errors and expedite ordering. Additionally, the business can provide extensive information on the product and save costly telephone inquiries.

Whenever possible, the business should have a customer prepay for an order or pay immediately upon receipt. Prepayment is standard for any industry where product is being customized for the customer. Because many fledgling businesses are creating unique products for their customers, it is possible to require prepayment or payment upon receipt.

If prepayment or payment upon receipt is not used, the business should bill the customer as soon as possible. Some firms will process and mail the invoice prior to shipping so that the invoice and the shipment will be received at the same time. It helps to maintain and monitor an accounts receivable aging report that shows money owed by the customer. The company should know which customers are most timely with payment. Late fees may be charged if payment is not received on time.

The company should have a debt collection procedure to insure that all debts are collected. Smaller businesses may be taken advantage of by customers who think small businesses do not have the resources to collect. The company should develop a system to collect debts. This includes sending monthly statements, late payment letters, and calling the customer. These are extremely effective in getting customers to pay.

Credit card systems provide timely cash turnaround and put the financing burden directly on the customer. Cost to set up credit card payment systems is sometimes seen as a barrier by small businesses. Setup costs are up to $500, and there is a cost of 10 cents per transaction, plus a monthly fee of about $10. Credit card companies charge from 1% to 2% of the purchase value. However, the ability to collect immediate payment without having the expense associated with staff time to collect debts can outweigh these costs.

A basic principle of cash management is to get it in the bank as soon as possible. The faster cash moves from the customer to the bank and into appropriate short-term investments, the better. Some small businesses consider a run to the bank every day a burdensome task and will collect checks over a few days. This has two drawbacks. First, money not in the bank does not generate interest. Second, this practice increases the possibility of loss or other bookkeeping problems. Once in the bank, large cash amounts can be swept into interest-bearing accounts. The business should work with a banker to insure that money does not accumulate without generating interest.

A small business should work very quickly to establish a good payment record so that it has a good credit history. This will allow the business to negotiate more favorable payment terms with creditors. Whenever possible the business should revisit these terms with the vendor. Often as a business grows and becomes more stable, better payment terms can be negotiated.

The business needs good receiving procedures so that payment is not made for a product that was not

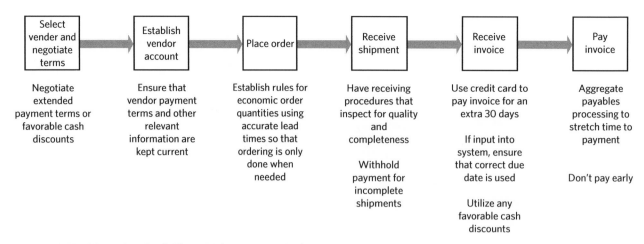

FIGURE 6-13. Managing Cash Flow: Disbursement Cycles

delivered. Once the invoice is received, accounts payable procedures should ensure that the business pays the invoice only when it is due. Some clerical staff will aggregate invoices and pay them weekly, often pulling in invoices that are due in a few days. Aggregating procedures should try to stretch time to payment out as long as possible without incurring penalties.

Managing the production process can do much to improve the cash flow within a business. Large enterprises like Dell have shown that changing the customer ordering process and working closely with vendors can cut production time. In most business models, the business makes a forecast of orders and manufactures to inventory according to the forecast. If the forecast is wrong, costs are incurred. If the forecast is too high, surplus inventory must be sold at deeply discounted prices. If the forecast is too low, expediting orders can cause production costs to go sky high.

Developing a business model in which goods are not manufactured until ordered can save considerable

expense and makes business sense if customers are willing to wait for their order. This strategy often involves working closely with vendors to reduce the lead time for getting raw materials. Establishing online ordering with vendors and having the ability to check their inventory via the web can assist in saving time in the production cycle.

Additionally, carefully controlling inventory so that only frequently turning items are stocked reduces the amount of money that is tied up in financing and maintaining inventory. In terms of the labor force, a core labor force with additional contract labor for peak times can save on labor costs, though it can reduce quality in some industries that require high skills.

Lack of tax planning and not filing tax returns in a timely manner is a sign of poor organization. Among business owners filing for bankruptcy, 20% gave the cause as problems with the IRS. Procrastination can be the downfall of small business owners. Taking the time to file the taxes gives the business a chance to review its performance for the year. Additionally, most bankers

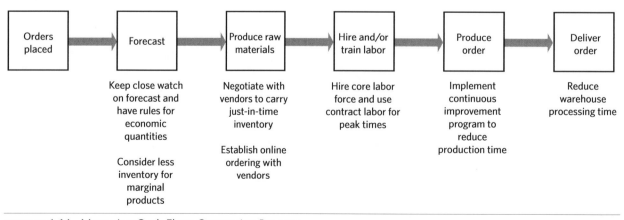

FIGURE 6-14. Managing Cash Flow: Conversion Process

look to timely filing of taxes as the first sign of financial responsibility.

Accounting and Financial Metrics

In addition to the financial analysis above, the student team may want to calculate the following ratios to determine trends in the company's financial performance:

- Horizontal analysis. Analysis of the growth rates (percent change from previous year) of revenues and net income for the company gives an indication about trends in the company's revenues and profits.
- Profitability.There are several measures of profitability. Merchandising firms typically examine gross margin or gross profit ratio (net revenues minus cost of sales divided by net revenues). This profit ratio indicates if a merchandising company is purchasing product effectively and getting a good price.
- Current, quick, and working capital. Current ratio (current assets divided by current liabilities) and quick ratio (current assets minus inventor divided by current liabilities) are liquidity measures and thus show the company's ability to meet its obligations.
- Inventory turnover. Inventory turnover (COGS divided by average inventory) measures how often a company sells its inventory.
- Receivables. Receivables turnover (net receivable sales divided by average net receivables) is a measure of the times, on average, that receivables are collected.
- Payables. Payables turnover is calculated by taking average payables and dividing by COGS. Payables days are calculated by taking 360 days and dividing by payables turnover. Typically a company will negotiate or take full advantage of any credit terms it receives.
- Debt-to-asset ratio. The debt-asset ratio (total debt divided by total assets) measures the amount of the company's assets that are a result of debt.

FINANCIAL PROJECTIONS

The consulting team may develop recommendations that involve both increased revenues and increased expenses. In small business consulting, financial projections that support the proposed expenditures or expected revenues should be in the final report.

Inherent in any projection is the risk that assumptions about revenues or expenses may not be accurate or per-fectly predictable. The risk of inaccurate assumptions is higher for smaller businesses than for larger firms, so special care should be taken in producing a financial pro forma for a small business.

Opportunity. The first order of business is to assess the size of the opportunity. This is best done by conducting the market and business research described earlier in this book. Potential revenues figure prominently in the financial projections. It is important to get evidence to support these projections. It is also important to be realistic about the business's chances. Even if the market potential is large and the opportunity looks attractive, if there are competitors it is unlikely that the business will be able to get a large share of the market.

Time frame. Projections for investments should be made to the end of the useful life of the investment. Many IT systems become outdated in three years, so financial analyses of computers and software should extend to three years. Other investments—for example, buildings and equipment—can extend further. The key for a consultant is to determine the length of the investment's value. The longer it takes to pay back the investment, the harder it is to project sales and expenses with any amount of certainty.

Gathering the numbers. Fledgling business owners with few resources are often more concerned with downside risk than with upside potential. They rarely invest large amounts of money in new opportunities. Instead they iterate their way to success with small investments.

The key to maximizing opportunities is to project the revenues accurately and ensure that all costs and risks are captured. Take the case of a small business considering e-commerce. When focusing on costs, the costs are first divided between the up-front investment and ongoing costs. In the example illustrated in Table 6-4, $10,000 is budgeted to develop the site and catalog, and an additional $5,000 is budgeted in one-time marketing costs.

Next, the cost of goods sold is examined. Although the business may have a storefront, the cost of goods sold may be different on the e-commerce site, because there may be additional costs in packaging, handling, and shipping and reduced costs in warehousing the inventory.

Selling on the Internet involves a new way of marketing to the customer. There are affiliate programs, new

Green Cleaning Seattle

The Triple Bottom Line

In 2006, Gea Bassett was completing a master's program in education. With just $25 and a prepaid cell phone, she started cleaning homes to earn extra money. It did not take long before she hired her first employee because of rapidly growing demand. By graduation, Bassett realized that this was a promising career opportunity. She focused her efforts exclusively on her new company, Green Cleaning Seattle—Eco-Maid Services™, which offers a variety of eco-friendly cleaning services

Why green? Bassett worked at Natural Foods when she was a teen; the experience sparked an interest in environmentally friendly products. She is intent on reducing pollution and chemicals in the environment, while supporting the local economy. For example, clients are grouped by location to reduce drive time. Bassett also recognized the high demand for green cleaning in the environmentally conscious Pacific Northwest, as well as a growing demand among parents and pet owners for chemical-free home cleaning products.

Bassett realizes the importance of delegating tasks. She primarily focuses her efforts on marketing and business operations. As with many new startups, her marketing budget was small; she initially used Craig's List and Google Ad Words to promote her business. In 2009, Green Cleaning was the second business in Seattle to be featured in Groupon. With very little competition in green cleaning at the time, she sold about 285 deals. The increased awareness due to this promotion was a turning point for the company. Today Bassett works exclusively with local advertisers.

Bassett focuses on developing and retaining employees. She offers flexible working hours to her employees with set days on, weekends off, and work days that end at 5 p.m. She uses a standard pay scale, paying more for longer-term employees. She has a handbook and policies to guide employees and two lead cleaners to provide supervision. All cleaning products are provided; employees are not allowed to use clients' products. She also takes the time to review client evaluations each week.

Bassett has grown her company through internal sources of capital and has strategically hired employees. Most of her company's revenues come through cash payments and from having only cleaning products as inventory and vacuum cleaners as assets; accounting is straightforward.

In 2011, a team of student consultants worked with Bassett to enhance her financial acumen. Although Bassett had recently hired an accountant, the students recommended that she strengthen her own accounting skills. They provided her with templates, including a step-by-step process on how to input data and calculate common financial ratios. The students reviewed her pricing strategy, created a model to forecast future growth, and calculated key financial metrics to be monitored. She implemented several of their recommendations, including changes to her website, building team spirit, and enhancing her employee incentive package.

Bassett attributes perseverance, creativity, and an interest in the local economy as her keys to success. She emphasizes the ethics behind the business. Green Cleaning's projected revenues for 2011 are nearly $390,000, with approximately 17 employees—impressive growth for a $25 initial investment.

TABLE 6-4. Sample Upfront and Variable Costs

	Year 0	Year 1	Year 2	Year 3
	Upfront Costs			
Marketing	5,000			
Site development	10,000			
Revenues		50,000	75,000	100,000
Cost of goods (50%)		25,000	37,500	50,000
Gross margin		25,000	37,500	50,000
Expenses		Costs by Year		
Hosting		3,000	3,300	3,630
Advertising		2,500	5,000	7,500
Ongoing maintenance		1,000	1,100	1,210
Personnel		10,000	11,000	20,000
Profit	-15,000	8,500	17,100	17,660

promotional programs, and advertisements that have to be developed. Additionally, there are site maintenance and hosting costs.

Once the costs have been determined for the first year, projections have to be made into the future. For some costs, such as hosting costs, the business might add an estimated cost increase based on a multiyear hosting contract or an analysis of past years' trends in hosting cost increases. Other costs, such as personnel, behave in a not strictly variable or step function way—they take a jump (additional person needed) when they hit a certain level of sales.

Payback Period

This is the simplest measure of return on investment and calculates the time to break even. With the investment of $15,000 in the example above, take the profit for each year and determine in what year the investment will be recouped. In this case, the payback period occurs in the second year. The year 1 profit of $8,500 plus the year 2

profit of $17,100 equals $25,600, which covers the original $15,000 invested.

When using the payback period of analysis, the faster the payback period, the better the investment is determined to be. Some enterprises require 18-month payback periods for certain levels of investment. While large enterprises, which focus on net present value calculations to make investment decisions, do not put much credence on payback, small businesses with scarce money resources and tight cash flow find that the payback period, simple as it is, is the main criterion for a go or no-go decision on an investment.

Net Present Value

Net present value (NPV) gives the size of the return from the investment. It incorporates the time value of money and the cost of capital to a firm. It is a tool to use in determining the long-term profitability of an investment. To construct an NPV analysis, a consultant will first determine the profit from each year in which a new product is available as a result of the investment. Following this, the profit from years beyond the first one are discounted back using this cost of capital. When the calculation is performed on the example in Table 6-5, the net present value is $21,586.

For small businesses, the cost of capital or discount rate is typically the interest rate they are charged for a bank loan. For large enterprises, the cost of capital is typically a weighted average of their borrowing costs and the cost of equity.

Net present value allows the business to evaluate whether the initial investment in the effort of setting up an e-commerce site is worth the return it will receive over three years.

Return on Investment

Return on investment (ROI) evaluates the results of an investment without factoring in the time value of money.

TABLE 6-5. Sample Net Present Value Analysis

	Year 0	Year 1	Year 2	Year 3
Investment	15,000			
Profit		8,500	17,100	17,660
Calculation of present value		$8,500/(1+0.08)^1$	$17,100/(1+0.08)^2$	$17,660/(1+0.08)^3$
Present value	$ (15,000.00)	$7,870.37	$13,574.53	$15,140.60
				$21,586
	Net Present Value			
	(-15,000 + 7,870.37 + 13,574.53 + 15,140.60)			

It is a useful way to help a small business decide between two different investments of the same size. To calculate an ROI, simply sum the total profits over a given period and divide this by the dollar amount of the investment.

TABLE 6-6. Sample Return on Investment Analysis

	Year 0	Year 1	Year 2	Year 3
Investment	15,000			
Profit		8,500	17,100	17,660
Return on Investment				288%
(8,500 + 17,100 + 17,660) / 15,000				

The drawback of ROI is that large projects are not differentiated from small projects. Also, it does not give any measure of how long it takes to achieve that return.

Internal Rate of Return

The internal rate of return (an iteration process) finds a yield that fits future earnings to the investment today. This is relevant when comparing investments against each other.

Internal rate of return does not give the magnitude of the investment or what the investment will bring in dollars to the business. Another drawback is that if there is zero cash flow in any year, the calculation does not work.

TABLE 6-7. Sample Internal Rate of Return Analysis

	Year 0	Year 1	Year 2	Year 3
Investment	15000			
Profit	-15,000	8500	17100	17660
Rate of Return (calculation iterates a return that fits the cash flow)				67%

Sensitivity Analysis

To anticipate the uncertainty of future revenues and expenses, most financial projections will include a view of different scenarios. The direction of this analysis should be to anticipate what downside risk the investment brings as well as the impact on the business should sales exceed expectations. When sensitivity analysis is done, the business owner and consultant are asking "what if" questions. What if sales do not take off? What if marketing expenses are higher? What if it costs more to buy the product? What if ongoing maintenance is higher? What if sales are higher than expected and I need to hire new staff?

In the example shown in Table 6-8, the analysis does some sensitivity analysis on the level of sales and the amount of advertising expenditures. This analysis shows that the business stands to lose $25,000 in the worst-case scenario.

Taking into consideration all the likely scenarios, the business owner can plot a distribution of the expected returns with assigned probabilities. Analyzing this distribution, the business owner can decide whether the investment is worth the risk.

Financial Plan for a New Business Opportunity

All entrepreneurs benefit from starting a business with a plan. Most investors and lenders know that the key people in the business are the main determinants of its success. They will look for people who are experienced in the industry and who have a track record of success. Usually these people are very cognizant of the business model, industry benchmarks, how to manage risk, and how to increase profitability.

In this example, the new business is a restaurant. Although student consulting teams rarely work with a start-up business, their work often involves evaluating a new business or product line. Compiling the financial plan would be similar to a financial plan for a new business. The financial plan will start with a detailed listing of the start-up costs. An entrepreneur knowledgeable about the restaurant industry knows what costs to include and how to minimize them. New entrepreneurs might spend more up front and take longer to generate sales. This is illustrated by the S-curve for experienced and inexperienced entrepreneurs shown in Table 6-9. As consultants, it is important to advise the business on how to minimize up-front costs without compromising quality and ramp up sales as quickly as possible to hit breakeven. Any new venture is risky. Adopting such a strategy will mitigate the risk to some extent.

Next, a detailed month-by-month projection of the income statement is prepared (see Table 6-10). Note that it is helpful to follow this conventional format when compiling the projections. The data collected start with daily projections of the number of covers or meals served and the average price of a meal. This comprises the unit sales and price data needed to calculate revenues. This is further multiplied by the number of days in a month to come up with the monthly unit sales. The business owner should be a good source for this information.

TABLE 6-8. Sample Sensitivity Analysis

Most Likely Case	Year 0	Year 1	Year 2	Year 3
Marketing	5,000			
Site development	10,000			
Revenues		50,000	75,000	100,000
Cost of goods (50%)		25,000	37,500	50,000
Gross margin		2,5000	37,500	50,000
Expenses				
Hosting		3,000	3,300	3,630
Advertising		2,500	5,000	7,500
Ongoing maintenance		1,000	1,100	1,210
Personnel		10,000	11,000	20,000
Profit	-15,000	8,500	17,100	17,660
Present value	-15,000	$7,870	$13,574	$15,140
Net present value	$21,585			
Worst-Case Scenario	**Year 0**	**Year 1**	**Year 2**	**Year 3**
Marketing	5,000			
Site development	10,000			
Revenues		30,000	45,000	50,000
Cost of goods (50%)		15,000	22,500	25,000
Gross margin		15,000	22,500	25,000
Expenses				
Hosting		3,000	3,300	3,630
Advertising		5,000	7,500	7,500
Ongoing maintenance		1,000	1,100	1,210
Personnel		10,000	11,000	20,000
Profit	-15,000	-4,000	-400	-7,340
Present value	-15,000	-$3,703	-$317	$6,292
Net present value	-25,314			
Best-Case Scenario	**Year 0**	**Year 1**	**Year 2**	**Year 3**
Marketing	5,000			
Site development	10,000			
Revenues		75,000	125,000	200,000
Cost of goods (50%)		37,500	62,500	100,000
Gross margin		37,500	62,500	100,000
Expenses				
Hosting		3,000	3,300	3,630
Advertising		2,500	5,000	7,500
Ongoing maintenance		1,000	1,100	1,210
Personnel		10,000	11,000	20,000
Profit	-15,000	21,000	42,100	67,660
Present value	-15,000	19,444	33,420	58,007
Net present value	$95,872.32			

TABLE 6-9. Sample Start-up Costs for a Restaurant

Start-up Costs	
Security	$10,000.00
Construction rent	10,000.00
Construction utilities	2,000.00
Licenses	5,000.00
Deposits	2,500.00
Marketing	5,000.00
Printing	5,000.00
Architects	10,000.00
Legal	3,000.00
Inventory	10,000.00
Furniture, fixtures	75,000.00
Leasehold improvements	60,000.00
Other	35,000.00
	$232,500.00

Seasonality has been incorporated in these projections, and this can affect cash requirements. In this case, the restaurant is assumed to have more revenue during the summer months. Payroll is projected from the number of workers needed, the hours they will work, and the appropriate pay rate. Other expenses are projected based on market rates or by accessing comparable financials from services like www.bizstats.com. The amount of detail necessary to make valid projections is critical. Student teams that are new to financial analysis can call on their mentors, advisors, and faculty to guide them through how to gather costs for financial projections.

After projections are compiled and verified, the expenses as a percentage of sales are compared to the industry benchmarks. In this case, a return on sales of about 5.7% is very close to the benchmark for restaurants with $1 million in revenues.

Adding back the depreciation and amortization, it appears that the business will have about $77,000 to pay interest and debt. The financial projection should factor in a ramp-up period when customers are just getting to know the restaurant; sales in the first few months will thus be less than they are when the restaurant is established. With many restaurants there is also a seasonality to sales, where December typically has a higher sales volume than January, for example. To cover the ramp-up period and the seasonality of sales, the business needs a cash reserve. If the business is able to achieve the projections used in this example, the payback period will be about five years.

Breakeven

In evaluating the investment, the concept of breakeven is important. Breakeven is defined as the time when total invested costs (both start-up and operating) equals the amount of revenue received. The breakeven is noted as the time when investment + operating expenses = total revenue.

For the small business, it is equally important to determine a breakeven on year-to-year or even month-

TABLE 6-10. First-year Projections - New Restaurant

Month	1	2	3	4	5	6
Seasonality	6%	6%	8%	10%	10%	8%
Covers	4,020	4,020	5,360	6,700	6,700	5,360
Revenues	60,300	60,300	80,400	100,500	100,500	80,400
Cost of Goods	24,120	24,120	32,160	40,200	40,200	32,160
Gross Profit	36,180	36,180	48,240	60,300	60,300	48,240
Management (Fixed)	3,350	3,350	3,350	3,350	3,350	3,350
Salaries and Benefits	13,266	13,266	17,688	22,110	22,110	17,688
Rents (Fixed)	5,443	5,443	5,443	5,443	5,443	5,443
Advertising	1,675	1,675	1,675	1,675	1,675	1,675
Other Expenses	11,474	11,474	11,474	11,474	11,474	11,474
Depreciation and amortization	1,675	1,675	1,675	1,675	1,675	1,675
Taxes	3,433	3,433	3,433	3,433	3,433	3,433
Total Operating Expenses	40,316	40,316	44,738	49,160	49,160	44,738
Net Profit	-4,136	-4,136	3,502	11,140	11,140	3,502

to-month fixed costs. In this way, the business can aim for the revenues (usually translated to the number of customers) it takes to get to breakeven and keep the business viable by having that sales goal in mind.

In the case of the new restaurant, it is helpful to calculate breakeven meals that need to be sold on a monthly basis. A monthly goal for meals helps the entrepreneur focus on profitability and take action as needed to increase the number of customers. To do this, break out monthly fixed costs. This includes rent, utilities, a core staff, marketing costs, and other costs that will be there as long as the business is open. In this case, assume that fixed costs are about $40,000 before depreciation and amortization.

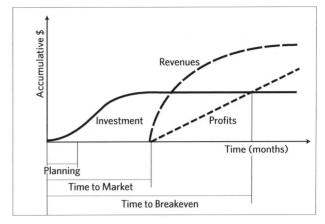

FIGURE 6-15. Breakeven Analysis

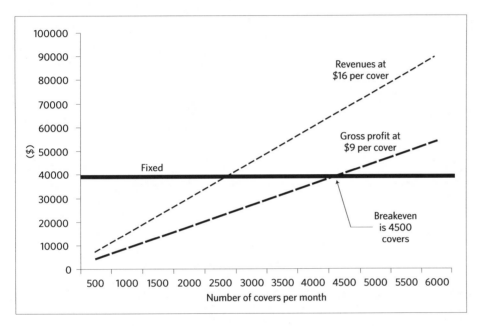

FIGURE 6-16. New Restaurant Breakeven Analysis

TABLE 6-10 (cont.)

7	8	9	10	11	12	Annual Total	
6%	8%	8%	10%	10%	10%		
4,020	5,360	5,360	6,700	6,700	6,700	67,000	Average Meal $15
60,300	80,400	80,400	100,500	100,500	100,500	1,005,000	
24,120	32,160	32,160	40,200	40,200	40,200	402,000	40%
36,180	48,240	48,240	60,300	60,300	60,300	603,000	60%
3,350	3,350	3,350	3,350	3,350	3,350	40,200	4%
13,266	17,688	17,688	22,110	22,110	22,110	221,100	22%
5,443	5,443	5,443	5,443	5,443	5,443	65,316	7%
1,675	1,675	1,675	1,675	1,675	1,675	20,100	2%
11,474	11,474	11,474	11,474	11,474	11,474	137,688	14%
1,675	1,675	1,675	1,675	1,675	1,675	20,100	2%
3,433	3,433	3,433	3,433	3,433	3,433	41,196	4%
40,316	44,738	44,738	49,160	49,160	49,160	545,700	54%
-4,136	3,502	3,502	11,140	11,140	11,140	57,300	6%

A gross profit of about $40,000 would be required to break even. Working backward from a 60% gross profit or $9 per cover, it is calculated that 4,500 covers or meals will be the breakeven number. (See Figure 6-16.)

OTHER TOOLS

Pareto Principle

Many business owners use a rule of thumb that 80% of the sales come from 20% of the customers. The rule of thumb, called the Pareto principle or the 80-20 rule, applies to other aspects of business as well. For example, 80% of sales may also come from 20% of inventory items. By classifying data into categories, it is possible to analyze a business and determine where it should focus attention for the greatest impact. For a consultant, however, it will be important to determine if the 80-20 rule applies or if it is actually 70-30 for a particular business.

The Pareto principle is applied by gathering data on the problem in question. For example, a business wanting to increase efficiency by reducing the number of calls to customer service could decide to log all calls and record the reason for the call for a two-week period. At the end of two weeks, a frequency bar chart could be constructed to present the data. If it turns out that 80% of the calls are from people who have lost instruction manuals, the business can then create a system where people can retrieve instructions via the web, saving considerable expense in the customer service area.

Inventory is another area where Pareto principle analysis is fruitful. In the case of a Thai gift shop, the owner was able to determine that of 14,000 items sold, 271 items (or 2% of all items) yielded 19% of profit for the store. The recommendations of the student consulting team centered on increasing sales of those items.

Cost-Benefit Analysis

Often a quick and simple cost-benefit analysis is a key part of the business case. Financial analysis to determine if a strategy, solution, or program generates more cash than it will cost is basic to most consulting projects. Yet it is surprising how often this analysis is left until the end of data gathering.

Basically, cost-benefit analysis takes the acquisition (fixed) costs of an investment and the projected benefits or cash flow generated and determines whether any financial benefit will be derived. A more extensive cost-benefit analysis will incorporate intangible benefits such as improved customer service, better competitive position, or better information. The example given in Table 6-11 covers the experience of a firm purchasing a special sweeper-blower truck to be used in parking lot cleaning.

Fishbone Diagram

Kaoru Ishikawa, a management consultant and professor, developed the fishbone diagram for cause-and-effect analysis. This is a technique used to explore all possible causes of a problem back to its root cause. Its value is that solutions will not focus on the first level of causes, which sometimes may be symptoms. For reasons of its uses and design, it is also called a cause-and-effect diagram.

The first step is to name or identify the problem. Second, suggest all possible causes for the problem. Next, suggest causes for the causes. This process can be repeated until the root causes are identified. In Figure 6-17, slow service is a problem with an African American fast-food restaurant. Notice that there are three main causes of the slow response time in delivering orders and within each there are further causes. Once identified, it becomes possible to "fix" the problem by correcting the causes. In this case, short staffing is a major cause. This in turn is caused by absenteeism and lack of motivation among the staff. By implementing a program to measure staff productivity and giving incentives for good service, the problem of slow service was resolved.

Force-Field Analysis

When working with small businesses, the proper identification of key issues does not always happen prior to the start of a consulting project. The force-field technique will be modified to help student teams identify key issues that need to be addressed.

Identifying issues. During this step, group members list all the issues facing the company. Student consultants are encouraged to include all the issues regardless of whether they are part of the scope of work for the consulting project. Student consultants may have discovered a key issue that the client might not be aware of that needs to be addressed. These issues should be listed on a flip chart or whiteboard so the entire group can see the list.

A student consulting team helped an African American–owned temporary employment company determine how to grow its market share. The company was in a catch-22 situation where they could not gain more clients

TABLE 6-11. Comparisons of Main Uses of Cost-Benefit Analysis

Purchase of a Special Truck

	Cost	Benefits	Financial Analysis
One time	Purchase or financing of a new cleaning truck costs $125,000.	Trade-in price received from an old truck (if any) or increased efficiency of the new vehicle (i.e., lower fuel costs, increase speed of project completion that reduces staff expenses)	Cash sufficient to cover purchase or cash flow sufficient to cover financing.
Continuing	Cost of maintaining, financing, and using the new truck in excess of the cost of the old truck. Depreciation of truck.	Increased revenue.	Net present value, return on investment, and internal rate of return may be used.
Time	Useful life of the new truck.	Longer life of the new truck.	Payback period.
Other factors	No increase in customers prompts competitive response (pricing), recession, quality issues, start-up problems.	High-quality service, customer satisfaction, customer retention, efficiencies with other product lines.	May not be included in financial analysis.

without hiring more employees, but they could not recruit enough workers to sign up with them without getting more clients. The team completed research among both potential workers and potential clients. The team members then met to analyze their research data and found that gaining new workers by focusing on recent university graduates was relatively easier than finding new business clients. By growing their pool of educated workers looking for placement, the company was able to leverage this into gaining new clients in knowledge-based industries.

Enumerating forces. Once the one or two key issues have been identified, the student consulting team should brainstorm two lists: one that will identify the forces that will drive the company to change and the other that will identify the forces holding back the change. It is important that the first step in this stage of analysis is brainstorming.

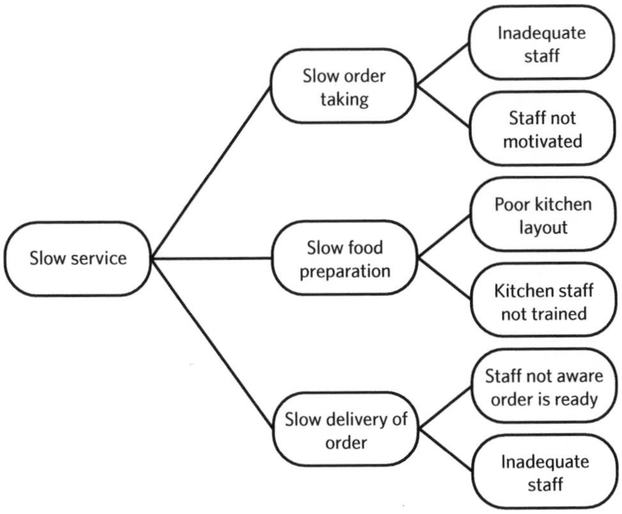

Clarifying forces. The goal of this step is to insure that all team members understand the concepts developed during the brainstorming session. The next step is to rank order the forces, so it is critical that all team members share an understanding of the list. If additional forces need to be listed to encompass all ideas, they should be included on the list.

Determining critical forces. Once all the possible forces are listed, the team should discuss the information gathered that either supports or refutes the inclusion of a force on the list. If there is insufficient data to warrant keeping a force on the list, it should either be removed from consideration or set aside for further investigation. When critical forces are determined, the student team may look at forces that restrain or work against the driving forces. This helps clarify what prevents the business from being successful in pursuing its strategies.

Now that the team has collectively narrowed down the list of driving and restraining forces to those that are supported by collected information, the team can use a variety of strategies. Using a five-point Likert scale, each team member ranks the importance of the force from 5 (very influential) to 1 (no force). If driving forces receive a cumulatively higher score than the restraining forces, the

FIGURE 6-17. Fishbone Diagram

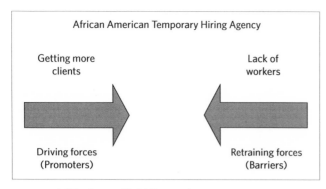

African American Temporary Hiring Agency

Getting more clients

Lack of workers

Driving forces (Promoters)

Retraining forces (Barriers)

FIGURE 6-18. Force-Field Example

team knows that accelerating change can most easily be accomplished by further strengthening the driving forces.

Using the Likert scale can also help determine which of the possible forces is most influential. In the temporary employment company example above, the students found that strengthening the knowledge about this company among university students preparing to graduate was the single most powerful factor for improving the company's ability to grow market share. They determined not only that the relative financial and time cost of reaching students was low but that the level of receptivity to information on employment opportunities was very high.

Benchmarking

Comparing a business with other businesses in the same industry, or *benchmarking*, is an important analysis for any business to perform. It can be done by gathering key financial ratios such as gross margin, profit margin, inventory turnover, receivables turnover, return on capital, return on equity, and revenues per employee. Benchmarking is not limited to financial data. Other key indicators to measure are new products developed, marketing programs, and distribution systems. Large enterprises might benchmark efficiency measures such as the number of transactions per employees in functions such as accounting and customer service.

When benchmarking, the business must be compared to similar businesses in terms of industry and size. Financial ratios for common businesses are available at websites such as bizstats.com. Some industry associations keep these statistics for their member businesses. A restaurant owned and run by a sole proprietor with $300,000 in annual sales would be benchmarked against similar-sized restaurants. It would not be compared to Starbucks or other large enterprises that have hundreds

of millions in revenues, nor would it be compared to a restaurant with annual sales of $75,000.

Such a comparison may yield areas of cost savings. For example, Figure 6-19 benchmarked an Indian restaurant against industry statistics for similar-sized restaurants. The restaurant was found to be high on both the cost of food and its payroll. This led the consulting team to recommend that the restaurant schedule waitstaff only when needed. It also pointed to the need for more spending on marketing.

Benchmarking can help the business set goals to help it become more competitive. For example, a business might have profit margins of 7%, but benchmarking lets it know that the best businesses in its industry have profit margins of 10%. The business can now set higher goals. Benchmarking can also point to strengths and weaknesses that should be exploited or corrected, respectively.

Best Practices

A best-practices analysis operates on the principle that the business should not reinvent the wheel. Taking the best company in the industry, it is possible to discern practices that are successful and implement these. For example, a visit to a successful competitor will give information on how it treats customers. Such a visit might reveal that customers are always greeted by name, that each salesperson has a complete history on customer sales, and that customer requests are dealt with quickly.

Best practices might also involve the deployment of specific technology. They might consider production processes or could revolve around how employees are compensated or rewarded. Generally the focus on this approach is to push firms to higher levels of performance. In the highest forms of practice, high-level firms would be referred to as being "world class." This might be well beyond a small or medium-sized firm. But the goal could still be to reach beyond other firms in their localized markets.

Secondary research and analysis could well identify performance goals and expectations that are appropriate for the client. If substantiated as true standards of the industry, they could be considered as part of the decision making that could be adopted by the client.

Organizational Analysis

Organizational analysis may be as straightforward as reviewing the skill sets of all the employees and determining whether all the skill sets needed to advance the

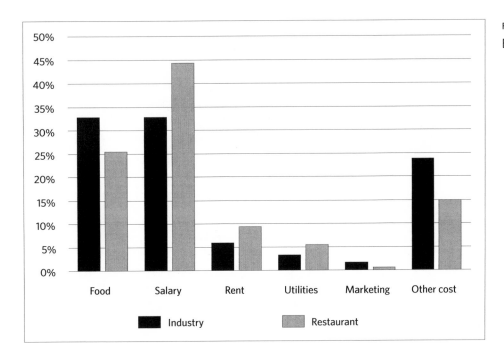

FIGURE 6-19. Benchmarking Business Costs

business are present. Sometimes employees may have to be reassigned or a new organizational structure developed. Operating procedures and policies may need to be standardized. Other organizational analysis may determine organizational readiness for technology adoption or other kinds of change. Organizational analysis may determine that the business needs training and education to succeed in its mission.

EVALUATING ALTERNATIVES

Once the critical issues are defined and agreed upon among the consulting team members (including faculty and advisors) and between the team and the client, the team enters the stage where it develops courses of action. A good action plan will specify what action, by whom, a time frame, what resources, and how performance will be measured. Since nearly all problems can be solved or opportunities capitalized on in multiple ways, alternative responses or solutions must be devised. This phase is a time when the client can be involved in the process. Since buy-in from the client is needed, it is important to get a sense of his or her risk tolerance, priorities in performance outcomes, and other factors that can influence the acceptance potential and feasibility of later implementation. Assessing a range of alternatives also forces the consulting team to test the strength of what will be included in its final recommendations. At the end of this process, the team should know and agree on the alternatives that will provide

the best solutions to the problems or opportunities that have been identified over the course of the consulting experience. How well this phase of the project is managed will in many ways be the ultimate test of how effective the consulting team will be as a change agent.

Recognize that in a typical management consulting situation there are many goals that a company is striving to achieve. However, given resource constraints, limited time, the priorities of management, and other factors, only a small number of actions or decision alternatives are likely to be effective in helping the company reach its goals. Whenever possible, stress that the criteria for evaluations should be measurable and quantifiable. Obviously in some areas this is more difficult to impose than in others. Some goals related to employee loyalty and commitment, for example, may be more difficult to assess than a comparison of wage rates and health benefits. The importance of "best customers" and "frequent buyers" may be quantifiable, but it may be more costly to actually measure than the turnover of high-margin products in a retail store. Make the comparison process as direct and cost-effective as possible.

A simple example of a descriptive method for comparing alternatives is presented in Figure 6-20. It is a plus-minus listing of alternatives with respect to selected criteria of interest; this clearly describes all the comparisons in descriptive and qualitative terms. They could be weighted or given a number so that choices or potential value could be calculated.

	Option A	Option B
Lowest startup cost	+	-
Lowest monthly operating cost	-	+
Highest sales volume	-	+
Least overhead	+	-

FIGURE 6-20. African American Service Company

In the case of the African American professional services company, shown in Figure 6-21, the consulting team needed to support the two best strategy choices for increasing sales revenue. The facilities cost for adding product lines along with the working capital requirements would amount to $8,000. Expected increases in sales over the course of a year would be under $4,000. It would take close to three years before the product development strategy would pay off.

Likewise, the diversification strategy would have required fees and other concessions that involved a $10,000 investment. But there was uncertainty over how well the response would be to a multiethnic clientele. Very likely it would have taken more than two years before sufficient revenue could have been produced. The team did not give a systematic estimate of payback expectation, and the owners were not enthusiastic about going outside the local community for attracting clientele in a service area that was new to the owners.

The team calculated that, using special offers to existing customers and building on relationships that were in place, the business could increase revenue on a monthly basis by $500–$1,000, and the price reductions would not exceed $400–$600 in lost revenue. The team estimated that within a year the market penetration strategy would generate $8,000–$10,000 in new revenue. The owners liked the festival idea. While it was unlikely to produce substantial revenue increases, it would provide community-wide exposure for the firm and at very low out-of-pocket costs.

The consulting team was able to present the ideas in terms that the clients understood and readily adopted. They decided to pursue marketing penetration and market development as their two main strategies for increasing customer flow and sales revenue.

Comparing alternatives is likely to provide stronger support for making recommendations to the business owner. These components are covered when using net present value and other financial analysis tools, but often it is necessary to lay out a simpler and more detailed analysis to educate and effectively communicate with the business owner.

The business owner for a manufacturing enterprise that creates labels for the food industry asked the consulting team to perform a feasibility study of purchasing a machine that would bring the business into a new market. With emerging businesses, the business owner often iterates his way to growth by evaluating opportunities in this way. The team's quick initial analysis suggested that the current sales infrastructure would not be able to break into the new market. It explored the possibility of using a broker to sell the product. The additional costs and benefits are presented in Table 6-12.

Once the alternatives have been compared, the team must go through a process of reaching consensus as to the "best alternatives" that will be presented to the client. Some kind of ranking and voting process should be devised. Weights assigned to different solutions will need to be evaluated with respect to what will ultimately be persuasive in getting the proposed solutions adopted. Often solutions obtained in this way count for less than what will ultimately get an adoption and buy-in from the client.

One further point: Recognize the importance of having confidence in the decision alternatives that are presented to the client. It is important that the consultant answer the following question positively: Were the

Current Products	New Products
Marketing Penetration Strategy	*Product Developmment Strategy*
Attract more Afro-centric customers through special lower prices and program membership (quarterly and monthly sessions)	Add product lines in scented and natural oils that have both male and female appeal
Market Development Strategy	*Diversification Strategy*
Increase market coverage by participating in community fairs and festivals	Partner with a fitness club to offer classes and other tension-reduction routines

Figue 6-21. Ansoff's Product/Market Expansion Strategy

TABLE 6-12. Option Analysis: New Equipment

	Current	With Broker	Increase
Benefits			
Monthly domestic sales	$90,000	$130,000	44%
Foreign sales	$10,000	$40,000	400%
Costs			
Production expense	$30,500	$41,000	34%
Production labor	$12,000	$12,000	0%
Sales staff expense	$40,000	$60,000	50%

best solutions the best possible, given the available information and circumstances? The selected solutions should be low cost/high benefit to the greatest extent possible.

Once the analysis has been completed, the team needs a method of determining the highest priority issues on which to focus. Often there is disagreement as to what they should be. It is important that the team discuss the issue and consider all points of view. At this point in the process, the greatest risk is to not give attention to innovative and creative solutions because the team is overwhelmed with data or fatigued with the issue. Here are a number of techniques to focus on the key items:

1. Rank order all ideas. If differences in rankings occur, discuss this fully.
2. Rank issues on a curve, with 1/6 as very important, 1/3 as important, 1/3 as somewhat important, and 1/6 as not important.
3. Create a matrix with the problems at the headings of both rows and columns. Rank the impact of solving the problem on all the other problems on a scale of zero (not at all likely) to nine (very likely). The problems with the highest scores are the source problems. Next highest are the secondary problems. The collateral problems have the lowest scores.

Remember that the goal is not to reach consensus, as often consensus is a suboptimal solution. The goal is to get to the best solution by fully considering all factors and feedback from team members. Then all team members must buy in to the direction the team has decided to pursue.

Focusing on Key Issues

Once all the data have been gathered and relevant analyses have been performed, it is the job of the team to begin focusing on key issues. In making business decisions, it is good to keep in mind the following:

1. Recognize pitfalls and biases in decision making. Too much ego involvement, excessive sense of ownership of a given idea or solution, and close-minded acceptance of a given tool or technique can misguide the process.
2. Be wary of using shortcuts and habit to guide decision making. They may be quick and easy to use but are likely to lead to more bad decisions than good ones.
3. Use rules of thumb when they are likely to support correct decisions. Average ratios or margins, generally accepted industry performance standards, or other rules of thumb may be appropriate for routine, frequently made decisions with low risk of much variability in outcomes. However, they should be evaluated critically and used selectively.
4. Make sure that the decision is directly linked to the specific problem(s) for which the analysis was completed. The right decision for the wrong problem is an obvious mismatch that should be avoided.
5. Process and integrate the best available data into the decision. These are the foundation of the analytical support for the decision.
6. Base decisions on an informed, rational choice-making process. Use a "bounded rationality" approach as a guide because it emphasizes analytical judgment based on facts, rational inferences, and consideration of other influences.
7. Recognize the value of intuition and creativity in the decision-making process. There are limits to analytical inferences and judgments. Insights and sound choice making can be formulated on hunches, imaginative insights, and other non-quantitative grounds.
8. Assess the value and impact of alternative decisions. Cross-check the analysis and results to ensure accuracy and consistency.
9. Evaluate expected outcomes and develop contingencies for the process. Recognize that assumptions can be inaccurate and that unpredicted and unexpected developments can block intended results.
10. Provide time, money, and other resources needed for implementation and follow-up on a decision to make sure that it produced the expected results. This should be done to make sure that the right decision was made and that corrections will be made as needed.

Prioritizing Findings and Analysis

The consulting team's research findings and analysis must be prioritized in order to make them understandable, acceptable, actionable, and usable for the client. A few guidelines should be of help to the consulting team. Group what has been done into general categories or topics, such as marketing, accounting, or finance. More specifically, the task could be problem focused on new customers, cash flow, increased services, reducing operational costs, etc. Using specific recommendations is another way of approaching the task. Getting suggestions from the faculty and mentors who have been there and done that should be helpful as well. Of course the team's own ideas are key. Based on the team's work and interactions with the client, what are the most persuasive or effective findings for what the team is proposing to the owner? Thinking along these lines should make a challenging task easier in gaining client buy-in and the implementation of the team's recommendations.

CREATING THE ACTION PLAN

Once the consulting team and the client have finalized a direction, the team needs to develop an action plan that will enable the company to reach its goals. Critical path analysis is an effective method of analyzing a complex project. It helps calculate the minimum length of time in which the project can be completed and which activities should be prioritized to complete by that date.

Critical path analysis recognizes that some activities in the plan will take longer than others, some activities in the plan are dependent on other activities being completed first, and the dependent activities need to be completed in a sequence, with each activity needing to be finished before the next activity can begin. To develop the critical path, the team would use the same procedure as in any project plan.

The basic concept is illustrated in the timed-layout of a human resource action plan shown in Figure 6-22. Whether using a formal critical path analysis or not, the team should be able to meet deadlines more consistently when tasks and activities are clearly delineated as to both people and time.

Action Steps

The ultimate test of a project's value will be determined by how well decisions and action steps are implemented by the client. Hence, it is very important that a detailed plan for decision implementation be articulated. Be clear about what the proposed action will require of the client, how the action taken is to be directed and measured, and what markers there will be to measure results. The business owner must know what is expected and how to determine what is, and is not, working over the course of decision implementation. In addition, the client or someone designated by her should be accountable for implementation. Therefore timelines, budgets, cash flow projections, or other measurement and control tools must be identified as part of the implementation process. If this is not done properly, it makes accountability and follow-up impossible.

If the client has been properly involved in the entire process, there should be approval and acceptance. But recognize that implementation of decisions will involve change. Some of those in the business who will be affected by the change are likely to resist it. This should be anticipated as an aspect of the implementation plan. In this regard, some measure of cooperation and incen-

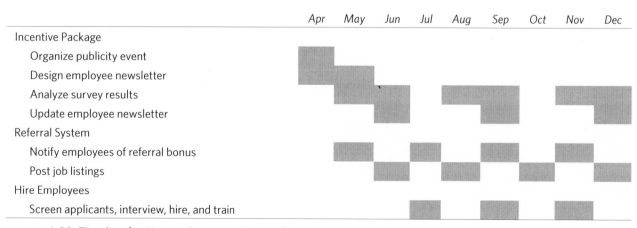

FIGURE 6-22. Timeline for Human Resource Action Plan

tives for participation will be needed. Overall, the benefits and gains to the individuals and to the firm are likely to be important in gaining acceptance and support.

Realistically, very few things in business are certain. Contingency should be built in for adjustments to the unexpected and some possible contingencies in the event that expectations are not met. The prospect of failure must be considered. Give thought to how the contingencies can be built into decision implementation. With such a consideration, the most relevant bases of decision implementation should have been covered.

In laying out the course of action, use these questions as a guideline:

1. What should the new arrangements/actions achieve? What level of performance? What quality of output?
2. How will the new situation differ from the old? Will there be different products, services, or activities, different processes, different equipment, different locations?
3. Are the effects likely to last? Are the business and the target market changing so quickly that there may not be a need for the new product or service? Is there the possibility that people will revert to present practices?
4. What difficulties will arise in implementation? Will there be employee resistance or shortage of materials or other resources?
5. Who and what parts of the firm will be affected? Are employees receptive? What should be done to prepare employees? Do matching changes need to be made elsewhere?
6. When is the best time to change? Should it be at the end of a season, during down time, at the close of a financial period, or at the beginning of the calendar year?

Once the answers to these questions have been formulated, the timeline for the action plan is developed. It should provide enough detail that the business owner can implement it fully. Included should be a visual representation of the timeline for implementation. Figure 6-22 provides an example of a human resource action plan.

FOLLOW-UP

The special nature of these consulting projects makes the follow-up essential. The purpose of the project is to effect fundamental and long-term change in emerging

businesses such that they will operate in parity with all businesses. This cannot be achieved without diligent follow-up to ensure that recommendations are followed and change happens.

Decision follow-up should be guided by the performance expectations promised in the written client report. There must be sufficient detail and documentation so that anyone not part of the detailed work of the project can understand what is to be accomplished. Clear and concise financial, marketing, or other operational reports and documents should be integral to the follow-up process.

The directions that the client will take following the completion of the project will depend heavily on the quality and persuasiveness of the recommendations made. A final check to ensure that recommendations follow guidelines is important. They should:

- Address project goals
- Be supported by the data and analysis
- Add value to the client and the operations of the firm
- Consider resource availability or provide means of getting resources
- Provide enough detail to implement
- Provide the metrics for measuring success

Plan evaluations are best organized around or focused on specific functional programs. Generally there would be an evaluation designed for each of the elements of the marketing mix. Sometimes separate reports are prepared for specific campaigns or parts of a program. Follow-up should include the specific goal, the completion date, who was responsible for the goal, and some reflection on the results.

Carter McNamara suggests using the following key questions for monitoring and evaluating plans. He also recommends that modifications be made to suit the circumstances and needs of the firm or organization.

A major question is: Are goals and objectives being achieved? If they are, acknowledge, reward, and communicate the progress. If not, consider the remaining questions.

- Will the goals be achieved according to the timelines specified in the plan? If not, why not?
- Should the deadlines for completion be changed? (Be careful about making these changes; know why efforts are behind schedule before deadlines are changed.)

- Do personnel have adequate resources (money, equipment, facilities, training, etc.) to achieve the goals?
- Are the goals and objectives still realistic?
- Should priorities be changed to put more focus on achieving the goals?
- Should the goals be changed? (Be careful about making these changes; know why efforts are not achieving the goals before changing the goals.)
- What can be learned from monitoring and evaluation in order to improve future planning activities and future monitoring and evaluation efforts?

The ultimate test of the worth or value of marketing and business plans must be measured in terms of how well they accomplish their stated goals and objectives.

COMMUNICATING RESULTS
The Presentation

The final presentation takes the place of the typical meeting with the client where consultants present a clear and simple picture of the situation and the recommendations. Generally the presentation is structured to show the analysis of the problem and opportunity such that it naturally leads the client to the recommendations. The presentation must iterate the benefits of the solutions so that it is a foregone conclusion that the client must implement them.

The purpose of the presentation is to focus awareness on a manageable number of dimensions. It is not possible to cover all the work completed for the project and doing so could overload the client. The presentation does not have all the answers. These will be provided in the final report. The final presentation is a key means to communicate the results to the client and provide a showcase for the team's work to mentors and advisors.

Plan as a group. Maintain constant and open communication with team members as the team prepares for its final presentation. This includes a commitment to strive to collaborate and actively listen. It is important that room is made for every team member's ideas to be shared; although there may not be consensus, there is buy-in for the team's recommendations. Keeping communication open at this late stage in the process will be difficult. Team members will be tired. There will be the urge to get it over and done. Rehearsals may run late into the night. Resist the urge to "satisfice," and instead choose excellence to the finish.

Analyze the situation. The occasion, setting, and purpose of the presentation along with the many reasons for making the presentation are all part of the situation analysis that should precede any oral presentation. For most project-related presentations, these elements are relatively straightforward. Early in the project experience, gaining agreements on project scope and priorities or defining problems more clearly are likely to be dominant issues and concerns. However, by the time of the formal presentation of recommendations as part of the final report, considerations of credibility, persuasive evidence, and reinforcing the client's buy-in are likely to become important.

Regarding the physical surroundings of the presentation, give attention to seating, lighting, and other factors that may influence the comfort and attention of those in the audience. Another factor to consider is making sure that the content and focus of the presentation are appropriate for the client's needs.

Know the audience. In approaching this part of the planning process, consider several aspects of what makes for effective interpersonal communications. Start with knowledge, education, and cultural background. Individuals must have some common ground in all these areas, at least with respect to language use and expectations. It is the speaker's responsibility to learn what the client knows about the subject and what he or she expects in the presentation. Additionally, to the extent that differences in age or other demographics affect the response to or understanding of the subject, adjustments will need to be made accordingly.

Also recognize that the team is being evaluated in the presentation process. Its ability to establish rapport or relationships along with cultivating confidence and credibility should be given consideration.

Identify the team's goal. Determine the purpose of the presentation by focusing on what the audience needs to know when they leave. Formulate a succinct statement that summarizes the basic point the audience must accept. The best presentations make the message stand out, easy to follow, and personally important to the audience.

Organize the body of the presentation. Once the key purpose is determined, select the main points to support the purpose, and determine the evidence that will be used to support the recommendations. Understand that the team will have an abundance of data and that it is important to select the findings and analyses that are the most persuasive in achieving the purpose of the presentation. Often team members will want to include the analyses that they invested the most work in or that result in the most interesting visual display. These can all be included in full detail in the final report. The findings, analyses, and recommendations in the presentation must serve the presentation purpose only. It must be organized in such a fashion that the audience will be persuaded to accept the team's recommendations.

Develop the introduction. The introduction must gain the audience's attention. It should preview how the team will proceed and tell the audience when questions will be taken. The most important element of the introduction is to establish credibility to the audience. If the audience does not perceive the team as honest and trustworthy, they are not likely to take the presentation seriously. When planning, ask how the team will be perceived and what can be done to enhance credibility. Determine similarities and differences between the team and the audience.

The introduction will include the full names of all the team members and the agenda for the presentation. It may acknowledge other mentors and advisors. Keep the introduction brief, yet complete.

Plan the conclusion. Recognize the importance of having a strong conclusion. It should accomplish several tasks. The conclusion reviews and highlights the main points of the presentation. The audience should be reminded of the importance and benefits. There might be some follow-up actions that should be conveyed as part of the conclusion. It should answer the question: "So what?" Be clear about what is in it for the client.

It is customary to acknowledge the team's gratitude to the client, mentors, and advisors. Often teams end with a memorable statement that brings the presentation to a close.

Practice the presentation In the case of presentations, the adage "practice makes perfect" is apt. Rehearse in front of others who are unfamiliar with the material. Each team member should develop and repeat the presentation outline until he or she is fluent. This often involves hours of rehearsal for a 20-minute presentation. Rehearsal should

be done under presentation conditions. All speakers should be checked for eye contact, gestures, and voice inflection. The rehearsals should be timed.

Reading the presentation is the least desirable choice because it tends to take away eye contact with the audience and reduces the likelihood that the presenter will be sensitive to audience feedback. Typically there is such a preoccupation with getting the words out that expressiveness and enthusiasm may be lacking. This method of presentation may also reveal a speaker's discomfort with a more conversational style. The delivery is likely to be stilted. It is best to avoid this manner of delivery. It tends to bring out the bad parts of public speaking and oral presentations.

The impromptu mode of delivery is one in which the team member speaks in a conversational tone with no notes. Eye contact is enhanced along with a likelihood of keeping in touch with the audience and following their reactions. There is likely to be a readiness to answer questions that may arise. But there are serious limitations, particularly for novice presenters. They may be prone to forget the order of the presentation or leave out key points.

The term *extemporaneous* is used to define a mode of delivery as speaking from prepared notes in a conversational manner. The speaker can adopt different methods that suit a particular presentation's need or situation. The use of the keyword outline is a staple. It can complement note cards and other devices that can provide aid and comfort to the speaker. Yet it can fit in with a conversational style of delivery. Audience contact can be encouraged. All forms of visual or other presentation aids can be incorporated into the presentation as well.

In most cases, the entire team will participate in the presentation. Determine the order of the speakers. Often team members will present the part in which they were most involved. Ensure that there is a smooth transition between speakers. In such a short presentation, it is usually not necessary to reintroduce the team members or say that the next team member will be presenting on a certain topic. This type of information can be easily communicated on the slides.

Use a keyword outline. As a way of bringing closure to the planning phase, it is suggested that a keyword outline of the presentation be prepared. These words can serve as cues for parts of the delivery phase. They can also reduce the reliance on memory at transition points or in other parts of the presentation. The outline can also serve as a checklist or reminder of the flow of the entire presentation.

Establish or reinforce your credibility. How much the attention of the audience is retained could rest on whether the team members indicate that they know enough and are prepared enough to deserve the attention of the audience for the duration of the presentation. The team may emphasize the depth and care of the research and analysis for the project. It can establish common ground. Showing a passion for the project goes a long way toward establishing credibility.

Use your body effectively. Body language is very important in public speaking. Standing rigidly behind the podium or slouching on it can be signs of needing it as a defense between the speaker and audience or indicate some discomfort at being in front of an audience. Do not use the podium as a crutch or point of separation.

It is usually suggested that the presenter stand up straight, arms at sides, and face the audience. Establish and maintain eye contact with the audience as a way to welcome audience members into the presentation and give them a sense of their importance. Use gestures to complement voice changes or points of emphasis. Gestures should help give energy to the presentation. Other tips for effective use of the body include moving around, standing erect but relaxed, and using a variety of facial expressions.

Use voice effectively. Avoid speaking in a monotone. The voice should enhance the message. Be sure that the presenter can be heard by everyone in the room. Speaking too softly will convey a lack of confidence. Speaking too loudly could give the impression of being too brash and pushy. Change the pace or rate of speaking. Pause to get attention and make a serious and complex point of information. Speed up the pace when there are details that do not need to be emphasized or remembered. Be clear and enunciate words clearly. If there is an accent in the presenter's speech, it may be necessary to slow the speech. Recognize differences between the articulation and the sounds that the audience will hear.

Preparing and using visual aids. Communication is usually best when it can be both verbal and visual. Visual aids should be an integral part of most formal presentations.

It is rare for a business presentation not to have visual aids. Unfortunately this practice has some undesirable side effects such as "information dumping." Presenters are so eager to get material before the audience that slides are overfilled with content. In preparing visual aids, be judicious in including only those that enhance the message.

It is prudent to check out the room prior to the presentation to be aware of any problems that might arise. Technical glitches can occur, and backup options such as additional laptops or projectors are handy to have on hand. In addition, it is a foregone conclusion that the most complex presentations with animation are the most likely to go wrong. Do not rely on the visual effects to give the presentation its punch. All slides in the presentation should be proofread several times. There should be *no* typographical, grammatical, or spelling errors.

Handling questions and answers. In terms of audience takeaways, handling questions and answers can be a very important complement to the presentation. It is best to try to anticipate audience questions and prepare answers before the presentation. Handling the question period well at the end of the presentation adds to the credibility of the team.

When answering the question, repeat it back to the audience. Be gracious, respectful, and positive, even if the question seems to cast doubt on credibility. Be truthful and sincere in answering the question. Defer longer questions until the team is finished with the presentation. It is important that the audience feels that all concerns will be addressed.

Nervousness and anxiety. Nervousness and anxiety are natural reactions to stressful situations. Even prominent entertainers and professional speakers report that they experience these emotions. The response and challenge for everyone is to find a way to cope with nervousness and anxiety. Extensive rehearsal is the best method for overcoming most of the problems with presentations. Taking long breaths (four-count inhalations and four-count exhalations) while imaging relaxing words before speaking can also have a calming effect. When it is time to present, enjoy the moment, as the team has worked hard to be able to shine.

In preparation for the final presentation, take the time

to watch several presentations at ted.com. Some of the best speakers present in that forum, which allows only 20 minutes for each presentation.

The Final Report

Report writing can be among the most challenging and demanding aspects of the project experience. It must be a total team effort. Yet the report must be written and presented in such a way that the client or reader sees it as a single voice of the team. To be really effective it must read as if one individual wrote it. Thus at the outset each team should develop a style sheet for the writing and have a primary editor.

Report writing is a process that should extend throughout the term of the project. Various assignments are intended to provide preparation for later integration into some part of the written consulting report. A very early part of the process should involve developing a report writing plan. This means outlining and organizing before the team writes. It also means that each team member is assigned tasks that will ensure that all the research, analysis, and problem solving that will go into the report will be defined and completed in a timely way.

This should also mean that workloads are allocated fairly and with regard to the skills and strengths of each team member. Particular attention should be given to determining who has the style that will best complement the writing of the team. That individual should be considered for the role of primary editor.

Most knowledgeable businesspeople agree that a project report should be about 30 to 50 pages. This means that the first draft may be significantly longer than the finished report. This length forces the team to sharpen its focus so that the resulting product will hold the reader's interest. This is not to say that the large amount of documentation that usually accompanies a project will be lost. Background materials can be contained in the appendices, and indeed some of the materials in this section may be vital to proper execution of strategies and programs.

Display of Data

To communicate clearly to a business audience, it is important to make effective use of graphics, data, and text. When the data details must be shown, text is the most efficient means of communication. However, graphics are likely to be more influential in getting and keeping the audience's attention. The visual display of information has the benefit of using many more elements, such as color, shape, pattern, texture, and dimension, to communicate. Graphs and text can be used to show relationships. Additionally, the creation of a visual display of information is in itself a means of critical analysis. Often, seeing data in the form of a map or other graphic can clarify the results of the analysis.

Pie charts. Pie charts are effective means of showing categorical data. An audience looking at a pie chart can see the relative proportions of each category quickly. Be careful to use the pie chart with a limited number of categories. Too many categories can overwhelm the display.

Bar charts. Bar charts are often used for frequency distributions of population in quantitative measures such as age or income. They also lend themselves well to showing year-to-year growth in measures such as sales and profit.

Line graphs. Line graphs are useful in communicating trends. A time series line graph is used to show what happens to a variable such as income over time. The horizontal axis is time or years, while the vertical axis shows variables such as income. Time series graphs are excellent for depicting patterns such as economic cycles.

Maps. By using a map and color coding, it is possible to show the geographic concentration of variables. Maps are also excellent for showing competitor locations and other geographic factors that might affect the profitability of a business.

Matrices. Matrices are tables that invite comparison. They are often used effectively as narrative tables. Matrices can be used to show what attributes competitors have as compared to the business. The key to an effective matrix is to select the attributes that are important to the analysis. For example, potential customers might be compared to where they source promotional products.

Use combinations or multiples. Types of graphs can be used in combination to show more variables.

Use color. Color is one of the most important elements of visual display. Unfortunately, using the default values of programs are sure to demonstrate "chart junk." With computer screens it is tempting to use bright colors. But the temptation should be resisted. A good guide to follow is to use colors found in nature. They tend to be muted. Bright colors used in moderation can be very effective in communicating. Also be careful of colors used in combination. They can have a subtractive effect or, worse yet, they can have an unsettling effect on the audience. Given that projectors can alter colors, it is typically safer to use a white background.

Use text. There is no rule that limits the amount of text in a visual display, yet many novices use short truncated titles that detract from good communication. Use the text to extend the explanation and make the analysis clear.

Keep display clear. Programs such as MS Excel make it easy to graph. Experts in the visual display of information say that this is very dangerous. It can lead to a proliferation of chart junk—that is, displaying images without much informational value. Chart junk is also about making the wrong choices and missing the mark in effective display. For example, using three-dimensional graphing does not increase the communication of information, nor does the use of strikingly bold colors or massive amounts of textures.

Be careful of the grid's impact on visual display. Often grids, labels, and titles can overwhelm the visual display with their intensity. Use them only when needed. Think carefully about the scaling of data. Not all charts have to start at zero. Start at a point that allows the audience to understand the relationships and to make meaningful comparisons.

Most sophisticated forms of visual display need to be on paper. Data density on computer screens is one-tenth to one-thousandth of a printed page. If providing complex evidence, put it in print and allow the audience to look at it carefully and in detail.

Show the data. It might sound obvious, but good visual display actually shows the data. The Challenger explosion immediately after takeoff was blamed on O-ring failure. But the main culprit was poor visual display of information. Although data were given, no one could see the clear pattern of O-ring failure in low temperatures. In order to show the data, understand the data. In fact, the Columbia explosion was blamed on simplified display of information through PowerPoint slides. Know the data inside out. This helps team members come up with the appropriate visual display. Experts in information believe that people with a passion for what the data show come up with the best form of visual display.

Eliminate ambiguity. Good visual display of information is clear. Even when there is extensive data, the presentation must still be clear. Relationships and conclusions should be logical and meaningful. The message should be precise. There must not be any ambiguity or confusion. The presentation should be efficient and show what is necessary with a minimum of effort on the part of the viewer.

Do not distort data. Data, like truth, must have integrity; otherwise it is misleading. There are many temptations to distort data in the business world. Sometimes it might appear that bending the evidence will ease the path for a recommendation. Or a marketer might want to put products in the best light. A client could pressure the team to show one thing while omitting another. In the long term, business relations are about trust, and distorting the data will erode that trust. Strive to obtain and present only the most relevant and accurate data. If the truth has to be bent to demonstrate a point, the wrong path of communication is being pursued.

Excellent visual display requires excellent command of the data and an in-depth understanding of design. To communicate what the data show, the visual display must have a purpose. Once the mission is clear, use color, shape, layout, comparison, layering, dimensions, and other elements to tell the story.

Elements of the Final Report

Cover letter. The cover letter serves at least three purposes. First, it acknowledges that the report is being submitted to the client. Second, it provides a brief description of the project along with a few highlights of the findings, conclusions, and recommendations. Finally, it expresses gratitude to the client for his or her cooperation, support, and contributions to student learning that have been made along the way.

Executive summary. The executive summary provides much more than a summary of the entire project. In fact it is the most widely read of any part of the plan, and its quality is often the deciding factor in whether the client will read the rest of the report. The executive summary succinctly focuses on what managers/decision makers need to know, yet it is complete enough that it is persuasive. Executive summaries are difficult to write, and the team should take the time to think through all the findings and recommendations before tackling it. Typically executive summaries are drafted after the body of the report is complete. They must provide the highlights of the work and the call for action. Good executive summaries undergo many revisions.

Table of contents. The table of contents shows how the report is organized. Major headings (and sometimes subheadings) are indicated so that readers can find the portions of the report that are of interest. If headings are properly formatted while drafting the report, a table of contents will be generated automatically.

Background and introduction. This section includes an explanation of the project's purpose and scope and presents the methods of research and analysis. It provides background information on the company, financial performance, and management biographies. The business model may also be included. The business model definition calls for thinking of the company in terms of what value is being provided, what benefits are being offered in the marketplace, and how the business will profit from it. Differentiation adds further content and context by considering how the delivery of these values and benefits will be designed for competitive advantage of a given company in comparison with its competitors.

Environment, industry/competitive, and situation analysis. An important part of any report is the assessments that are made of the external and internal environments in which the firm operates. Such assessments must include the challenges, constraints, and influences that will determine the outcomes of the plans that are implemented. A detailed SWOT analysis may be included here.

Findings and analysis. This main section of the report will include data analysis and presentation of findings on competitive analysis, business process analysis, market analysis, financial analysis, and other discussion. As there can be many findings, it is important to group similar findings together and to prioritize the categories. In assessing the value of this section, readers will ask the following questions:

- Was the research sufficient, or was key information not sought?
- Was the methodology sound? Was the analysis done correctly?
- Were the conclusions drawn supported by the evidence?
- Were patterns or conclusions missed? Were incorrect conclusions drawn?

Recommendations. The recommendations that the consultant team makes to its client are critically important to the overall success of the project. They are the result of many hours of hard work. Recommendations should not be presented to the client before they are in final form. Past experience with novice consulting teams shows that often they have not completed all the necessary analysis or communicated the findings in such a way that the client will readily accept them. In these cases, it is important to review the findings and recommendations with faculty, advisors, and mentors before going to the client.

Recommendations should:

- Address project goals
- Be supported by data and analysis
- Add value to the client's firm
- Consider resource availability or provide means of getting resources
- Provide enough detail to implement
- Provide the metrics for measuring success
- Be fully documented in the report

Recommendations should be grouped by category and prioritized. Often teams will have recommendations follow the findings and analysis. Questions to be asked include:

- Were the recommendations supported by the evidence?
- What benefits will the recommendations provide to the business?
- Were costs and benefits quantified?
- Do the recommendations fit with the mission and vision of the business?
- Does the business have access to the resources necessary to implement the recommendations?
- Is there sufficient detail in the report for the business to know how to implement the recommendations?
- Were the recommendations time bound?

- Have the risks been analyzed?
- How will the business measure whether it has been successful in implementing the recommendations?

Appendix materials. Copies of surveys, summaries of raw data, transcripts of focus groups, or significant interviews should be included in this section. Student teams often include data sets that provide valuable information to the business, such as potential customer lists. These should be included in their entirety in the appendices.

Style, Layout, and Presentation

The report should be written in a clear, concise, and direct style. Short sentences are usually better than longer sentences. Long sentences with clauses are harder to follow, since they are likely to contain more than one complete thought. Use bullet points any time there are three or more items in a sequence or list. This is more appealing than using a sentence containing a lot of commas.

Avoid complicated language that has to be explained or that is likely to require a great deal of effort to read and understand. When technical or complicated words must be used, provide an accompanying clarification or illustration. Avoid sending the reader to a dictionary. Be sure to keep the client in mind as the primary reader. Recognize that if the client is going to have difficulty reading the report, its usefulness to him or her is likely to be limited. Moreover, it could reduce the likelihood of getting ideas and solutions adopted or implemented.

Keep in mind that the report informs, advises, persuades, and possibly even warns the client about some important issues that need his or her attention. In order to be clearly heard, make sure all findings and recommendations are expressed as positively as possible. For example, instead of describing the business as disorganized, specifically address what has to be improved, such as having a better database or documenting procedures.

The final report is often the part of the project that endures. Business owners may retain the project report and implement the recommendations over a long period of time. They may use elements of it to apply for financing. It is important documentation of the team's hard work. Often team members will show the report as evidence of the quality of work they can achieve. The team should take the time and effort to make it the best possible product.

REFERENCES

Block, P. *Flawless Consulting: A Guide to Getting Your Expertise Used.* 3rd ed. San Francisco: Pfeiffer, 2011.

Guess, Vincent. *CMII for Business Process Infrastructure.* Scottsdale: Holly Publishing, 2002.

Kaplan, Robert S., and David P. Norton. *The Balanced Scorecard.* Boston: Harvard Business School Press, 1996.

Porter, Michael E. *Competitive Strategy.* New York: Free Press, 1980.

Porter, Michael E. *Competitive Advantage.* New York: Free Press, 1986.

See kpilibrary.com for an extensive listing of key performance indicators by function.

See ted.com for examples of speeches.

DISCUSSION

1. Select two presentations from ted.com. Analyze the introduction and conclusion. How did the speaker establish credibility? What did the speaker do to grab interest at the beginning? How did the speaker make a persuasive and memorable point in the conclusion? Assess the speaker's style. Was eye contact maintained? Was the speaking style extemporaneous? What did you learn that you will consider using when you make your oral presentation?

2. Complete a process map of a key process in the client business.

3. Compute and interpret several balance sheet, income statement, and cash flow financial ratios for the client business. What conclusions would you draw from your analysis?

4. Complete a breakeven analysis on the client business using an online coupon such as Groupon. Specify what level of new business (number of customers) is necessary to break even.

5. From your consulting project experience, write brief statements explaining at least two lessons or take-aways that you learned from your team members and your client/business owner.

Appendix: Business Plan

Most small firms do not have a written business plan. Yet they expect to be around for a while, and most of them will be. Most founders of gazelles acknowledge that they had no strategic plan in the early stages of their businesses. Plans play a relatively small role in the early stages of a business when market requirements are fuzzy or when the business owner is bootstrapping from day to day.

However, in the experience of the student consulting teams, for businesses moving from promising to long-lived, creation of a strategic vision is crucial. A plan is also important to the survival of businesses with strong competition or low barriers to entry. Without the direction that a plan provides, business owners are often distracted by the unevaluated opportunities presented to them. This creates a number of pitfalls, including pursuing unprofitable opportunities, taking resources away from key goals that will advance their long-term success, or stretching their attention so that strategies are not pursued to completion. A plan keeps the business owner focused on the mission of the business. It means that the firm has a destination in mind, and the plan provides direction and guidance for getting to it. Further, having a plan should increase the effectiveness of efforts to achieve business success.

In one project's experience with a restaurant, the owners wanted to expand into the ancillary business of catering. Yet they also faced other challenges with respect to improving their facility and determining ways of building customer volume in a community with changing demographics. Sorting out the options and opportunities clearly represented a situation in which a business plan was needed to determine what would be the best course of action for their business.

Here are five reasons why a firm should have a business plan:

1. A business plan will help the owners and managers determine where the company should go given its strengths, resources, and other capabilities.
2. The process of developing the plan will identify possible obstacles as well as opportunities that are in the marketplace, along with ways of responding to them. By knowing what the obstacles are, a firm can better prepare to overcome them. Similarly, more of the available opportunities are likely to be realized if they can be anticipated as a result of having a plan.
3. Developing contingencies and alternatives for responding to the market environment can best be accomplished through a business plan.
4. A plan is usually required in order to obtain a loan or other sources of financing for a business.
5. Since the plan is a kind of guide for showing where a business is headed, it should be possible to stay on track (or at least avoid being derailed) as a result of having a plan. The destination is likely to be reached sooner by having and following a well-developed business plan. Finally, an effective plan will help the firm reduce the risks of failure.

Mission. This is the broadest, most forward-looking expression of where the business is headed and what its future is expected to be. It can be represented as a theme for the future. For one home health care provider, its mission was to be the preferred provider of home-based health care. A mission could be expressed in a period of three to five years or much longer periods,

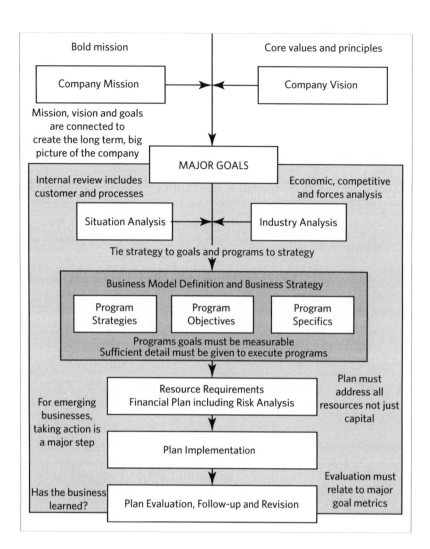

FIGURE 7-1. Business Planning Process

Bold mission

Company Mission

Core values and principles

Company Vision

Mission, vision and goals are connected to create the long term, big picture of the company

MAJOR GOALS

Internal review includes customer and processes

Situation Analysis

Economic, competitive and forces analysis

Industry Analysis

Tie strategy to goals and programs to strategy

Business Model Definition and Business Strategy

Program Strategies

Program Objectives

Program Specifics

Programs goals must be measurable
Sufficient detail must be given to execute programs

Resource Requirements
Financial Plan including Risk Analysis

Plan must address all resources not just capital

For emerging businesses, taking action is a major step

Plan Implementation

Has the business learned?

Plan Evaluation, Follow-up and Revision

Evaluation must relate to major goal metrics

such as ten or more years. Despite its long-term orientation, a mission should be based on and informed by realistic assessments of the possibilities of what can be accomplished. Those responsible for leading the firm should share in the development and pursuit of the mission. It is expected that they too will be committed to doing what is necessary to realize the vision.

Vision. This encompasses the core values and guiding principles of the firm. Often small businesses, like many large enterprises, have core values that involve giving back to their communities or otherwise supporting underserved populations. An African American home health care company's vision is that all its workers should have a good living wage. This works to its benefit because, in an industry where there is high turnover, the company is able to retain its workers because of higher wages. Similarly, tribal enterprises have core values that are different

from other enterprises. The core values of tribal enterprises are to lift their communities economically and provide employment to tribal members. Although tribal enterprises can hire outsiders who are initially more qualified, they choose to hire tribal members so that they can develop their own. These guiding principles can figure prominently in a company's major goals and are not necessarily counter to profitability.

Situation and industry analysis. Generally, this part of business planning covers industry analysis, an internal analysis of the firm, and an evaluation of the market conditions and circumstances facing the company. This is the section where various stakeholder groups and influences are acknowledged. Of special importance are competitors, customers, suppliers, government regulators, technological developments, and any other influential groups or factors that will affect how the company performs over time.

Goals. Goals are general outcomes and expectations of results. They are also stated as ideal end-states that may not be achieved within a specific time frame. For the African American home health care company, in the past its goal was to become the home health care market leader in the state. The company accomplished that by taking on large urban markets in its first years of business. Then smaller cities became the target markets.

The purpose of establishing major goals is to enable the company to then align all its actions and dedicate all its resources to reaching these goals. If a small business has a major goal, once a consulting team collects data and information, the team's challenge is to determine actions that the company needs to take to align all its resources to help it reach its goal. Thus, it is crucial for student consulting teams to either fully understand the existing major goals or help the company define goals prior to its work to plan a course of action to move the company forward.

Strategy. Strategy is the term applied to the approach, guidelines, and goal-directed actions that are followed in order to achieve stated goals. It is very important that a firm find ways to differentiate itself from the competition as an important aspect of market strategy. Entrepreneurs are often enticed by the many business opportunities that present themselves. Unless these opportunities align with the strategic focus and core competencies of the business, they can be detrimentally distracting to the business's success. For the African American home health care company, the move into a pharmacy business was a means of diversifying into another business within health care. This move would leverage its home health care business, which provided the pharmacy with a ready customer list. It was part of a long-term strategy to selectively enter other related businesses that allow it to establish a dominant position as a diversified quality health care provider.

When creating a strategy, the focus is on intention and direction. Intention defines what is to be accomplished, and direction includes the action steps that will be followed to achieve the goal. A strategic plan is one that embodies the pathways that will be followed in the pursuit of those objectives. When done properly it should be conceptual, visionary, and directional. Conceptually, it captures the essential characteristics of the firm as a successful enterprise. In being visionary the plan would reflect the future directions and aim beyond the current business thinking. An effective plan will give direction to those responsible for pursuing the firm's objectives.

The strategic plan serves as a framework within which management decisions are made. Its content makes clear to all the business's stakeholders what it is about. Besides informing them, it may help to build relationships that will improve the performance of the business.

Program. The term strategic is associated with thinking, acting, or making decisions that are focused, forward-looking, company-wide, and directed toward specific performance objectives. Usually these outcomes are viewed as being beyond one year in duration. For within-year activities, the terms program or tactics are applied. A program is a defined set of steps that in aggregate are part of an overall strategy to achieve business goals. Examples of programs include an advertising campaign, a direct mail campaign, public relations events, or a web marketing program.

Resource requirements. Note that when a business plan is created, it is important to determine whether resources can be obtained to achieve the plan. Emerging businesses always grapple with limited resources. If the business does not have the resources to implement the programs, alternatives must be sought.

Objectives. Objectives, by contrast, are the measurable performance results or metrics that are expected to be achieved within a given time period. They are most commonly stated with respect to such outcome measures as sales, market share, profit, return on investment, or other performance measures for a given time, such as month, quarter, or year. Objectives are also stated as changes and improvements. An example could be a 3% increase in same-store sales over the previous year.

Risks. Typically when financials for a business plan are compiled, sensitivity analysis is done to accommodate for uncertainty. However, there may be other risks that cannot be translated to financial statements. It is incumbent upon the business to list all the risks and consider contingency plans to mitigate or deal with the risk.

Evaluating the plan. A good plan will always include a comprehensive method for measuring its success. Any feedback about the plan should be incorporated into future versions in a continuous improvement loop.

REFERENCE

SBA. *How to Write a Business Plan*. http://www.sba.gov/category/navigation-structure/starting-managing-business/starting-business/writing-business-plan.

Index